GEORG LUKÁCS

GEORG LUKÁCS

THEORY, CULTURE, AND POLITICS

Edited and with an introduction
by
Judith Marcus and Zoltán Tarr

Transaction Publishers
New Brunswick (U.S.A.) and Oxford (U.K.)

Copyright © 1989 by Transaction, Inc.
New Brunswick, New Jersey 08903

All rights reserved under International and Pan-American Copyright Conventions. No part of this book may be reproduced or transmitted in any form or by any means, electronic or mechanical, including photocopy, recording, or any information storage and retrieval system, without prior permission in writing from the publisher. All inquiries should be addressed to Transaction Books, Rutgers—The State University, New Brunswick, New Jersey 08903.

Library of Congress Catalog Number: 88-20125
ISBN: 0-88738-244-4
Printed in the United States of America

Library of Congress Cataloging in Publication Data

Georg Lukács : theory, culture, and politics : a centenary volume / edited and
    with an introduction by Judith Marcus and Zoltan Tarr.
        p.   cm.
    Includes index.
    ISBN 0-88738-244-4
        1. Lukács, György, 1885–1971.   I. Lukács, György, 1885–1971.
    II. Marcus, Judith.   III. Tarr, Zoltán.   IV. Title:
    Theory, culture, and politics.
    B4815.L84G42   1988
    199′.439–dc19

Contents

Acknowledgments

Our greatest debt goes to the sponsors of the Lukács Centenary Conferences from which most of the papers are drawn: the New School for Social Research, Graduate Faculty of Political and Social Science in New York City, the Hungarian Academy of Sciences in Budapest, the Goethe Institut and l'Ecole des Hautes Etudes en Sciences Sociales et la College International de Philosophie in Paris, the Inter-University Centre of Post-Graduate Studies in Dubrovnik and the Universidad Autonoma Metropolitana—Xochimilco in Mexico, and Mr. Henry Voremberg.

We are indebted to those scholars, critics and friends who helped us in more ways than we could publicly thank them for. We are grateful to Professors István Deák, Ira Katznelson, Edith Kurzweil, Hans Vaget, Alexander Vucinich, Harry Zohn, and Mr. Alex Heller in the United States, to Ferenc Jánossy, László Sziklai, Mihály Vajda, Èva Gábor, Erzsébet Vezér, and the late György Ránki in Hungary, to Nicholas Tertullian, Francois Fejtö, Joseph Gabel, and Gerard Raulet in Paris, to Gvozden Flego and Gajo Petrović in Yugoslavia, to Graciela Borja, Gilberto Guevara Niebla and Adolfo Sanchez Vazquez in Mexico, and to Ze'ev Levy in Israel.

Thanks are due to Mrs. Hope McAloon for her prompt and careful technical assistance. At Transaction thanks are due to Ms. Anita Stock.

Needless to say that the chief responsibility lies with the editors for the selection, editing and in many cases for the translation of the material.

Introduction

By Judith Marcus and Zoltán Tarr

Ein grosser Mann verdammt die
Menschen dazu ihn zu explizieren.
Hegel

Lukács remains the most enigmatic and double-faced figure of the modern Communist movement. While some of the features of his thought have been clarified by recent scholarship and by the discovery of early manuscripts which had been thought lost, a full appreciation of the man and the work is still missing.

So wrote Lewis A. Coser, the distinguished American sociologist, in a recent review. Indeed, Georg Lukács—considered by many the most important Marxist thinker of this century—remains an enigma to most people. What kind of a man was he? Why were his theories so important to modern social and political thought? Why and in what way did his lifework exert such influence on so many people over such a long period? And why—at the same time—did many of his writings infuriate readers and critics? Finally, what is the significance of his work for us today?

Until recently, before the publication of the selected correspondence of the young Lukács, the man's life remained undisclosed; his enigmatic personality and the beginnings of his intellectual and personal development remained hidden behind the work. And even some of his most significant works remained unapproachable to all but a few of the Lukács scholars and critics possessing the knowledge of Hungarian.

On the occasion of the centenary of Lukács's birth (1985), there were symposia held in many countries on several continents attended by hundreds of Lukács scholars, students, critics, and others interested not only—or even mainly—in Lukács and his work but also in his time and its ideas. Papers read and heard in the East and the West, from New York and Budapest to Paris and Dubrovnik, Rome and Mexico City—just to name the main international events—shed new light on Lukács's work, dealt anew with some of his most controversial concepts, ideas, and theses, gave account of newly discovered data and writings, made known theretofore unknown preoccupations in Lukács's career, or just "revisited" old works and ideas.

This centenary volume brings together some of the original papers expressly written for the occasion by participants in the centenary in New York, Paris, Budapest, and Mexico City—along with a few older contributions that the editors considered to be worthy of introduction to a larger public. Some of the contributions are sharply critical, others are clearly admiring, and quite a few take an objective but nevertheless severe second look at diverse aspects of Lukács's work. Together, they amount to a close examination of the lifework of the man Thomas Mann called "the most important literary critic of today," Jean-Paul Sartre, "a significant modern philosopher," and Irving Howe, "a major force in European intellectual life" for the past half-century.

If this or that paper settles some old controversies or introduces new ones, it is quite in the spirit of the centenary; the authors were, in fact, encouraged to do so by the editors. It is no less in the spirit of Lukács, who knew all his life how to incite controversy or to live with it.

The Man: In Lieu of a Biography of Georg Lukács

Georg Lukács was born György Bernát Löwinger in Budapest on April 13, 1885, into a wealthy assimilated Hungarian-Jewish family. His father, a self-made millionaire and director of the Hungarian General Credit Bank, changed his name to Lukács in 1890; he became ennobled (szegedi Lukács or *von* Lukács) in 1901. Lukács grew up bilingual (German-Hungarian) and at an early age learned French and English as well. The father's very generous support enabled Lukács to live as a member of the *freischwebende Intelligenz* (free-floating intelligentsia).

Lukács went to Berlin in 1905 and attended the lectures of Wilhelm Dilthey and the private seminar of Georg Simmel. He received his (first) doctorate in law from the University of Kolozsvár (now Cluj-Napoca, Romania) in 1906; his second Ph.D. was in philosophy (Budapest University, 1909). His first publication appeared when he was 17. Two years later, in 1904, he founded the Thalia Theater, introducing avant-garde authors along with the classics; he instituted performances for workers at a very low price. His prizewinning *History of the Development of Modern Drama* was published in Hungary in 1911. During the same year, a collection of his essays, *Soul and Form,* was published in Berlin. The book was favorably received and helped Lukács's entry into German intellectual circles. Thomas Mann, the supreme stylist, called it "a beautiful, profound book."

Following a futile attempt to embark on an academic career in Budapest, the suicide of his love, Irma Seidler, and the death of his closest friend, Leo Popper, from tuberculosis, Lukács moved to Florence and started work on a systematic *Aesthetics.* His then friend, the German-Jewish philosopher Ernst

Bloch, persuaded him to move to Heidelberg in 1912, where he lived until 1917. During the Heidelberg period, Lukács worked away on his *Habilitationsschrift*, became a valued member of the Max Weber Circle and a trusted friend to both Max and Alfred Weber, to Emil Lask, and to Emil Lederer, among others, published an autobiographical novelette, *On Poverty of Spirit* (1913), and married a Russian anarchist-artist, Yelena Grabenko, to whom he dedicated *The Theory of the Novel* (1916).

At this point in his thinking he was influenced by Hegel, Dostoevsky, Max Weber, and Marx, the latter mediated through Simmel and Weber. His opposition to World War I made him an outsider among German intellectuals and a leading figure among young Hungarian intellectuals, after he returned to Budapest in 1917. In 1918 he made a last, unsuccessful attempt at a university career in Heidelberg. Although residing in Budapest, Lukács submitted his formal application on May 25, 1918, complete with the topic of his *Habilitation* presentation; quite a few faculty members were vigorously campaigning on his behalf, among them Weber, Gothein, and Rickert. Lukács was informed by the dean of Heidelberg University on December 7, 1918, that his application had been rejected.

In December 1918 Lukács joined the Communist party of Hungary and in spring 1919 became People's Commissar of Education under the short-lived Republic of Councils; after its defeat, he took refuge in Vienna. His theoretical and practical involvement with Marxism and revolutions gave birth to his essay collection *History and Class Consciousness*. Before leaving his Vienna exile, he was sent back to Hungary for underground party work; he managed to ''survive'' this mission by being ''cool'' and ''cunning,'' Lukács remembered fifty years later.[1] He spent a year in Moscow, working in the Marx-Engels Institute alongside Mikhail Lifshitz; they were, as Lukács recalled, the first to speak of a specific Marxist aesthetics that ''did not have to be borrowed from Kant or anyone else.''[2] He went on to Berlin in 1931, where he became one of the leaders of the left-wing group in the German Writers' Association while writing and teaching at the Marxist Workers' Academy. Following Hitler's seizure of power in January 1933, Lukács emigrated to the Soviet Union (in March).

During his exile in Moscow, Lukács abstained from political activity and devoted himself to scholarship, writing the first drafts of *The Destruction of Reason* and treatises on literary themes (Goethe, Thomas Mann, realism), and to finishing his book *The Young Hegel*. Lukács considered himself ''lucky'' in that he was arrested only in 1941 when the executions had stopped; thus, he survived ''one of the greatest purges known to history.''[3]

At the end of World War II, Lukács returned to Budapest and became a university professor, a public figure, an academician, and a member of the Parliament. He believed in the possibility of a long (transitional) period of People's Democracy, characterized by a kind of Popular Front policy; he envisioned it as a new form transitional to socialism that went parallel with the chance for long-term peaceful coexistence and competition between capitalism and socialism on the international scene. Consequently, he was actively engaged in promoting the vanguard role of the Communist party at home while participating in numerous international conferences abroad. After the commencement of outright Stalinism in Hungary in 1949, many of its architects became its victims and were either executed or imprisoned. Lukács fared better: he was only "purged" from his university post as the result of an "intellectual show-trial" of criticism and self-criticism. He retired into his study to pursue "pure" scholarship, and emerged as a public figure again in 1956 in the wake of the Twentieth Soviet Party Congress and Khrushchev's revelation of Stalin's crimes. From then on, Lukács became a critic of Stalinism—from a Leninist position. The combination of theory and practice in Lukács's critique of Stalinism came to a head in October 1956 when he became a member of Imre Nagy's government.

After the defeat of the 1956 revolt, Lukács was interned in Romania until April 1957. In the late 1950s he returned to active scholarship and supported the new Hungarian reformist liberalization movement in the 1960s. He was fully in favor of the new economic policy, because he held that it "necessarily implied democratization of the party and a renewal of Marxism."[4] Duly celebrated toward the end of his life as "the greatest living Marxist," Lukács died at the age of 86, on June 7, 1971. His *Collected Works,* some twenty-five volumes, are being published in both Hungary and West Germany.

Lukács's Works and Ideas

The seven decades of Lukács's creative intellectual life can be conveniently divided into four phases, complete with transitional stages: first, the pre-Marxist romantic anticapitalist period; second, a messianic-utopian-revolutionary Marxist period; third, the Stalinist years; and finally, a critical-reformist Marxist period subsequent to Stalin's death.

Lukács's contributions touch upon many branches of the social sciences and humanities, such as the sociology of art and literature, aesthetics, political philosophy, ethics, ontology, history of philosophy, and philosophy of history. It would be a mistake, however, to cut the Lukács opus into pieces, and to speak of the "young Lukács" and the "old Lukács," making them separate entities as some interpreters do. Lukács himself emphasized the dialectical unity of continuity and discontinuity in his lifework. A periodization merely serves as a guide to the thought of an intellectual who was always preoccupied with the political and cultural problems of his age and with the search for solutions.

The romantic anticapitalist Lukács rebelled against what he perceived as the oppressive and backward conditions of East-Central European societies and joined the progressive-democratic intellectual forces of pre–World War I Hungary in their search for theoretical and practical solutions. In the face of the onslaught of the crude positivism and vulgar Marxism of his time, Lukács searched for a method, a way out of the crisis of the social sciences and humanities, thus in close association with someone like Max Weber, who had similar aims, albeit from a different perspective. The uncertainties of the old, disintegrating European social order caused Lukács to yearn ''for certainty, for measure and dogma.'' He expressed his longing for ''value and form, for measure and order,'' believing in the redeeming power of form and proclaiming that ''aesthetic culture is the formation of the soul.''⁵ Two major works of this period, *Soul and Form* and *The Theory of the Novel,* reflect both personal and cultural crises; they influenced some of the best minds of Europe, from Max Weber and Thomas Mann to the theorists of the Frankfurt School (Horkheimer, Marcuse, Adorno). Lucien Goldmann correctly called Lukács the founder of modern existential philosophy.

Lukács's messianic-utopian-revolutionary Marxist phase was precipitated by such historical events as the outbreak of World War I and the Russian Revolution of 1917, followed by a wave of Central European revolutions, which gave him a new perspective, that is, the possibility of the ''leap'' from the realm of capitalist *Sein*/Being (''the age of absolute sinfulness'') to the realm of *Sollen*/Ought (socialism) or a more humane society. The theoretical thrust of this phase led to several essays on politics and culture, most notably ''Bolshevism as a Moral Problem'' and ''Tactics and Ethics,'' and to the collection *History and Class Consciousness.*

Lukács's shift is marked by a change in style from a romantic-poetic to a Hegelian-Marxist one, with strong ethical undertones. Certain Weberian and neo-Kantian elements were retained, however, such as Weber's notion of capitalism with the concomitant theme of rationalization/reification and the neo-Kantian epistemology in his critique of Engels's ''dialectic of nature.'' *History and Class Consciousness* serves as a starting point for rethinking and restructuring Marxist social theory (for the Frankfurt School, for example) and has been an inspiration for generations of leftist intellectuals in the twentieth century. The following five propositions sum up the main theses of *History and Class Consciousness:*

1. ''True'' Marxism is but ''orthodox Marxism,'' that is, a return to Marx's method, which emphasizes the primacy of totality.
2. Marx's dialectic is a method to be applied to historical-sociological studies of society, in opposition to Engels's ''dialectic of nature.''
3. The phenomenon of ''reification'' is the essence of capitalist society, permeating all human relations.
4. The proletariat is the agent (''subject-object'') of the world-historical process and is destined to eliminate the evils of capitalist society and to bring about the salvation of humankind.

5. The Communist party represents "the objectification of the proletariat's will," mediating between the realms of *Sein* and *Sollen*.

From the Nazi takeover in Germany dates the third period; the developments in Germany precipitated Lukács's third exile to Moscow. As an immediate and lasting response to the worldwide danger of fascism, he investigated the intellectual roots of the Nazi Weltanschauung. Lukács used the dichotomous terms "rational/irrational" in tracing German philosophical developments from the earlier, mystical-irrational strands to the most recent, most barbarian, and most vulgar manifestation in the irrational Nazi Weltanschauung. This endeavor resulted in *The Destruction of Reason,* a work that so enraged Adorno, for example, that he characterized it as the destruction of Lukács's own reason. Sartre and George Steiner, on the other hand, found more positive things to say about the work, especially its intentions.[6] In addition, two smaller, posthumously published monographs deal with the same problem complex. Lukács complements his analysis of the genesis of the Nazi Weltanschauung with a defense of the progressive, "real" German cultural tradition in numerous essays devoted to Goethe, Hegel, Heine, Büchner, Thomas Mann, and others.

Concurrently, Lukács worked out a theory of realism while testing it on specific "case studies" devoted to Balzac, Walter Scott (and the historical novel), Zola, and Tolstoy. His monograph *The Young Hegel* earned him the degree (his third doctorate!) of doctor of the Soviet Academy of Sciences. Finally, Lukács worked on the reconstruction of Marxian aesthetics, based on scattered remarks by Marx and Engels.

Lukács's accommodation with Stalinism is a rather complex issue that still awaits its chronicler. To be sure, he wholeheartedly supported Stalin vis-à-vis Trotsky and in regard to the Ribbentrop-Molotov pact; he also paid lip service to Stalinism in his writings of that period. Justifying his stand, he stated that the defeat of fascism, the main enemy of humankind, was the order of the day and that the Soviet Union was the most committed to this task. Nevertheless, he criticized Soviet bureaucracy and dealt with taboo topics such as Hegel, Dostoevsky, and giants of Western "bourgeois literature." He was supposed to have said (to Victor Serge) that one should not be "silly" and get oneself deported "for the pleasure" of being defiant. "Marxist revolutionaries need patience and courage; they do not need pride." Since the "times are bad," Marxists should "reserve" their strength, as "history will summon [them] in its time.'"[7] To be sure, Lukács survived the Stalinist purges; he was jailed in Lubyanka for a short period (about two months) in 1941.

In the last, the critical-reformist Marxist phase of his career, Lukács again combined theory and praxis. His many interviews and statements and his participation in the 1956 events in Hungary provided inspiration and ammunition for Eastern European reform movements of the 1960s. As a summation of his lifework and a last attempt at systematic Marxism, he finished his Marxist

Aesthetics (1964) and the *Ontology,* published posthumously. The two theoretical works represent a return to his youthful interests and "verify" Lukács's statement in regard to the continuity of his lifework: "With me, everything is the continuation of something. I believe, there is no non-organic element in my development."[8]

Lukács's ontological theses represent a return to the earlier theme of totality, a kind of holism, which has now become an organistic and historical category. He asserts that epistemology must be replaced by a historicized ontology and so form the basis of a modernized Marxism. Lukács continued to believe that a renaissance of Marxism would occur. He also emphasized two earlier themes, the first relating to the role of the intellectuals who bring class consciousness to the masses "from without," and the second concerning the workers' councils that "spell the political and economic defeat of reification," thus leading to a just, socialist democracy.

Notes on the Papers

Three of the papers of part 1 (Kline, Rockmore, and Kelemen) revisit *History and Class Consciousness.*

George L. Kline, philosopher, in his critical comments on Lukács's "will to the future," asserts that while Lukács had a better understanding of the thought of Kant, Fichte, and Hegel than any other twentieth-century Marxist, his theoretical position in *History and Class Consciousness* is beset by a number of tensions and contradictions, such as the tension between the Hegelian and the (Engelsian) scientific strands in his thought. Lukács is reprimanded for "terminological laxity." Kline finds Lukács's orientation toward the world-historical future—his "will to the future"—most un-Hegelian, theoretically problematic, and above all, politically dangerous.

The majority view of Lukács interpreters argues for a certain continuity of thought in that his Marxism retained baggage (idealist, existentialist, etc.) from his pre- and early Marxist periods. Philosopher Tom Rockmore is ready and willing to accept the continuity thesis; however, he reverses the sequence and projects back Lukács's Engelsian reading of German philosophy in the 1930s and 1940s onto *History and Class Consciousness.* While Lukács is scorned for having considered in *History and Class Consciousness* bourgeois philosophy from the classical Marxist standpoint as a form of ideology, that is, in the Engelsian reductionist sense, he is credited for having a "highly original approach" to classical German thought. The "outstanding trait" of Lukács, which distinguishes his approach from all other Marxist approaches, is his informed concern to demonstrate through specific interpretation the truth of the Marxist claim that philosophy is ideology. Rockmore is aware that his reading of Lukács's approach to the history of philosophy is controversial—in fact, he emphasizes it by his forceful line of argumentation.

János Kelemen, Hungarian philosopher of science, looks at Lukács's philosophy of science as presented in *History and Class Consciousness* in light of the developments in the modern philosophy of science. To be sure, when writing *History and Class Consciousness,* Lukács's primary interest was related to the ongoing revolutions. Yet a perusal of the various essays in the volume reveals that he touches upon almost all of the central issues of the philosophy of science. Indeed, the book contains a remarkable array of themes related to it, such as methodology of social science, the epistemological and methodological dualism of the natural and social sciences, the relationship between science and society, the nature of historical knowledge, and the relationship between empirical data and theory, just to mention some important ones. Thus, Lukács's answers add up to a coherent theory of science. *History and Class Consciousness* was a revolt against positivistic philosophy of science, which heightens its relevance for our post-Kuhnian antipositivistic era.

Joseph B. Maier's essay touches on two of the most important issues of the Lukács *Problematik*: his Jewishness and his impact on the Frankfurt School. He rightly points to the linguistic obstacle that most Anglo-American readers find difficult when they encounter Continental thinkers, the likes of a Lukács, Horkheimer, or Adorno. These three men wrote in a German that has a special *Wahlverwandtschaft* (elective affinity) to philosophy, a fact constituting an insurmountable barrier for many readers. Maier's exposition of the sociological and philosophical interconnections between Lukács and the Frankfurt school is a piece of grand scholarship in the European tradition of *Geistesgeschichte*. The inquiry into the impact of Judaic thought on the thinkers mentioned—making use of the relevant analysis of Werner J. Cahnman and Jürgen Habermas—is the most enlightening and fascinating part of the essay.

Harry Liebersohn, a young American historian well versed in European inellectual history, retraces Lukács's argument with three leading German sociologists of his time, Tönnies, Simmel, and Weber, and his rejection of their "Lutheran pessimism." Tönnies's nostalgia and the stance of Simmel, an assimilated Jew who chose to ally himself with Germany's hegemonic Protestant culture, are contrasted with Lukács's utopian orientation. Liebersohn also contrasts Weber's agnostic position about the chances for a return to *Gemeinschaft* and his tragic affirmation of modern individualism with Lukács's determined efforts to find a way to a new collective order. While the three Germans had a fixation on past and present, *Gemeinschaft* and *Gesellschaft,* Lukács in his *History and Class Consciousness* went beyond them by starting to talk about a future to be shaped.

In part 2, the Hungarian-American philosopher and aesthetician Laurent Stern attempts to solve the riddle that though a rather conservative thinker, Lukács taught a generation of rebels. In Stern's opinion, Lukács's views deserve close scrutiny "primarily for the questions he raised concerning the formative principles that are at the foundations of literary artworks.'' Stern analyzes Lukács's classic essay ''Narrate or Describe?'' (1936) and demonstrates that Lukács's distinction between narration and description is fully vindicated in the context of writing on history. What Lukács had to say about narration applies more to historiography than to literature. Stern is a severe critic of Lukács's (Leninist) theory of reflection of the 1930s, which of course set severe limits on his approach to the arts and literature. As has been shown by other studies, Lukács, as an exile from Hitler's Germany to Stalin's Russia, took up this position in order to be able to publish—or simply, to survive; under more benign circumstances, Lukács developed a more sophisticated notion of reflection. In his magnum opus, *Aesthetics* (1963), he differentiated between three forms of reflection of reality: reflection in everyday life, reflection in science, and reflection in art.

Ehrhard Bahr, German-American literary scholar, demonstrates the continuity of Goethe's role for Lukács and its influence on his work. He addresses himself to the problem of how Goethe served as the model for Lukács's literary theories—a role that constitutes a continuity in the lifework of Lukács. Goethe's influence reached from Lukács's youthful work *Soul and Form* through a series of essays written much later in the Stalinist Soviet Union, up to his late *Aesthetics*. Here Lukács's aim was twofold: ''to mobilize the traditions of the Enlightenment and humanism against the heritage of fascism'' on the one hand, and to influence ''the democratic renovation of contemporary culture'' on the other. From a strictly (literary) theoretical perspective, Lukács's option for Goethe coincided with his preference for ''closed'' works of art of classicism as opposed to ''open'' works of art of modernism or the avant-garde.

Robert Lilienfeld, sociologist, musicologist, and philosopher, makes a unique contribution to our understanding of the relationship between music and society in the twentieth century, as he compares the ''sociology of music'' of Lukács, Adorno, and Ernst Bloch—a comparison never before made. First, he gives a brief sketch of the sociology of music in the nineteenth and twentieth centuries, and moves on to the discussion of his three subjects. Lilienfeld's exposition of the sociology of music of Lukács, who was admittedly musically untrained yet sensitive to basic problematics, is truly original. He concludes that Lukács's sociology of music is ''broadly aesthetic, historical, and philosophical.'' His analysis of Bloch's theories regarding music is equally innovative. Lilienfeld's summary states that Bloch's writings on music deserve close study but will be difficult, as his essays are not systematic or logical but poetic and profound. He acknowledges that of his three subjects, Adorno was the most highly trained musically. He lists as major features of Adorno's musical sociology (1) his rejection of the dominance of the culture industry, which transformed music into a commodity; (2) his rejection of a sociology of music that took the form of market research; and (3) his embracing of the twelve-tone system of Schoenberg and his alliance with certain forms of the avant-garde. In addition, Lilienfeld points to Adorno's misjudgment of Bartók, whose work was more correctly perceived by Bartók's countryman Georg Lukács.

Judith Marcus, literary scholar, sociologist, and historian of ideas, investigates the complex and intricate process of reciprocal interaction between Thomas Mann, the bourgeois creative artist, and Georg Lukács, the Marxist philosopher and literary critic—an interaction that began before Lukács's conversion to Marxism and continued throughout their long and productive intellectual careers, which included two personal encounters. Marcus traces the genesis of Mann's "grand novel of ideas," *The Magic Mountain* (1924), and examines in some detail how Lukács's intellectual personality contributed to Mann's portrayal of Leo Naphta, the Jewish-Jesuit-Communist character of his novel.

In part 3, the political scientist and cultural critic Marshall Berman begins his essay with a lively story of how he, as a young student, "encountered" Georg Lukács in Manhattan's Washington Square Park in the late 1960s. He then moves on to discuss Lukács's reification theory and its redeeming message for the generation of Berman, who perceived Lukács as a "great modernist." Yet Lukács's indictment of the ideology of modernist writers served to temper his enthusiasm greatly. Berman assesses the greatness as well as the shortcomings of Lukács, whom he sees as one of the great messianic figures of modern times.

The Hungarian academician Ferenc Tökei tackles the complex issue of Lukács's "Hungarian roots" and ties with Hungarian culture. With heavy reliance on Lukács's autobiographical sketches and on his own many talks with Lukács, Tökei discusses two aspects of Lukács's relation to Hungary and Hungarian culture: the early and lasting impact of the revolutionary twentieth-century poet Endre Ady, and Lukács's mediating role between the two antagonistic groups of Hungarian literary life, the "urban" (Jewish) writers of Budapest, and the "populist" writers originally from the countryside. Both groups opposed and criticized the existing social and political conditions of pre-World War II Hungary, but envisioned different ways out of the backward conditions. The "urbanists" opted for Western-style liberal-bourgeois development, while the populists envisioned a national regeneration based on the peasantry, the majority of the country's population. (The case is somewhat analogous to the Russian case, Westernizers versus Narodniks. Albeit with a different content, the oppositional grouping has been revived in the cultural life of Hungary in the 1960s.)

Lee Congdon, historian, traces the development of Lukács's political theory and praxis from the messianic utopianism of *History and Class Consciousness*, inspired by the post–World War I revolutions, to his "romantic realism" of the late 1920s after the ebb of the revolutionary wave, as present in two theoretical masterpieces, the essays on Ferdinand Lassalle and Moses Hess. Congdon emphasizes Lukács's "sense for continuity and tradition"—so highly praised by Thomas Mann—that applies to both politics and culture. What Congdon has in mind is Lukács's idea of reaching back to the progressive bourgeois traditions of the nineteenth century, such as the 1848 Hungarian revolution, as the "only soil in which the new, proletarian culture could be nurtured and grow." He convincingly argues that Lukács's famous Blum Theses must be studied in connection with the literary theory that Lukács was working out in the late 1920s.

In his essay, the young Hungarian political philosopher József Bayer argues for the continuity of Lukács's thought. He outlines Lukács's idea that in our age the strategy of the fight for progress may not necessarily be linked directly with the problem of the alternative of capitalism versus socialism, but may relate to other problems or alternatives, such as the question of fascism and antifascism as in the 1930s and 1940s, or the attitude toward war and peace, that is, the issue of coexistence today. Bayer elaborates on Lukács's constant search for a *tertium datur* that would replace false extremes in both theory and praxis, such as socialist democracy between Stalinism and manipulative bourgeois society. Bayer pulls together from Lukács's scattered writings and numerous interviews the unifying theme of his later political philosophy, the imperative for the struggle for socialist democracy in the socialist countries.

The French sociologist Michael Löwy believes that the notion of romantic anticapitalism is the key to understanding the young Lukács, as well as to his development from bourgeois aesthete to Marxist theorist and activist. He then meticulously traces Lukács's stance on romantic anticapitalism with regard to its leading representatives in Western, particularly German, thought as well as regards Dostoevsky and Tolstoy; Lukács's shifting attitude is characterized as a "tormented and contradictory path" and a "mystery." Löwy finds Lukács's continuously oscillating position comparable to that of Hans Castorp, the hero of Lukács's favorite novel, *The Magic Mountain,* who was torn between two oppositional forces, Enlightenment (Settembrini) and messianism (Naphta).

The Italian critical sociologist Franco Ferrarotti visited Lukács in Budapest in 1970 and had a three-hour conversation with him on topics ranging from sociology to science and politics. The appendix offers this exhange (edited) because it can be considered an important document: it brings us closer to the working of the mind of one of the remarkable thinkers of the century. It matters little here whether one can accept all or most of Lukács's arguments; his dogmatic antisociologism is certainly an objectionable position. Lukács elaborates in detail on the need for a general (critical-Marxist) theory for the understanding and interpretation of capitalist, socialist, and non-Western societies, as well as on the imperative of the primacy of this theory before praxis, and that of strategy before tactics.

Lukács's talk with Ferrarotti was one of the last interviews he was permitted to give on account of his rapidly deteriorating health. His very last conversation took place on May 7, 1971, one month before his death of lung cancer, with the editors of his centenary volume, Judith Marcus and Zoltán Tarr. On this occasion very little was said about Marx, theory, or politics—it was mainly devoted to Lukács's lifelong fascination with, respect for, and admiration of Thomas Mann's artistry.[9]

Notes

1. For Lukács's account of this incident, see *Georg Lukács: Record of a Life: An Autobiographical Sketch*, ed. István Eörsi, trans. Rodney Livingstone (London: Verso, 1983), pp. 81–84.
2. Ibid., p. 86.
3. Ibid., p. 98.
4. Ibid., p. 168.
5. See György Lukács, *Esztétikai kultura* (Aesthetic Culture) (Budapest: Athenaeum, 1913), p. 28.
6. See George Steiner, "Making a Homeland for the Mind," *Times Literary Supplement* (January 22, 1982), p. 68. Steiner writes, "Though bitterly attacked for its partisan crudity, *Die Zerstörung der Vernunft* still strikes me as a challenging indictment. Lukács asks: what are the affinities between the continuities from German Idealist and post-Idealist metaphysics and psychology (Schopenhauer, Nietzsche) and the barbarism which ensued? The tone in which he poses the question is, too often, one of vulgar simplification and philippic. The question, however, is fundamental."
7. See Victor Serge, *Memoirs of a Revolutionary* (Oxford: Oxford University, 1963), pp. 161–162.
8. Lukács, *Record of a Life*, p. 81.
9. Judith Marcus, *Georg Lukács and Thomas Mann* (Amherst: The University of Massachusetts Press, 1987).

Generations

*You did see the forest for the trees, and now in
    your old age
You also see the trees for the forest, but without
    terror,
Growing taller as you move away among stumps
    and logs.*

*Old age is nothing enviable, but we envy you
    nonetheless,
For we, too, grow old, but do not become
    contemporaries of time;
Cannot mould flesh on the skeleton of ideas—
While you, from under the shadow of a winter
    tree,
Behold both fruit and foliage naturally.*
        István Eörsi *Translated by William Jay Smith*

Part I
THEORY AND INTELLECTUAL LINKAGES

1

Class Consciousness and the World-Historical Future: Some Critical Comments on Lukács's "Will to the Future"

By George L. Kline

In 1923, when he published *History and Class Consciousness*, Lukács had read and pondered every word of Marx's that had then seen the light of print. He was both adroit and resourceful in finding the most appropriate Marxian text to support the point he was making at any given moment. And he had a better understanding of the thought of Kant, Fichte, and Hegel than any other twentieth-century Marxist with whose work I am familiar.

At the same time, despite the impressive erudition and the marked theoretical power of *History and Class Consciousness* and other works of the 1920s, Lukács's theoretical position is beset by a number of tensions and contradictions.

I

First, there is what I would call the tension between the "Hegelian" and "scientistic" strands in Lukács's thought.[1] Lukács was one of the first theorists to attempt to waken Marxists from the "Hegel-amnesia" or forgetfulness of Hegel and the "dialectical principle," as Karl Korsch had called it.[2] This forgetfulness had been induced by Engels but was continued, and deepened, in different ways by Eduard Bernstein, Karl Kautsky, and the Lenin of 1909 (of whom more below).

The "Hegelian" strand is expressed in a series of concepts, among them:

(1) Consciousness (*Bewusstsein*), self-consciousness (*Selbstbewusstsein*), and a series of related concepts—which take their origin from Kant and Fichte

as much as from Hegel himself: activity, creativity, purposefulness, freedom. But Lukács's central concept of "objective, imputed class consciousness" (*objektives, zugerechnetes Klassenbewusstsein*), which stems from Lenin rather than either Hegel or Marx, involves a deliberate neglect of the "merely empirical" consciousness (as Lukács scornfully calls it) of particular factory workers: their feelings, wishes, attitudes, and values. (Cf. *HCC* 493/325.) Lukács explicitly denies that the Communist party should display an "unconditional willingness to implement the momentary desires of the masses," asserting that "it is sometimes forced to adopt a stance opposed to that of the masses" (*HCC* 498/328–29).

As a recent commentator aptly puts it, "Proletarian class consciousness in the *subjunctive mood* serves as a substitute for Hegel's notion of the cunning of reason. If the proletariat *were* fully aware of its role, it *would* become the subject of history."[3]

Sometimes Lukács appears to "out-Hegel Hegel"—he himself uses the expression *Überhegeln Hegels* in his self-critical 1967 preface to *History and Class Consciousness* (*HCC* 25/xxiii)—by treating proletarian class consciousness as a kind of supraindividual class self.[4] Thus, he speaks of the "becoming conscious of proletarian class consciousness" (*Bewusstwerden des proletarischen Klassenbewusstseins*), an expression that makes sense, though sense of a mythological kind, only when interpreted to mean the "becoming conscious of the (collective) proletarian class *self.*" This in turn looks suspiciously like a hypostatization, even a reification (*Verdinglichung*) of proletarian class consciousness, something that Lukács, a sworn enemy of all "bourgeois" reification, would presumably be committed to avoiding at all costs.

I shall return briefly to this question in section V, in connection with my scrutiny of Lukács's account of the "world-historical" role of the Communist party and its leadership.

(2) Lukács's distinctive notion of the "identical subject-object" that is realizing itself in the historical process (*das im Geschichtsprozess sich realisierende identische Subjekt-Objekt*) (*HCC* 24/xii [from the 1967 preface]) is, strictly speaking, more Fichtean than Hegelian: "self-creation" of and by the "proletarian class self" is identified with "world-transformation" where, of course, the "world" in question is social and historical rather than natural.[5]

As Lukács puts it in a key passage, "Only when the consciousness of the proletariat is in a position to point out the step to which the dialectic of [historical] development objectively compels it, . . . will the consciousness of the proletariat grow into a consciousness of the [historical] process itself, and only then will the proletariat appear as the identical subject-object of history whose praxis will change [historical] reality" (*HCC* 339/197; translation revised).[6]

This posited, or projected, subject-object identity is intended, in a broadly "Hegelian," or at least post-Kantian, way, to overcome the (nondialectical) epistemological and ontological dualism that, in the Marxist tradition, springs mainly from the later writings of Engels, especially *Ludwig Feuerbach and the Outcome of Classical German Philosophy* (1888) and the *Anti-Dühring* (periodical publication 1877; first book publication 1878). Engels's position is in fact much closer to that of Locke than to that of either Hegel or the young Marx. It involves a primitive copy theory of knowledge, and equally primitive materialist ontology, and a clumsy generalization of the dialectic from human history to the whole of nature. All three of these points were notoriously taken up and dogmatically defended by Lenin in *Materialism and Empiriocriticism* (1909).

Difficult as it is for us to imagine a time when Lenin's book had not yet become a household item, translated into all the world's tongues from Armenian to Yakut—there was such a time, and in fact it lasted for eighteen years: from 1909 until 1927. In the latter year the first translation into a foreign language appeared: the German version in Lenin's *Sämtliche Werke*, volume 13, published in Vienna.[7] Thus, as of 1923, when he published *History and Class Consciousness*, Lukács remained in blissful ignorance of the painful fact that his political and ideological hero, the leader and thinker whom he viewed as infallible in both theory and practice, had accepted and defended precisely those naive and undialectical positions in epistemology and ontology that Lukács himself impatiently (and quite justifiably, from his "Hegelian-Marxist" point of view) rejected when he encountered them in the works of Engels. However, the bliss was short lived. As soon as he read *Materialism and Empiriocriticism* in the 1927 German translation, Lukács made a 180-degree doctrinal shift in both epistemology and ontology. But that melancholy story must be reserved for another occasion.

(3) A related Hegelian term is "concrete totality" (*konkrete Totalität*), where Lukács uses the much abused adjective "concrete" in Hegel's speculative sense, to mean "many-sided, fully related, complexly mediated."[8] Even more explicitly and clearly than for Hegel himself, "totality" for Lukács—as Lucien Goldmann has emphasized—means a "process of totalization." The stress on process is Hegelian enough, but Lukács's use of this concept—with its powerful orientation toward the world-historical future—is wholly contrary to the spirit of Hegel's philosophy. (See section IV below.)

In any case, Lukács leaves no doubt as to the centrality of the category of totality (or totalization) in his philosophy of history. He insists that historical reality (*Wirklichkeit*) "can only be understood [*erfasst*] and penetrated as a [concrete] totality, and only a subject which is itself [such a] totality [viz., the collective proletarian self] is capable of this penetration" (*HCC* 111/39).

(4) Although it was Hegel who introduced, or at least made philosophically

current, the notion of historical transition (*Übergang/Übergehen*) and of "transitional periods" or "times of transition" (*Übergangsperiode, Übergangszeit[en]*), Hegel was always scrupulously careful to locate such transitions in the historical past. For example, the end of the fifth century B.C., according to Hegel, was a time of transition in Athens; Socrates was a transitional—and tragic—figure. In sharpest contrast, Lukács follows Marx in locating the historical transitions and periods of transitions with which his works are crowded between the historical present and the historical future.[9]

II

Yet there is in this, Lukács's most "Hegelian" work, a countervailing "Engelsian" strand, both reductionist and "scientistic." As we have seen, traces of this have penetrated even into his most Hegelian terms and concepts. In at least three respects Lukács attaches himself unapologetically to the Marxist tradition that springs from Engels and runs through Dietzgen and Plekhanov to (relatively early) Lenin.

First, although Lukács makes it abundantly clear that he is aware of the sharp doctrinal differences that separate Marx from Engels on such questions as the universalization of the dialectic and the cognitive grasp of the *Ding an sich* through technology and industry, he nevertheless speaks repeatedly of the position of "Marx *and* Engels." He thus takes a long step on that fateful path that, in the late 1920s, became a King's Highway (or rather, a Commissar's Freeway!), institutionalizing the fusion of Marx and Engels into a single hyphenated author-authority.

Second, in a related terminological move, Lukács frequently refers to Marx's own philosophical position as "dialectical materialism" and more than once implies that Marx himself used this expression to characterize his own position.[10] Of course, Marx did no such thing; the expression "dialectical materialism" (*der dialektische Materialismus*) was first used by Joseph Dietzgen four years after Marx's death.[11] This is more than a matter of careless terminology; anyone who calls Marx's position "dialectical materialism" is tacitly equating it with that of Engels. This in turn amounts to tacitly attributing to Marx the three-pronged Engelsian doctrine: the copy theory of knowledge, a materialist ontology, and the universalized dialectic ("of nature," as Engels would have it). Yet it is a matter of record that neither Marx nor the Lukács of 1923 accepted any of these three positions.

Lukács's unfortunate usage cannot, as of 1923, be blamed on the sad example of Lenin. As we have just seen, Lukács was, during the entire period in which *History and Class Consciousness* was being written, in the enviable position of not yet having read *Materialism and Empiriocriticism*, the work in which Lenin stated flatly, and quite falsely, that both Marx and Engels "scores of times" referred to their (allegedly common) philosophical position as "dialectical materialism."[12] In fact, neither Marx nor Engels ever used that expression, although it was indeed Engels who laid the doctrinal foundation for what Dietzgen, Plekhanov, Lenin, and later Soviet-Marxist-Leninists came standardly to refer to as "dialectical materialism."

Third, somewhat less serious, but still terminologically and conceptually misleading, is Lukács's repeated use of the expression "historical materialism" to characterize Marx's own "unadulterated" and "unfalsified" method of historical investigation and explanation (cf. e.g. *HCC* 103/33). In fact, Marx himself did not use this expression either; it was introduced by Engels nine years after Marx's death.[13] To be sure, Marx did use the expression *die materialistische Geschichtsauffassung* ("the materialist conception of history"), and Engels considered this a synonym for "historical materialism." Perhaps, in a sense, it is; but such "materialism" does not—as Engels claimed—have anything to do with a materialist ontology ("philosophical materialism"). In the expression *die materialistische Geschichtsauffassung* the term *materialistische* means simply "economic," not "physical" or "spatio-temporal." Such "materialism" has nothing whatever to do with "matter in motion" or "atoms in the void."[14]

It must be said that Lukács is dismayingly lax when it comes to distinguishing the various distinct senses of the term *materiell* as used by Marx. Elsewhere I have distinguished seven of them.[15] The details are not appropriate in the present discussion, but I wish to stress that, *pace* Marx, Engels, Lenin, and most Marxists, emphatically including Lukács, there is nothing peculiarly "material" in the sense relevant to a materialist ontology about the forces and relations of economic production.

III

Although the terminology and rhetoric of heresy hunting is not unique to Engels—there is a fair amount of it in Marx and an overabundance in Lenin—it belongs, in my judgment, on the anti-Hegelian side of the tension that I have been attempting to adumbrate. Following the Lenin of the political pamphlets, Lukács makes copious use of such terms as "revisionist," "opportunist," and "renegade" in strongly pejorative senses.[16]

But all independent philosophical thought involves "revision" in the double sense of critical scrutiny and doctrinal modification of received theoretical positions. Engels and Lenin were revisionists of Marx; indeed their revisionism merged into eclecticism and even syncretism. That is, they attempted to combine incompatible elements: on the one hand, a materialist ontology and copy theory of knowledge; on the other, Marx's Fichtean stress on activity and self-creativity and his Hegelian stress on the central role of consciousness and self-consciousness in social praxis.

It seems tolerably clear that what Lukács really objects to is not revisionism as such but "revisionism from below."[17] He has no objection to "revisionism from above," namely, that which is initiated by what he likes to call the "classics [i.e., classical authors] of Marxism-Leninism." With respect to political rather than philosophical revisionism, Lukács made this point crisply and without qualification in 1963:

> Khrushchev's 1956 speech breaks with Lenin's thesis, now overtaken [and made obsolete] [*überholt*] by history, that world war is inevitable as sharply as Lenin in his time had broken with Marx's thesis that proletarian revolutions can start only in developed countries and can succeed only on an international scale.[18]

In other words, Khrushchev was justified in "revising" Lenin's doctrine of the inevitability of world war, just as Lenin was justified in revising Marx's doctrine of worldwide proletarian revolution and substituting the doctrine of "socialism in one country." The alert reader will have noticed that in this essay, published at the summit of Khrushchev's power, Lukács is an orthodox Khrushchevian in two respects: first, in endorsing Khrushchev's "revision" of Lenin's doctrine concerning the inevitability of world war, and second, in following Khrushchev's lead in falsely attributing to Lenin the doctrine of "socialism in one country." That was the Stalinist doctrine, as both Khrushchev and Lukács well knew, and it was forged in the face of bitter resistance from such good Leninists as Leon Trotsky. Indeed, in his pre-Stalinist period, Lukács made it clear that Lenin was an orthodox, not a revisionist, Marxist on this point, holding that the "revolution can only be victorious *on a world scale*" and "it is only as a *world proletariat* that the working class can truly become a class."[19]

IV

But what is the most un-Hegelian, theoretically problematic, and politically dangerous about Lukács' position—although it is entirely in the spirit of Marx—is his powerful orientation toward the world-historical future, his "will to the future." This is a complete reversal of Hegel's position. The task of the speculative philosopher of history, according to Hegel, is to discern and exhibit the rational, "dialectical" pattern of past historical development, that development which has brought world history to this present (the "rose in the cross" of the present), and not to predict, or to advocate, how the historical future will or should develop.[20] Lukács joins Marx in heaping scorn on Hegel's *post festum* ("after-the-party-is-over") historical consciousness.[21] And in two specific respects he joins Marx in "standing Hegel on his head":

First, as I have already indicated, Lukács shares Hegel's fascination with transitions and times of transition, but reverses Hegel's treatment, shifting such transitions from the historical past to the historical future.

Second, like Marx, but rather more explicitly, Lukács treats the future as actual, knowable, determinate, and structured. In a word, he follows Marx in committing what I have elsewhere called "the fallacy of the actual future."[22] Like Marx, he holds that his projected historical future is in some queer sense "already there"—that, in effect, future communities, cultures, practices, and especially, persons are (in a tenseless sense of "are") just as actual (*wirklich*), determinate, and valuable as present communities, cultures, practices, and, especially, persons. Indeed, in an important sense, those future entities are (again, tenseless "are") significantly more valuable than their present counterparts in the alienated, reified, commodity-ridden historical present, because they will have been perfected and purged of the failings, distortions, and weaknesses that plague everything in this historical present.

Moreover, Lukács goes on—again quite in the spirit of Marx—to commit, in effect, the related "fallacy of deferred, or historically displaced, value." That is, he defers all positive social, political, personal value to an "actual future"—hundreds or even thousands of years hence—and correspondingly devalues and instrumentalizes present communities, cultures, practices, and—especially—persons. This position has two unacceptable corollaries: (1) the claim—which Lukács had made publicly—that "the worst socialist state is better than the best capitalist state"; and (2) that present, actual, living individuals may justifiably be instrumentalized, sacrificed for the sake of the future, merely possible, individuals.

Echoing Marx, Lukács expresses hatred and contempt for the historical present (*HCC* 8/xi), a present mutilated and dehumanized by the system of capitalist production and exchange. Echoing Nietzsche, who preached the "overcoming of [present] mankind," Lukács preaches the "overcoming of the [historical] present" (*das Überwinden der Gegenwart*) (*HCC* 481/316). With respect to the specific question of freedom and its attainment, he declares bluntly,

In order to achieve the social preconditions necessary for real freedom battles must be fought in the course of which present-day society will disappear [or "go under"], *together with the race of men it has produced.*

"The present generation," says Marx, "resembles the Jews whom Moses led through the wilderness. It must not only conquer a new world, *it must also perish* in order to make room for people who will be equal to a new world (*einer neuen Welt gewachsen sind*)." For the "freedom" of the men who are alive now (*die "Freiheit" des gegenwärtig lebenden Menschen*) is the freedom of the individual isolated by the fact of property which both reifies and is itself reified (*den verdinglichten und verdinglichenden Besitz*). . . . . To wish to breathe life into this [present, abstract, mutilated] freedom means in practice the renunciation of real [i.e., future, socialist] freedom. (*HCC* 479–80/315; italics added)

Much of what Lukács has to say about the actuality and knowability of the future is contained in a 1926 article in which August von Cieszkovsky and Moses Hess are set in opposition to Hegel and in (partial) parallel to Fichte. Since much of the article is expository, it is not always easy to discern precisely what Lukács's own position on a given question is. However, I take him to be making all of the following claims:

The historical future is "there" as an "object of dialectical thought," which can be "grasped concretely." As "knowable," the future is the "concrete intentional object of the philosophy of history." The future is "an epoch which is just as concrete [i.e., determinate and actual] as the epochs of the past."[23] But it seems unlikely that Lukács would claim that we can, in the present, discern or construct the "narrative of the future."[24] At least, such a claim would fall of its own weight.

For Lukács, "objectivity must . . . be comprehensible as a constant factor mediating between past and future"; and the "series of mediations" must be a "movement of mediations advancing from the present to the future" (*HCC* 282/159; 311/179). In his book on Lenin he singled out for praise Lenin's "relationship to the present whole and to the question of development central for the *future*—to *the future in its practical and tangible totality [in ihrer praktisch-ergreifbaren Ganzheit]*."[25]

"Becoming [*das Werden*]," Lukács insists, "is . . . the mediation between past and future. But it is the mediation between the concrete, i.e., historical past and the *equally concrete*, i.e., *historical future*" (*HCC* 348/203; italics added). This bizarre claim appears to be a consequence of Lukács's attachment to the notion of "concrete totality": if world history is to be grasped as a totality, all of it must be included—not just the past and present, but, especially, the future, in which the transition to socialism and communism will have been completed.

> Man must be able [Lukács continues] to comprehend the present as a becoming. He can do this by seeing in it the tendencies out of whose dialectical opposition he can *make* the future. Only when he does this will the present be a process of becoming that belongs to *him*. Only he who is willing and whose mission it is to create the future can see the present in its concrete truth (*Nur wer die Zukunft herbeizuführen berufen und gewillt ist, kann die konkrete Wahrheit der Gegenwart sehen*). (*HCC* 348/204)

The joint stress that Lukács places upon transition, totality, totalization, and the world-historical future, together with his contempt and hatred for the historical present, opens the Marxist door to the theory and practice of what I have elsewhere called "transitional totalitarianism." It is no accident that

Lukács in 1923 defended Trotsky's defense of Bolshevik terror against the probing and, to my mind, convincing objections of both Karl Kautsky and Rosa Luxemburg. And by the 1930s and 1940s Lukács was extending his full intellectual and (so far as one can judge by the available evidence) emotional embrace to the "transitional terrors" of high Stalinism.

For Lukács the "creation of the world-historical future" is not a spontaneous or undirected process; it is closely and powerfully guided by the leadership of the Communist party.

It is noteworthy that, in his detailed discussions of both the Russian and Hungarian parties, and in particular of Lenin, Lukács the ironist, the acerb critic of the bourgeois present, reveals not the least trace of irony, not the least hint of criticism. One might detect a kind of meta-irony in the fact that in his pre-Marxist days Lukács had written knowledgeably and sensitively about those two master ironists, Søren Kierkegaard and Thomas Mann.

Conclusion

As we have already seen (section I and n.4), Lukács characterizes the Communist party as "a conscious collective will" (*HCC* 480/315). The essence of that party is defined in grandiose terms as the "concrete principle of mediation between man and history" (*HCC* 488/321; cf. also 484/318). It inspires and directs the proletariat (sometimes, as we have seen, opposing the masses' "wishes of the moment") in carrying out the latter's "world-historical mission" (*weltgeschichtliche Sendung*) (*HCC* 493/325). Echoing the interpretation, suggested above, that proletarian class consciousness is a kind of collective class self, Lukács insists that party members must "enter with their whole personalities into a living relationship with the whole of life of the party" (*mit ihrer Gesamtpersönlichkeit in eine lebendige Beziehung zu der Totalität des Parteilebens*) (*HCC* 508/336).

It is in his treatment of the Russian Communist party and Lenin, its "world-historical leader," that Lukács lapses most obviously and painfully into the "conceptual mythology" (*Begriffsmythologie*) of which, in another connection, he had accused Hegel.

Notes

1. I do not disagree with Kilminster's claim that, for Lukács, in the period before World War I, "scientism and irrationalism formed the twin horns of an intellectual dilemma, the solution to which he sought in a new totalizing perspective with the aid of the philosophy of Hegel." See Richard Kilminster, *Praxis and Method: A Sociological Dialogue with Lukács, Gramsci and the Early Frankfurt School* (London: Routledge & Kegan Paul, 1979), p. 29. But I see the Marxist Lukács of the interwar period as wavering between this "totalizing [Hegelian] perspective" and a position that, on key points, is strikingly close to scientism.

2. Korsch's terms are *Vergessen* and *Vergessenheit*. See Karl Korsch, *Marxismus und Philosophie* (periodical publication 1923; book publication 1924), 2d ed. (Leipzig: Hirschfeld, 1930), pp. 54–55. Cf. Lukács's own comments in the course of his severe 1967 critique of *History and Class Consciousness*: "The revival of Hegel's dialectics struck a hard blow at the revisionist tradition. Already [Eduard] Bernstein had wished to eliminate everything reminiscent of Hegel's dialectics in the name of 'science' [*Wissenschaftlichkeit*]. And nothing was further from the mind of his philosophical opponents, and above all Kautsky, than the wish to undertake the defence of this [Hegelian] tradition'' (*HCC* 21/xxi). In this and subsequent references in the body of this paper, *HCC* will stand for *History and Class Consciousness*; the first page number will refer to the German edition (*Geschichte und Klassenbewusstsein* (Neuwied and Berlin: Luchterhand, 1970) and the second page number, following a slash, to the English translation by Rodney Livingstone (Cambridge, MA: MIT, 1971).

3. Laurent Stern, "On the Frankfurt School," *History of European Ideas* 4(1983): 87ff. Italics added. In this connection Stern goes on to quote Connerton, who had written that, for the present and the indefinitely extensible future, "the party undertakes the administration of [the proletariat's] class consciousness, [thus] guaranteeing that identity of the subject of History with itself which does not yet empirically exist." Paul Connerton, *The Tragedy of Enlightenment* (New York: Cambridge University, 1980), p. 118.

4. Lukács appears to extend this hypostatization to the Communist party, defined as "a conscious collective will" (*ein bewusster Gesamtwille*) (*HCC* 480/315) when he refers to individual party members as the "members of a collective will" (*Glieder eines Gesamtwillens*) (*HCC* 511/337). The use of *Glied*, rather than the more usual *Mitglied*, for "member" (of an organization) strongly suggests that the relation of party member to party is like that of organ to organism, or perhaps of microcosmic self to macrocosmic self.

5. Lukács follows Marx uncritically in treating the Hegelian idea as a "disembodied spirit-object" standing over against the (social and historical) world. In fact, as another commentator has emphasized, "The very core of Hegel's mediations, the pith and marrow of his whole philosophy, is that it is embodied in and articulates the self-changing [social] world in its historical development" (Kilminster, *Praxis and Method*, p. 57). The same author pointedly adds that Hegel rarely speaks of "subject-object," but often of subjectivity and objectivity, and characteristically of the reconciling of substance and subject (ibid., pp. 61–62). Hegel "certainly never . . . tried to search for the identical subject-object in history. It was not an issue for him" (p. 64).

6. Livingstone's version of this passage is surprisingly inaccurate: he appears to have mistaken the verb *erwächst* (grows or develops) for *erweckt* (wakens), and thus renders the expression *erwächst das Bewusstsein des proletariats zum Bewusstsein des Prozesses selbst* as "will the consciousness of the proletariat *awaken* to a consciousness of the process" (italics added).

7. The editors of this edition express their intense regret that this important work has hitherto remained unknown outside Russia, together with their satisfaction that its appearance in German will now make it available for the first time to Western European readers. Here is the opening paragraph of the *Vorwort zur deutschen Ausgabe*: "Das vorliegende Buch W.I. Lenins bildet einen ausserordentlich wertvollen Beitrag zur Geschichte der philosophischen Begründung des russischen Marxismus und Leninismus. Es ist aufs lebhafteste zu bedauern, dass diese Arbeit Lenins ausserhalb Russlands bisher unbekannt geblieben ist. Allein

besser spät als nie. Lenins 'Materialismus und Empiriokritizismus' erscheint nun in deutscher Sprache und wird dadurch auch den westeuropäischen Lesern zugänglich gemacht.'' See Lenin, *Sämtliche Werke* (Vienna: Verlag für Literatur und Politik, 1927), 13:ix.

8. However, even here Lukács is inconsistent, repeatedly using "concrete" in the quite un-Hegelian "ordinary" sense of "particular" or "down-to-earth" in such expressions as "concrete situation" and "concrete analysis." Confusingly, in a number of passages both the Hegelian and the un-Hegelian senses appear. "Concrete" in the "ordinary" non-Hegelian sense appears, e.g., at *HCC* 55/xlvi, 189/97, 194/100, 200/104, 225/121, 231/125, 245/134, 264/146, 269/150, 305/175, 309/178, 310/179, 331/192. This careless usage continues in Lukács's book on Lenin. Cf. *Lenin: A Study on the Unity of His Thought* (1924), trans. by Nicholas Jacobs (London: NLB, 1970), e.g., pp. 79, 83, 84, 85, 88.

9. References to transitions or periods of transition occur at *HCC* 9/xi, 33/xxix, 61/3, 381/240, 389/246, 390/246, 393/249, 399/253, 427/276, 467/306, 475/312, 476/313, 509/336. During our conversations in Budapest (in 1960, 1964, and 1967) I was struck by the number of times Lukács referred to the 1960s as an *Übergangszeit* or *Übergangsperiode*.

10. By 1933 Lukács was referring flatly and unequivocally to *der dialektische Materialismus* as *die Lehre von Marx* (cf. "Mein Weg zur Marx," in *Schriften zur Ideologie und Politik: Werkauswahl*, vol. 2, selected and introd. Peter C. Ludz (Neuwied and Berlin: Luchterhand, 1967), p. 328.

11. Cf. Josepf Dietzgen, "Streifzüge eines Sozialisten in das Gebiet der Erkenntnistheorie," in *Schriften in drei Bänden* (East Berlin: Akademie, 1965), 3:61, 75, 79. The expression *dialektischer Materialismus* occurs on each of these pages; the expression *dialektischer Materialist* occurs on p. 62. This work, written in Chicago in 1886, was first published in Zurich in 1887. In a much better known work, Plekhanov, four years later, used the expression *dialektischer Materialismus*; cf. his "Zu Hegels sechzigstem Todestag," in *Die neue Zeit* (1891), English translation in G.V. Plekhanov, *Selected Philosophical Works in Five Volumes* (Moscow: 1961), 1:478, 741. However, Engels had come fairly close to using the expression a decade before Dietzgen, characterizing what he called *der moderne Materialismus* as *wesentlich dialektisch*; cf. *Anti Dühring* (periodical publication 1877; book publication 1878), in *Marx-Engels Werke* (hereafter *MEW*) (East Berlin), 20:24. It seems likely, though the evidence is only circumstantial, that Dietzgen's 1877 use of the expression *dialektischer Materialismus* was inspired by Engels's 1877 characterization of modern materialism as *wesentlich dialektisch*; and that Plekhanov in 1891 was (perhaps unconsciously) echoing the usage that he had found in Dietzgen (certainly not in either Marx or Engels) in 1887.

12. Lenin, *Materialism and Empiriocriticism* (New York: International, 1927), p. 9.

13. See the preface to the English translation (1892) of Engels's *Socialism, Utopian and Scientific* (Chicago: 1903), p. ix. German text in *MEW*, 22:292. In private correspondence Engels had used the expression *historischer Materialismus* at least as early as 1890; but that was still seven years after Marx's death. For his 1859 use of the expression *die materialistische Geschichtsauffassung* see *MEW*, 13:469.

14. For details see my essay, "The Myth of Marx's Materialism," *Annals of Scholarship* 3, 2(1984): 1–38, esp. 1–11.

15. See ibid., esp. pp. 3–4.

16. In this connection Lukács in 1945 even had recourse to the ugly Stalinist term

"liquidation," urging the Hungarian Communist party to liquidate "sectarianism" within the party in "Partköltészet" ("Party Poetry"). For German translation see Ludz, ed., *Schriften zur Ideologie und Politik*, p. 397.

17. See my article "Leszek Kolakowski and the Revision of Marxism," in *European Philosophy Today*, ed. G.L. Kline (Chicago: Quadrangle, 1965), esp. pp. 113–22.

18. Lukács, "Zur Debatte zwischen China und der Sowjetunion. Theoretisch-philosophische Bemerkungen" (periodical publication 1963), rpt. in *Schriften zur Ideologie und Politik*, p. 683.

19. Lukács, *Lenin*, p. 86; italics added. In fairness to Lukács we should note that in his 1963 article he attributed two distinct "revisions from above" to Lenin and that only one of them ("socialism in one country") was Stalin's. The other revisionist thesis—that proletarian revolutions can after all take place in underdeveloped countries like Russia in 1917—was indeed Lenin's own.

20. G.W.F. Hegel, *Philosophy of Right*, preface. In this connection it should be noted that Livingstone's readable and tolerably accurate translation of *History and Class Consciousness* is marred by a striking error in the rendering of a celebrated passage from this same preface (the "Owl of Minerva" passage), which Lukács quotes (*HCC* 138/59). Lukács obviously assumed that his readers would recognize the passage without a citation of chapter and verse. Equally obviously, Livingstone failed to recognize it; if he had, he would surely have used the perfectly adequate Knox translation. Instead, when Hegel describes the speculative philosopher of history as painting his *Grau in Grau*, Livingstone renders the expression quite arbitrarily and quite wrongly as "gloomy picture." In fact, as Hegel scholars well know, the first "gray" is the "gray-hairedness," that is, the old age, of a culture or *Gestalt des Lebens* that has passed its historical prime; the second "gray" is the gray of theory—an allusion to Goethe's celebrated line, "Grau, teurer Freund, ist alle Theorie."

21. In 1926 Lukács branded as "reactionary" Hegel's "Stehenbleiben . . . bei der Gegenwart als Sich-Selbst-Erreichthaben des Geistes," rpt. in *Schriften zur Ideologie und Politik*, p. 245. Italics added.

22. Cf. my articles "Was Marx an Ethical Humanist?" *Studies in Soviet Thought* 9(1969):91–103, and "Was Marx von Hegel hätte lernen können und sollen," in H.G. Gadamer, ed., *Stuttgarter Hegeltage 1970* (Hegel-Studien BeiHeft 11) (Bonn: Bouvier, 1974), pp. 497–502.

23. Lukács, "Moses Hess und die Probleme der idealistischen Dialektik" (periodical publication 1926), rpt. in *Schriften zur Ideologie und Politik*, pp. 243–44. English translation of this essay by Michael McColgan in *Tactics and Ethics: Political Essays 1919–1929*, ed. and introd. Rodney Livingstone (London: NLB, 1972), pp. 181–223.

24. Cf. János Kelemen, "*Philosophy of Science and Its Critique in Georg Lukács's History and Class Consciousness*," chapter 3 of this volume. The same author concludes, "Historical knowledge is knowledge *post festum* and . . . no fact will attain its final form until the end of history, that is, until the totality of history becomes actual. . . . The present is therefore always in need of the future dimension in order to provide the suitable context for knowing historical facts. . . . [T]his means that the totality in which we incorporate the partial phenomena of history is always virtual [that is, potential], not actual." The last point is a sensible revision of Lukács's position, but I doubt that Lukács himself would have accepted it.

25. Lukács, *Lenin*, p. 85; italics added.

2

Lukács and Marxist History of Philosophy

By Tom Rockmore

This paper concerns the Marxist character of Lukács's reading of the history of philosophy, with special attention to his interpretation of German idealism. Although his thought has been the topic of much discussion, and has attained almost the status of a cottage industry, culminating in the recent publication of Lukács bibliography,[1] at least in the West this aspect of his position has not received adequate attention. In fact, for various reasons, in part because of its unattractive character, Marxist history of philosophy in general has long languished since its creation by the *Urvater des Marxismus*, Friedrich Engels.

The unattractiveness of much Marxist history of philosophy is not due only to the fact that since its inception Marxists have in the main had little good to say about the philosophical tradition. Obviously, it is not necessary to be laudatory; nor is it requisite that one hold compatible opinions to be interesting. But that is not the problem. Rather, with rare exceptions, Marxists since Engels have seemed to know little about a rich intellectual tradition, which they have been mainly content to weigh in an abstract balance in order to find wanting. For the most part Marxists have appeared unconcerned to acquire more than a superficial acquaintance with a field that they already "know," through an a priori analysis sharply divergent from the Marxist stress on practice, to be intellectually bankrupt. Now it would be hasty to deny the conceptual ties that bind Lukács to orthodox Marxism, whose extent has often been incorrectly underestimated. Yet it is precisely from that perspective that we can best appreciate the specific character of his own reading of the history of philosophy, which differs from other forms of Marxism less in intent than in the detailed nature of his knowledge of the topic.

In view of the dimensions of Lukács's corpus, it will be wise to limit the present inquiry. The general interpretation of the history of philosophy is a continuing feature of Lukács's lengthy Marxist period in all its phases, beginning roughly with *History and Class Consciousness*. In the present context, I shall concentrate mainly on Lukács's approach to so-called classical German philosophy, his term for German idealism including Kant's position, as elaborated in *History and Class Consciousness*. But in my opinion it would be an error to regard Lukács's later writings as the source of a distinctly different perspective. Although there is indeed an important elaboration of the argument in his later thought in various ways, the basic Marxist insight remains unchanged. For Lukács never abandons, or even restricts, the view that Marx's thought is the truth of idealism, even if he finds different ways to make this argument. The points I shall raise in the discussion to follow will mainly concern the initial form of that argument. But to the extent that they count against it as such, and not its specific form, they are pertinent to Lukács's later thought as well.

I

In order to evaluate Lukács's particular approach to the history of philosophy, it will be convenient to relate it to other approaches, including other forms of Marxism. It is obvious that the concept of the history of philosophy is related to a concept of philosophy; it is equally obvious that there are many different views of the nature of philosophy as well as of its relation to history and to the history of philosophy.

In the nineteenth-century German philosophical tradition, there is a clear dispute about the relevance of the history of philosophy for philosophy. This dispute opposes Kant and Hegel. Kant's well-known distinction between a priori and a posteriori forms of knowledge clearly suggests that epistemology concerns the former only. In fact, he explicitly draws this inference in the *Critique of Pure Reason* at B 864 when he distinguishes between *cognitio ex datiis* and *cognitio ex principiis*. Certainly, the critical philosophy was intended by him as an example of the latter type, since the transcendental approach deals only with the conditions of the possibility of knowledge whatsoever in total abstraction from experience. Kant's negative attitude toward the relevance of historical considerations was widely influential in later thought. Two examples will suffice to make this point: Husserl's assertion of the need to start over again from the beginning, for although much has been attempted nothing has in fact been accomplished;[2] and Quine's reported distinction between those interested in the history of philosophy and those interested in philosophy.[3] Hegel, on the contrary, denied sharply that philosophy as such could successfully be isolated from its previous forms, upon which it must build and whose task it was to complete, however imperfectly it might be aware of its own past. A clear illustration of Hegel's view is found in Kant's position. Despite its systematic intent, the critical philosophy clearly presupposes as an integral part of the argument—as its existential reason, so to speak—interpretations of the positions of relevant predecessors.

The dependency of Marxism on Hegel is difficult to overestimate. In particular, Marxism shares with Hegel the belief that thought is inseparable from time, in fact is indivisibly related to the social context in which it appears. For Hegel, thought remains partially true because of its link to its historical moment; but for Marxism, which here follows Marx, it is because of that link, as analyzed in terms of the concept of ideology, that thought is false. The result is a difference in attitude toward the history of philosophy, which from both perspectives remains relevant. For Hegel, philosophy is concerned with the completion of an ongoing task within the philosophical tradition, through the elaboration of an allegedly highest form of philosophy that takes up in a single synthesis all that is of value in the preceding tradition. On the contrary, Marxism, at least on one prominent interpretation, is concerned to complete the philosophical task from an extraphilosophical perspective, that is, from a vantage point outside the philosophical tradition. On the latter view, philosophy is held to concern real problems, of which it is symptomatic, but that it is incapable of resolving, since philosophy itself is part of the problem. In short, for Hegel the correct theory that resolves the problems of philosophy differs from its predecessors merely in degree; for Marxism it must further differ in kind.

In Lukács's initial interpretation of classical German philosophy, the Marxist theory of philosophy presupposes as an integral element the Marxian view of ideology. Although not often noted, the concept of ideology has its roots in the philosophic tradition as early as the Greek view of nonbeing. In modern times this view was restated on the basis of presuppositions that hinder the subject's apprehension of the object. This analysis was initially formulated by Francis Bacon in his theory of the *idolae tribu*; it was later restated by the French sensualists and materialists. Marx's reformulation of the concept of ideology breaks significantly with the line of thought initiated by Bacon. According to Marx, the misapprehension of the object of knowledge is due not to the subject, but to the object's effect upon it. Marx's view of ideology can be said to rest upon a causal theory of perception. In simplest terms, the object, or social context, which is distorted with respect to the realization of human potential, causes a distorted apprehension of itself on the level of conscious thought.[4]

Since Lukács proposes a theory of consciousness with a clearly epistemological intent, it should be noted that Marx's view of ideology has an epistemological thrust. More precisely, it can be regarded as a contribution to what

Hegel understood as the traditional epistemological concern, present through-out the history of philosophy, to grasp the relation between thought and being. Marx's theory presupposes a distinction between the economic base and the cultural superstructure, in Hegelian terms the *Bildung*, from whose perspective society can be known. According to Marx, in a society whose economy is based on commodity exchange, awareness of that society is distorted in a manner that tends to support the existing state of affairs. From an epistemological perspective, this view can be expressed in terms of three related propositions: (1) being determines thought, not thought being; (2) distorted social being distorts thought about it, impeding its apprehension and resulting in false consciousness; and (3) thought can correctly grasp or know being.

The difficulty lies in the application of this perspective to the history of philosophy. Marx does not provide a detailed philosophy, and his own view of philosophy is at least ambiguous. His writings, especially the early "Critique of Hegel's Philosophy of Right: Introduction," can be read as suggesting that it is not philosophy as such, but a form of it, that is ideological; this way of interpreting his attitude leaves open the question of the relation of his own position to the philosophical tradition. On this interpretation, it is at least consistent to regard Marx's own position as a form of philosophy while noting that he rejects some types of philosophy as ideological. In practice, however, since Engels most commentators have tended to read Marx as rejecting all philosophy as such nonscientific ideology. This in turn suggests that his own view must be some form of nonphilosophical science, and hence external to the philosophic tradition, whose problems it resolves on an extraphilosophic plane.

The latter interpretation, which is widely favored in the Marxist tradition, has traditionally functioned as the basis for a Marxist reading of the history of philosophy. Engels's pioneer Marxist reading of philosophy as ideology, which in basic ways diverges from Marx's thought, presupposes both the Marxian concept and his own early defense of Hegel against Schelling, prior to his encounter with Marx. Engels's polemic with Schelling, which developed after his attendance of the latter's lectures in Berlin, resulted in a series of three articles. In the second article, "Schelling und die Offenbarung. Kritik des neuesten Reaktionsversuchs gegen die freie Philosophie" (March 1842), Engels maintained that philosophy must be monistic. Here he attempted through a simple reductio ad absurdum to refute Schelling's basic distinction between positive and negative forms of philosophy. He further argued, on this point following Hegel's students, notably Heine, that philosophy reaches a peak in Hegel's view, which brings to a close the Protestant approach to philosophy set in motion by Luther.[5]

This simplistic reading of Hegel's position as the highest and final form of philosophy was combined with the suggestion that as ideology philosophy must be superseded on the plane of science. Engels developed this suggestion in a series of writings. In *Anti Dühring*, he argued that Hegel brought philosophy to an end in his system, which has since been superseded by modern materialism; and he further argued that to Marx we owe the discovery of historical materialism, or the science of society. Engels later repeated this point in *Ludwig Feuerbach and the Outcome of Classical German Philosophy*. Here he maintained that historical materialism puts an end to philosophy in the realm of history. A similar point emerges from the posthumously published, incomplete *Philosophy of Nature*.

Within Marxism, Engels's approach to the history of philosophy is widely influential, but not universally followed. Despite its stress on orthodoxy, Marxism is in many ways pluralistic. Engels's reading of the history of philosophy is extreme. By equating philosophy with ideology, he denied any positive epistemological content to philosophy. This same point has recently been restated forcefully in the French discussion by Althusser.[6] But there are also weaker forms of orthodox Marxism that maintain the quasi-Hegelian claim for Hegel's thought as the peak of classical German philosophy and adopt a materialist perspective—which avoid a reductive approach to philosophy as mere ideology. An excellent example of a nonreductive form of orthodox Marxism is furnished by Manfred Buhr's recent survey of classical German thought.[7] Buhr's discussion is directed toward the clarification of the social-historical presuppositions of classical bourgeois philosophy. The basic assumption of this form of thought is that reason rules the world. According to Buhr, Marx's insight is not to move to an extraphilosophic plane, as Engels suggests and Lukács, following him, asserts. Rather, Marx's insight is to argue that history must be consciously made by man.

The difference between the two Marxist readings of the history of philosophy proposed by Engels and Buhr are as interesting as they are illustrative of the range of opinion found in orthodox Marxist circles. In simplest terms, Engels proposes an a priori, reductionist scheme, based on little knowledge of philosophy. According to Engels, philosophy must give way to historical materialism, which differs from it in kind. On the contrary, Buhr offers a nonreductionist, deeply informed reading of classical German philosophy. Rather than a demonstration of the ideological status of philosophy as such, Buhr is interested in eliciting the roots of the various positions in the social context and in arguing for the relative preeminence of the Marxist approach.

The range of Marxism from Engels to Buhr provides an appropriate framework for understanding Lukács's own reading of the history of philosophy. Lukács's approach to classical German thought combines elements characteristic of both Engels and Buhr. They include the former's reductionist concern to treat philosophy as a mere superstructural phenomenon and the latter's deep acquaintance with the entire range of German idealism. Despite Lukács's later, perhaps tactical, self-criticism for an alleged neglect of labor in *History and Class Consciousness*, he considered bourgeois philosophy there and elsewhere from the classical Marxist standpoint as a form of ideology, or at least as basically flawed by its bourgeois perspective. From this angle of vision, the conceptual impotence of bourgeois philosophy is due to the neglect, or at least incomplete appreciation, of the economic basis of capitalism. In this sense, Lukács follows classical Marxism and does not break new ground. But in another sense, Lukács's approach to classical German thought is highly original. Its outstanding trait, which distinguishes it from all other Marxist approaches with which I am familiar, is the informed concern to demonstrate through specific interpretation, as opposed to mere assertion, the truth of the Marxist claim that philosophy is ideology. In a word, although otherwise original, the main thrust of Lukács's interpretation of German idealism, especially in *History and Class Consciousness*, is to provide a demonstration of Engels's asserted, but unsubstantiated, view of philosophy.

II

At this point, some obvious objections to my reading of Lukács's approach to the history of philosophy can be considered. I have stressed the continuity between Lukács's approach, despite some important innovations, and classical Marxism, since I believe that an appreciation of this relation is crucial to comprehending Lukács's efforts in this domain. This controversial claim appears to contradict numerous contrary indications, some of which are due to Lukács himself. They include the significance of his early criticism of Engels; Lukács's reputation as the founder of so-called Western Marxism; and the widely remarked evolution of his position, which is often described in terms of pre-Stalinist, Stalinist, and post-Stalinist phases.

I believe that none of these objections is well founded. In fact, when we examine the situation more closely, a somewhat different image, less flattering to Lukács, begins to emerge. To begin with, the early criticism of Engels for the extension of dialectic to nature and for his inadequate remarks on the thing-in-itself—the concept upon which Lukács's own reading of classical German philosophy turns—is significantly relativized by him in the new preface written for the second edition of his magnum opus. To put the point in Kantian terms, although there is clearly a difference as regards the interpretation of the letter of Kant's view, there is none at all as concerns the spirit of the response that needs to be given. In fact, in later writings Lukács aligns his position ever more closely on Engels' thought. This reappraisal of his attitude toward Engels results in the abandonment of every significant criticism initially raised. It is accordingly significant that in the uncompleted, posthumously published *Zur Ontologie des gesellschaftlichen Seins* Lukács explicitly presupposes a dialectic of nature as the foundation of a Marxist ontology.

Second, despite the obvious differences in various phases of his position, their "discontinuity," widely represented in the secondary literature, is highly exaggerated. For no thinker of any stature simply abandons his previous thought; and all changes in orientation are always carried out on the basis of a deeper continuity. As concerns Lukács's position, the general continuity of the pre-Marxist and Marxist phases, whose relation had been unintelligible, has been clearly shown by Congdon recently.[8] Further, the specific continuity of the Marxist phase, throughout its complicated evolution, is revealed in the lengthy, unvarying commitment to orthodox Marxism, already evident in "Bolshevism as a Moral Problem,"[9] published in December 1918 shortly before his adherence to the Hungarian Communist party. Lukács never wavered from this commitment, which he maintained until the end of an exceptionally lengthy intellectual career.

Third, I am skeptical about the concept of Western Marxism. The influence of Lukács on the evolution of the later Marxist debate is enormous, and probably even greater than has yet been realized. But the concept of Western Marxism propagated by Merleau-Ponty[10] and taken up again by Arato and Breines[11] is meaningful only as a geographical designation, roughly in Perry Anderson's sense.[12] If it is meant to refer to a nondoctrinaire form of Marxism, distinct from either its classical or later Soviet varieties, it is clearly mythological.

The general continuity mentioned here is specifically evident in the reading of classical and postclassical European philosophy. Lukács stressed the formulation of the so-called Blum Theses, written in 1928, as signaling a significant change in his outlook. But as concerns the history of philosophy, no such change can be detected in his later writings. After the original reading of classical German thought takes shape, it never undergoes basic alteration. Both early and late, Lukács varies the form of the argument, but never modifies the fundamental claim, that is, that Marx is the truth of German idealism.

The basic Marxist reading of the history of philosophy takes shape in *History and Class Consciousness*, especially in the celebrated central essay, "Reification and the Consciousness of the Proletariat." The essay is divided into three parts, including a discussion of reification, a related description of the antinomies of bourgeois thought, and a statement of the proletarian standpoint. Simply stated, classical German philosophy is analyzed from a closely Marxist perspective, which then provides the key to an interpretation of Marx's position.[13]

In later writings, Lukács demonstrated wide acquaintance with the entire German idealist tradition. In this essay, classical German philosophy is described mainly through the positions of Kant and Hegel as a form of bourgeois ideology. I stress this latter point, since the reductive nature of Lukács's interpretation of idealism as ideology has on occasion been overlooked in the secondary literature. But Lukács's approach to German idealism as ideology is clear, for instance in contrast to his view of Marxism as the objective alternative to a merely subjective stance. In a description of his discussion, Lukács writes,

> Our intention here is to *base* ourselves on Marx's economic analysis and to proceed from there to a discussion of the problem growing out of the fetish character of commodities, both as an objective form and also as a subjective stance corresponding to it. Only by understanding this can we obtain a clear insight into the ideological problems of capitalism and its downfall.[14]

Lukács's claim for the ideological nature of bourgeois thought, as reflected in internal antinomies, is restated by him in a series of later writings. In each case these texts further elaborate, but do not basically alter, themes already sounded in *History and Class Consciousness*. Since Engels there was a pronounced tendency within Marxism to interpret Marx's thought as arising through the "negation" of Hegel's position. Prior to Lukács, there was as yet no substantive Marxist study of the Hegelian view. In *Der junge Hegel* Lukács provided the initial Marxist reading of Hegel's position, focusing on the relation of dialectic and economics, in order to locate the roots of the Marxian concept of alienation in Hegel's thought. In a discussion of existentialism entitled *Existentialisme ou Marxisme?* he defended Engels's view of the exclusive alternative between idealism and materialism through an attempted refutation of the existentialist endeavor to define a third position. In an often scurrilous work from his so-called Stalinist period, he described the rise of irrationalism in German thought, beginning with the later Schelling, as contributing to National Socialism. Finally, in his monumental, unfinished study, *Zur Ontologie des gesellschaftlichen Seins*, he returned again to the theme of the contradictions in bourgeois thought, especially in Hegel's position, before elaborating a Marxist theory of ontology based on the concept of work.

As concerns German idealism, I have already noted that Lukács's specific contribution lies in a perhaps unprecedented effort to go beyond a mere assertion through a concrete demonstration of its ideological nature. His demonstration of what he calls "the antinomy of bourgeois thought"[15] is based on an interpretation of the relation between the problem of system and the Kantian concept of the thing-in-itself. According to Lukács, classical German philosophy is characterized by the discovery of the principle of complete system, which results in an antinomy between the drive toward system and the recognition of facticity. As he writes in an important passage,

> The greatness, the paradox and the tragedy of classical German philosophy lie in the fact that—unlike Spinoza—it no longer dismisses every *donné* as non-existent,

causing it to vanish behind the monumental architecture of the rational forms produced by the understanding. Instead, while grasping and holding on to the irrational character of the actual contents of the concepts it strives to go beyond this, to
overcome it and to erect a system.[16]

The antinomy, then, lies in the tension between the demand for universal system and the impossibility of its fulfillment.

The proposed demonstration of the ideological character of classical German philosophy rests on an analysis of Kant's concept of the thing-in-itself.
Lukács links this concept to the idealist tendency toward system. Common to
the various aspects of this Kantian concept, which Lukács considers to be
"the fundamental problem of bourgeois thought,"[17] is the designation of a
limit, that is, an irrational content that cannot be known.[18] The consequence is
an incompatibility in Kant's thought between form and content, which Lukács
interprets from a neo-Kantian perspective as an incommensurability between
the categorical structure of thought and the given that is not cognizable. Nor
does Hegel's concept of the absolute as a concrete totality of the historical
world provide a satisfactory resolution of the problem, even if he perceives
the need to construct an identical subject-object. For in the effort to discover
the unity of rational form and irrational content in an extrahistorical concept
of the absolute, Hegel is driven beyond history to mythology.[19]

Lukács later attributed the insight into the antinomic structure of classical
German thought to classical Marxism, especially to Engels. In fact, the source
of this approach lies elsewhere. It is no accident that Lukács's demonstration
strongly resembles German neo-Kantianism. It is well known that Lukács
studied in Heidelberg, where he was close to a number of neo-Kantians,
above all to Emil Lask.[20] The efforts of such thinkers as Windelband, Rickert,
and Lask to analyze the duality of fact and value, content and form, universal
and particular, culminated in the latter's brilliant discussion of Fichte's position. According to Lask, Fichte's thought combined an analytic method and a
speculative, or synthetic, approach, that were obviously incompatible.
Lukács's demonstration of the antinomy of bourgeois philosophy is not borrowed from Engels at all; rather, it is an extension of Lask's reading of Fichte
to classical German philosophy as a whole. This extension is based on the
conviction that the idealist drive for system fails in the recognition that the
object is not cognizable, that is, in the incompatibility between rational form
and irrational content.

By virtue of the antinomic structure, bourgeois thought cannot provide a
solution to the problem posed by the irrationality of the thing-in-itself, which
is its central concern. A satisfactory analysis, which reveals the rationality,
and hence cognizability, of the only apparently irrational given is available
only from the perspective of commodity analysis. This perspective is further

adequate for the solution of any and all contemporary problems.[21] In a word, the difficulty with which classical German thought is centrally concerned, and which reflects the real structure of the social context, cannot be resolved within philosophy; rather, it can be resolved only on the economic plane of historical materialism. For it is only when the proletarian class transcends German philosophy in the awareness that it produces its own social reality that it will be able, through consciousness of this fact, to abolish commodity fetishism.

III

The novelty, depth, and significance of Lukács's reading of Marx's position have often been celebrated in the secondary literature; they need not to be mentioned again here. I have already stressed the continuity between his reading of classical German thought and classical Marxism as concerns Lukács's specific understanding of Marx's thought as historical materialism as an inverted Platonism, which denies the idealist separation of thought from reality.[22] According to Lukács, thought and reality are interrelated—in what parenthetically is a quasi-Spinozistic form of Marxism—as aspects of a deeper, dialectical process. Although this quasi-Spinozistic form of Marxism is better known in the French discussion, particularly in Merleau-Ponty's writings, its origin is in Lukács's approach to Marx.[23]

The obvious result is to contradict two basic Marxist dogmas concerning the relation of thought and being. On the one hand, thought cannot be dependent on being, which is independent of it, as the reflection theory of knowledge holds, since in that case knowledge would be impossible; for by virtue of its independence from thought, there would be no conceptual link to being, which accordingly could not be known. On the other hand, being cannot determine thought, as the theory of ideology holds, since thought must also be able to determine being. The proper understanding is as an interaction, in which each determines the other. This is similar, it can be noted, to Fichte's interactionist view (*Wechselbeziehung*). For it is only on this hypothesis that a conscious awareness of social conditions can be effective in bringing about social change.

There is little doubt that the kind of reading of Marx that Lukács here adumbrates is more interesting than most forms of Marxist orthodoxy. But it would be an error to overestimate the significance of Lukács's insight into Marx's thought for his own writings, for he never drew the consequences that follow from that insight. The limited differences between Lukács and classical Marxism indicate the acuteness of his intellect, which is obvious, but not an inclination, which was never present, to renounce basic orthodoxy. Unfortunately, in a profound sense Lukács's reading of Marx and philosophy in general remained Marxist. In *History and Class Consciousness*, the Marxist perspective is clearly evident in the explicit intent to show that classical German philosophy is ideologically incapable of resolving its central problem, which is, however, solved by Marx on the plane of economic science.

In that book, Lukács's approach to Marx's position as a form of political economy, which is widespread in the secondary literature, is based on the view that commodity fetishism underlies reification. Although he continued to believe that Marx's view was the truth of idealism, in later writings Lukács softened the original sharp opposition between philosophy and economics. Obviously, it is well that he did so, since an opposition of this kind is not an accurate description of Marx's position. Perhaps it is this that Lukács had in mind when, in the new preface to this work, he conceded that intellectual genesis and historical genesis do not coincide, even in Marx's view. The reason, of course, is clear, as a glance at Marx's thought will show. For even if in practice reification results from commodity exchange, in theory the concept of the commodity presupposes the labor theory of value, which in turn rests on the theory of alienation. To put the point simply, Marxian political economy is not separable, but conceptually inseparable, from Marxian philosophy.

Althusser notwithstanding, there is no break between the earlier philosophical and later economic aspects of Marx's thought. For were such a break to exist, then its cost would be to render Marxian political economy unintelligible by depriving it of its conceptual basis in Marxian philosophy. Beyond the significance for the interpretation of Marx's position, which cannot fairly be interpreted through one of its parts, this point is further significant for Lukács's reading of German idealism. For his approach to bourgeois philosophy as ideology in terms of a constitutive antinomy requires that its problem be resolved on the extraphilosophic plane of science; but the interpretation of Marx's position indicated that its claim to that exalted status is not pure, but rooted in a philosophical anthropology.

There is further an irony to be noted in view of Lukács's obvious lack of sympathy concerning idealism. For his pretended demonstration of an antinomy in German thought consists mainly in the assertion of the widely criticized idealist doctrine—whose roots lie in Plato's thought—of the unlimited character of knowledge. This point is significant; it means that Marxism, at least on this reading, is as idealist as any form of idealism. In fact, it is more idealist than all forms of German idealism. For although German representatives of this tendency are routinely and frequently reproached for their exaggerated epistemological claims—which are also held to mark the divide between Kant and later thought—none of the so-called German idealists, including Fichte, Schelling, or Hegel, ever held that knowledge is in principle limitless.

Moreover, Lukács's criticism of classical German philosophy in terms of the thing-in-itself invokes a questionable reading of this controversial concept. Here several points need to be distinguished. Lukács appears to conflate the cognizability of the given with the thing-in-itself. But this is a clear misunderstanding of Kant's position. For the thing-in-itself, which does not appear in experience, is hence not a given at all. It is further not cognizable since, according to Kant, cognition is limited to objects of experience. And by the same token it is not irrational, but arational, that is, beyond the sphere of the proper application of the categorical framework, which according to Kant is confined to the contents of experience only.

Lukács is further in error as concerns the centrality of the thing-in-itself in classical German thought. It is correct that this problem reappears in different ways in later German idealism. But it is not clear that this is the central problem of the period. Lukács offers no argument on this point, which is crucial to his interpretation, other than the bare assertion. Yet if this point is not demonstrated, then the proposed reading of the thought of this period in terms of this supposed "central problem" must fail.

Lukács further confuses Kant's doctrine of the limits of knowledge with Marx's concern to pierce the ideological veil of illusion through a theory of commodity analysis. He correctly notes that in all its forms the thing-in-itself refers to a limit. But it is a mistake to interpret what in Kant's terminology is mere appearance, and hence fully cognizable, with its putative source in the thing-in-itself, which does not itself appear, is uncognizable, and cannot be known. I believe that there is no contradiction on this point between Kant and Marx, as a closer look will show. It is perfectly compatible to assert with Kant that the thing-in-itself is uncognizable, since it does not appear, although it is not therefore irrational, and further to recognize the importance of Marx's efforts to penetrate beyond ideological appearance to social reality.

I am further doubtful about the accuracy of Lukács's description of classical German philosophy as a tendency toward system blocked by a recognition of the irrationality of the given. In this regard, it is useful to distinguish between the concept of system and its intended use. The latter is, of course, meant to result in knowledge of the content of experience against the framework of a categorical structure. Although the aim of the framework is to provide for knowledge of being as given in experience, the extent to which system is elaborated, or whether it can be completed, or even whether that is the intent, is not related to the status of its possible content.

To avoid the charge of substituting one assertion for another, some illustration, which should not be confused with a sketch of the history of German idealism, even in outline, will be useful. In general terms, the entire post-Kantian phase of what Lukács, in Marxist language, refers to as classical German philosophy is concerned with the restatement of the results of the critical philosophy in systematic form. Kant's view of system, which is evoked briefly in the chapter on the "Architectonic of Pure Reason" toward the end of the *Critique of Pure Reason*, contains an important ambiguity. This ambiguity can be described in Kantian language, as a distinction between constitutive or regulative views of system as a requirement for philosophy.

From this perspective, the post-Kantian reaction to the critical philosophy can be divided into two opposing camps. Each of these two camps claimed to continue the critical philosophy in orthodox manner; but they disagreed about the correct interpretation of the concept of system and hence further disagreed about the proper manner in which to reformulate the critical philosophy. This point is easy to illustrate. Reinhold, who argued for a quasi-rationalist, foundationalist view of system, was opposed by Fichte, and later Hegel, both of whom argued for a quasi-rationalist, but antifoundationalist interpretation of the same concept. It is only if the concept of system is interpreted constitutively, not regulatively, that it becomes problematic. But it should be noted that the arguments for the latter interpretation made by Fichte, and later Hegel, concern the problem of the presuppositionless status of theory, and in no sense depend on the alleged cognizability of a possible or actual given of experience.

IV

This closes my brief discussion of Lukács's Marxist reading of the history of philosophy, with particular attention to classical German thought. It is obvious that there are many issues that could not be explored in such brief compass. I shall conclude with a comment about the usefulness of the Marxist reading of the history of philosophy. Lukács's own discussion is ambivalent on this point. For he suggests in *History and Class Consciousness* that he is only interested in the basis of thought in existence, although he in fact endeavors to reduce the former to the latter.

In my opinion, it is the second tendency that must be resisted. For to argue that thought is nothing but the expression of its social context is to miss the way in which ideas are determined by preceding ideas and to abandon the concept of truth. But the weaker claim, that is, that ideas are also influenced by social being, or the social context in which they emerge, is not to be neglected. It should further be stressed against the widespread, but rarely challenged, and indemonstrable assumption that thought appears in, but is unlimited by, time. In this weaker sense, as recently developed by Buhr, a Marxist reading of the history of philosophy is useful, provided that one acknowledges the limits of its lack of attention to the manner in which thought is also determined by other thought. A full reading of the history of philosophy would need to perform both tasks, including in the context of a single analysis the Marxist concern to relate thought to social being and the so-called bourgeois desire to grasp thought in respect to prior thought.

Notes

1. See François H. Lapointe, *Georg Lukács and His Critics: An International Bibliography (1910–1982)* (Westport, CT: Greenwood, 1983).
2. See especially Edmund Husserl, *Philosophie als strenge Wissenschaft* (Franfurt am Main: Vittorio Klostermann, 1965).
3. This *boutade* is reported by Richard Rorty. See his *Consequences of Pragmatism* (Minneapolis: University of Minnesota, 1982), p. 211.
4. For a discussion of Marx's concept of ideology from this perspective, see my "Idéologie et herméneutique," *Laval théologique et philosophique* 40, 2(June 1984):161–73.
5. For a brilliant statement of this interpretation, see Heinrich Heine, *Zur Geschichte der Religion und Philosophie in Deutschland*, vol. 7 of *Werke und Briefe*, ed. Hans Kaufmann (Berlin: Aufbau, 1961).
6. For a classic example, see Louis Althusser, *For Marx*, trans. Ben Brewster (New York: Vintage, 1970).
7. See Manfred Buhr, *Vernunft, Mensch, Geschichte. Studien zur Entwicklungsgeschichte der klassischen bürgerlichen Philosophie* (Berlin: Akademie, 1977).
8. See Lee Congdon, *The Young Lukács* (Chapel Hill: University of North Carolina, 1983).
9. See Georg Lukács, "Bolshevism as a Moral Problem," trans. and introd. Judith Marcus Tar, *Social Research* 44, 3(Autumn 1977):416–24; rpt. in Judith Marcus, *Georg Lukács and Thomas Mann: A Study in the Sociology of Literature* (Amherst: University of Massachusetts, 1987), pp. 155–59.
10. See Maurice Merleau-Ponty, *Les aventures de la dialectique* (Paris: Gallimard, 1955), ch. 2, "Le marxisme 'occidental.' "
11. For a sympathetic development of Merleau-Ponty's point, see Andrew Arato and Paul Breines, *The Young Lukács and the Origins of Western Marxism* (New York: Seabury, 1979).
12. See Perry Anderson, *Considerations on Western Marxism* (London: NLB, 1976).
13. On the circularity of Lukács's reading of the relation of Marx and classical German philosophy, see my "La philosophie classique allemande et Marx selon Lukács," *Archives de philosophie* 41, 4(1978): 569–97; cf. "Lukács on Marx and Classical German Philosophy," *Idealistic Studies* (September 1980), pp. 209–31.
14. Georg Lukács, *History and Class Consciousness*, trans. Rodney Livingstone (Cambridge, MA: MIT, 1971), p. 84.
15. Ibid., p. 113.
16. Ibid., p. 117.
17. Ibid., p. 150.
18. See ibid., pp. 113–14.
19. See ibid., p. 147; cf. p. 187.
20. For an indication of Lask's influence on Lukács, see his important article, "Emil Lask. Ein Nachruf," *Kant-Studien* 22(1918):349–70.
21. See Lukács, *History and Class Consciousness*, p. 83.
22. See ibid., p. 202.
23. For a quasi-Spinozistic approach to Marx, obviously dependent on Lukács's suggestion in *History and Class Consciousness*, see especially Maurice Merleau-Ponty, *Adventures of the Dialectic*, trans. Joseph Bien (Evanston, IL: Northwestern University, 1973), p. 40: "The two relationships—consciousness as a product of history, history as a product of consciousness—must be maintained together."

3

Philosophy of Science and Its Critique in Georg Lukács's *History and Class Consciousness*

By János Kelemen

The limitation of my discussion to one single aspect of Lukács's *History and Class Consciousness*[1] constitutes an immediate offense against the basic methodological principle of that work: the principle of totality. In defense of my choice of this theme I should like to point out that, for the past couple of decades, the focus of philosophical discussions has largely shifted toward the philosophy of science. Very often it is within the framework of philosophy of science that different "world outlooks" clash over questions about the whole of human life, such as the enduring debate between rationalism and irrationalism. One may ask, however, whether this choice of a universe of discourse will prove relevant to a reading of *History and Class Consciousness*. Is the framework suggested not alien to the purpose and problematic of Lukács's approach? It may be objected in a similar fashion that Lukács's primary interest was in the revolution, and this work of his is to be taken as documentary of his efforts to appropriate revolutionary Marxism—as he himself remarked later. It might be a vain attempt, then, to present Lukács in the guise of a philosopher of science.

The objection may be countered in various ways, of which let me mention only the most obvious. A perusal of Lukács's various essays in the volume is enough to reveal that he touches upon almost all the central problems of philosophy of science, problems that were rooted in the social and intellectual context of the day and that still occupy a prominent place after the recent "Kuhnian turn" in that branch of philosophy. Seen from the angle of the history of science, that period was characterized by a revolt against positivism,

41

as today's post-Kuhnian tendencies are strongly antipositivistic. *History and Class Consciousness* was also a product of that revolt against positivist philosophy of science, among other things. This is testified to by the fact that Lukács, like many of his contemporaries, held the positivist ideal of science to be identical with the idea of science. His criticism of positivism is thus significantly framed as the criticism of science. On the other hand, he also identifies the positivist ideal of science with bourgeois rationality. Consequently, his criticism of science and of positivism is transposed into the criticism of bourgeois reason. Again, this is well demonstrated by his reliance on the tradition of the *Geisteswissenschaften* and contemporary antipositivist authors (most visibly on Max Weber) in criticizing bourgeois rationality and science.

The variety of themes related to philosophy of science in *History and Class Consciousness* is indeed remarkable: methodology of social science; the epistemological and methodological dualism of natural and social sciences; the problem of scientific facts; the relationship between science and society (the internal link between the structure of scientific knowledge and the fundamental traits of capitalism); the nature of historical knowledge, the relation of philosophy to the special social sciences; the nature of scientific laws; the relationship between empirical data and theory; and so on. To this list, far from being complete, one could add the problem of scientific rationality as well as the question whether the terms and concepts employed in the scientific description of facts ought to fall in with the subjective representations of those facts, that is, with the terms in which the producers of the facts interpret their situation, and within it, themselves. The metaphysical and historical-philosophical thesis that historical knowledge is self-knowledge and that knowledge formed of an object changes the object itself can also be viewed as pertaining to the philosophy of science.

The logical domain of the answers to these questions is defined along the dimensions of appearance and reality, externality and internality, part and whole. To these can be added the dichotomy of statics and dynamics (factual and processual character). The answers Lukács gives along the different dimensions are consistent and, as a whole, form a coherent theory of science. In the first analysis, this theory simply appears to be antipositivistic, for a number of Lukács's assertions (in proper logical reconstruction) are also found in the core of other antipositivist philosophies of science, both traditional and modern. The kind of dualism that he embraces in firmly contrasting natural with social science is no less part of a more general antipositivism than his negation of the isolated or theory-independent nature of facts. (Lukács's position concerning the relationship between empirical data and theory can be translated into the language of today's philosophy of science as denying the existence of an empirical basis independent of theory as well as the possibility of a neutral language of observation, and asserting the "theory-ladenness" of the empirical terms, etc.)

Apart from the commitment to revolutionary practice, the philosophy of science discernible in *History and Class Consciousness* is theoretically distinguished from other brands of antipositivism by the use of the categories of reification, the identity of subject and object, and totality on the one hand, and on the other, especially by the way in which Lukács relates science to the structure of a given society and to a socially and historically distinguished point of view.

In what follows, I wish to take up a few problems that receive specific and original treatment in Lukács's work in contrast with mere antipositivism. Along this line, I hope to highlight both the merits and the disadvantages of his philosophy of science.

I

Some words, first of all, about the Lukácsian form of a dualistic philosophy of science. What his Eastern European critics took for the negation of natural dialectics in his work is in fact the manifestation of that dualism. Setting aside the question of the relationship between natural and social dialectics, let me point out now that Lukács asserts more than the mere autonomy of social scientific knowledge. He explicitly claims the autonomy of social science with regard to the model of natural science to be characteristic of proletarian science, ignoring thus the fact that he himself adopted the idea from bourgeois thinkers seeking independent grounds for social science. His stance is based on the assumption that natural science is intrinsically related to capitalism. From this, it immediately follows for him that it is a typically bourgeois attempt to extend the ideal of natural scientific knowledge to the study of society: "When the ideal of scientific knowledge is applied to nature it simply furthers the progress of science. But when it is applied to society it turns out to be an ideological weapon of the bourgeoisie" (p. 10). Thus, the emancipation of proletarian class consciousness presupposes the independence of societal knowledge from natural science.

It emerges by now that, as has been mentioned, Lukács necessarily regards positivism as the typical philosophy of capitalism. But what should the affinity between natural science and capitalism mean? For Lukács, it basically means that capitalism produces phenomena in reality in the same way as natural science produces its "pure" facts in the cognitive sphere. Both spheres resort to the method of isolating abstraction "when a phenomenon of the real world is placed (in thought or in reality) into an environment where its laws can be inspected without outside interference." Both areas are also characterized by "reducing the phenomena to their purely quantitative essence" (p. 6).

Lukács's analysis seems to be correct; it essentially carries the insight that natural science represents a type of rationality that is the historical product of the capitalist organization of society. There remain, nevertheless, certain questions open in respect of the affinity between natural science and capitalism and the relationship between natural and social science.

Such questions are whether natural science depends on capitalism only for its origin or also as a precondition of its possibility. Therefore, if the facts of natural science are analogous to the facts of the social world of reification, does then the abolishment of reification not remove the grounds of the natural scientific attitude? Can natural scientific knowledge be adequate at all if it is itself the product of a particular, socially determined perspective? Or is it the case that the bourgeoisie is incapable only of comprehending its own social relationship while its particular class position and point of view enable it to develop adequate natural scientific methods?

Lukács does not raise such questions explicitly, but he seems to recognize the validity of natural science and uncritically to endorse the generally accepted conception of its development. He writes,

> The methodology of the natural sciences which forms the methodological ideal of every fetishistic science and every kind of revisionism rejects the idea of contradiction and antagonism in its subject matter. If, despite this, contradictions spring up between particular theories, this only proves that our knowledge is as yet imperfect. Contradictions between theories show that these theories have reached their natural limits; they must therefore be transformed and subsumed under even wider theories in which the contradictions finally disappear. (p. 10)

All this corresponds well to the traditional positivist conception, surviving almost up to our day, that the progress of science is a cumulative development that leads to more and more general theories, while earlier theories are incorporated as parts in the later ones. Lukács's strategy does not differ in this respect from that of such thinkers active at the turn of the century as Rickert, Dilthey, or Weber, who called for the independent grounding of the social, cultural, or historical science without challenging the received view of natural scientific knowledge. However, contrary to the neo-Kantian and *geisteswissenschaftliche* approaches, Lukács seeks the specific difference of social scientific knowledge from natural science not in "individuating concept formation" or in understanding as opposed to explanation but in the fact that "in the case of social reality these contradictions are not a sign of the imperfect understanding of society: on the contrary, they belong to *the nature of reality itself and to the nature of capitalism*" (p. 10).

Let me summarize the main features of the dualistic philosophy of science that Lukács endorses. He holds that natural science, in spite of its fundamental affinity to capitalism, is a source of adequate knowledge. On the other hand, social science can have no claim to validity unless it transcends capitalism. To achieve this, it must part with the ideal of natural scientific knowledge, which is based on the structures of reification and which essentially cannot accommodate contradiction. The proper knowledge of the structure of society presupposes the unveiling of reification on which natural science is based and demands the acceptance of contradictions as real contradictions.

The way Lukács opposes natural to social science explains the fact that the real target of his radical criticism is social science conceived as dominated by the methodology of the natural sciences. We can only remark here that, according to his critique of science, the social preconditions to statistical or other sorts of exactitude is "the fact that capitalist society is predisposed to harmonize with scientific method" (p. 7). The striving for exactitude causes "science" to be ahistorical and, on the other hand, runs the risk that "it thereby takes its stand simply and dogmatically on the basis of capitalist society" (p. 7). To make matters worse, science remains a captive of appearance, of "the form in which the phenomena are immediately given" (p. 8). It is easily recognized that, from the epistemological point of view, the real target of this critique of science is first and foremost empiricism and that the conception Lukács opposes to bourgeois science is deeply antiempiricistic. His critique finds its continuation in the antiempiricism of later radical critics of scientific methodology. What Lukács did not realize was that a criticism of empiricism cannot be partial and restricted only to the social sciences. It is no accident that today's radical philosophies of science attack empiricism in its safest stronghold, natural science.

The rightful claim of social science to autonomy does not imply that the extension of natural science qua natural science to the societal sphere is responsible for the distortion of social scientific knowledge. In other words, the fact that an ideal of science stems from natural science does not guarantee the applicability of that ideal even to natural science itself. A scientific ideal as a framework of general epistemological presuppositions is liable to criticism independently of its application in either the natural or the social sciences. If, for example, the ideal proves to thwart social science, this helps to identify it as untenable in general. In this respect, among others we may refer to Collingwood.[2] He was right in maintaining that it is an epistemological model incompatible with the mere existence of history that places in the starting point of every cognitive situation the simultaneous presence of the subject and the object of cognition, observational descriptions and actual sense-data. That model taken from natural science indeed misrepresents natural science itself.

At any rate, Lukács's critique of science turns out to be justified in several respects. The twentieth-century development of science has shown a tendency to a greater and greater degree for research to be partitioned into isolated areas that can rarely, or often not at all, be seen to be interdependent. The drawbacks, such as the futility of segments deprived of their contexts, need not be detailed here. They are no less characteristic of natural science than of social science.

However, the conception of science traceable to *History and Class Consciousness* has also initiated a rather problematic tradition to Marxism. The dualistic philosophy of science analyzed above greatly contributed to establishing the view that the social sciences are of a merely ideological and class character while the natural sciences are free from any social or ideological determinants. (This kind of scientism became an element of Stalinism even though various branches of natural science were also labeled "bourgeois pseudo-science" in the Stalinist era.)

II

"It is not the primacy of economic motives in historical explanation that constitutes the decisive difference between Marxism and bourgeois thought, but the point of view of totality" (p. 27). This statement, which opens the essay on "The Marxism of Rosa Luxemburg" and became one of the targets of Lukács's later self-criticism, is one of the clues to *History and Class Consciousness*.

Within that work, the category of totality appears to have special functions. It serves as a basis of the theory of possible consciousness and of the thesis that the adequate knowledge of society is at the same time the self-knowledge of the proletariat. (On a more general level, this thesis entails that adequate knowledge is only possible as adequate self-knowledge: "For every piece of historical knowledge is an act of self-knowledge" [p. 237]. Only the proletariat is capable of this.) It is widely known that within these interrelations the category of totality is the main analytic tool applied to proletarian consciousness, this function of it having been studied by many, from Lucien Goldmann to István Hermann.[3] But the function it plays in the field of philosophy of science in the more specific sense has received less attention.

Speaking in terms of philosophy of science, we may say that the point of view of totality is first of all an expression of Lukács's antiempiricism. The main function of that category in this area is to serve as the foundation of Lukács's idea of science. More precisely, he intends to infer from it the possibility of a social science that applies the methodology of natural science and thus is trapped within the limitations of mere facticity and reified appearance.

As latter-day methodological debates (like the so-called *Positivismusstreit* et al.)[4] indicate, many authors doubt if the category of totality can be invested with some nonmystical, scientific sense. I myself would not go as far as that. Nowadays, when the hermeneutic approach is making its comeback, it is easier to argue that any empirical investigation can only take on significance within a wider context of sense. Conceiving any results of observation, measurement, or experiments as data requires interpretation that is only possible through that wide context of sense. It remains a problem that it is very difficult to specify the conditions under which "totality" or the "wide context of sense" can become operational, that is, translated into practical procedures. *History and Class Consciousness* offers few guidelines in this direction. One rather finds in it problematic claims that, for the most part, were not confirmed by subsequent scientific developments.

One aspect of the problem of totality on the concrete methodological plane is involved in the relationships among the special social sciences and their interrelation with philosophy. About the latter interrelation, *History and Class Consciousness* pronounces the traditional view that the social and historical sciences, unlike the natural sciences, bear a specifically intimate relation to philosophy because societal and historical knowledge is philosophical by nature. As Lucien Goldmann puts it, "For Lukács, historical knowledge and historical action can only be philosophical."[5] But while Croce takes the postulated identity of history with philosophy as his point of departure, and more recently, Peter Winch has focused on the subject matter of sociology, both of them seeking to derive the inherent unity of philosophy and special social sciences, Lukács rather posits that unity as a mere requirement. "Hence only by overcoming the—theoretical—duality of philosophy and special discipline, of methodology and factual knowledge can the way be found by which to annul the duality of thought and existence" (p. 203). It must be noted that the unity is only required of proletarian science, for within the limits of bourgeois thought" philosophy stands in the same relation to the special sciences as they do with respect to empirical reality" (p. 110).

Applied to the interrelation among the special social sciences the principle of totality leads to the union, at least as a requirement, of the individual discipline and indivisible social science. "In the last analysis Marxism does not acknowledge the existence of independent sciences of law, economics or history etc.: there is nothing but a single, unified—dialectical and historical—science of the evolution of society as a totality," states Lukács (p. 28).

Even the recent tendencies calling for interdisciplinarity and scientific integration cannot deny the fact that no such unified science has been developed even in areas under predominant Marxist influence. The institutional segregation and the differentiation according to subject matter and method of the special disciplines seem in fact to be increasing. Needless to say, Lukács speaks of a "single unified" science "in the last analysis" only, and he recognizes the practical need for the "abstraction and isolation" of fields of research. Through his claim for unity he wants the abstraction and isolation of individual areas to be the means of knowing the whole and not to become ends in themselves. But he says little of how an integration of the sciences is supposed to take place concretely. Beside the crucial category of mediation and the general principle that the "totality of an object can only be posited if the positing subject is itself a totality" (p. 28), many other conditions must be fulfilled in order for partial research results to make up knowledge of the whole in a testable manner. For example, we must be able to connect the image of the totality as a theoretical construct to the individual part areas. Unless this is done, no partial result can become part of the whole and no empirical research can justify and serve as a foundation for our knowledge of the totality.

It can be objected here that Lukács wanted to fulfill precisely this task through the critical application, based on Marx, of the dialectic of "immediacy" and "mediation." For example, he succeeds in analyzing the bourgeois consciousness tied to the immediately given forms of objectivity as false consciousness, that is to say, as a necessary element, consequence, and functional precondition of social totality. Thus he can actually show a sphere of empirical phenomena to be part of the whole. This example illustrates, too, how the scientific explanation of empirical social phenomena can be based on totality. Our problem stems from something else, though: it must be recognized that knowledge of the totality as well as the relationship found between totality and the partial areas as itself in need of justification. Linking proletarian consciousness as a totality with society as a totality (unlike the connection between bourgeois consciousness and social totality) means linking two theoretical constructs together. Since both constructs are of the same origins, there is a risk that their relationship takes the form of *praestabilita harmonia*, that is, that the class consciousness of the proletariat as coordinate consciousness must be considered as an a priori correct reflection of social totality. In that case, the truth of a scientific theory will depend on the extent to which it expresses the possible class consciousness of the proletariat. If the theory (in our case, historical materialism) is found to be a proper expression of proletarian class consciousness, then its truth will count as a priori truth, that is, the a priori correct theory of social totality. But in this way there will be no place left for justification or refutation. That this is a real risk can be judged from the way Lukács treats criticism of historical materialism coming from the sociology of knowledge. He merely declares, after all, that the truths of historical materialism "are truths within a particular social order and system of production," and, as such, "their claim to validity is absolute" (p. 228).

Naturally, such difficulties do not only arise with regard to the Lukácsian principle of totality. (As is well known, for example, the problem of priority endangers Weber's ideal types too.) In fact, social science has found no final solution to these problems. Still, it must be acknowledged, and we have to emphasize this, that only in view of the whole, that is, of the social totality, is it possible for empirical research to attain significance. Under this aspect,

Lukács's principle of totality vindicates the conviction that just as there is no revolutionary practice without the vanguard of theory, there is no scientific practice without wide-ranging theoretical foundations either.

Such an array of contradictory requirements will presumably force us to accept the following situation. Empirical research that is supposed to yield knowledge of the whole can focus only on temporally fixed states of affairs while social reality continually undergoes change. A mere summing up of state descriptions would never lead to a comprehension of the whole: totality would, as it were, escape us. If only for that reason, the comprehensive result expected of empirical research must be, so to say, preconceived (and also for the other, quite obvious reason that empirical research necessarily presupposes a prior point of view or conceptual framework). Part and whole, the empirical and the theoretical thus enter into a vicious circle.

Such a circularity appeares inadmissible, however, only to formalistic thought. As a matter of fact, empirical research conducted in proper perspective may perform a twofold role. On the one hand, it may provide new factual knowledge and thus enrich our comprehensive knowledge of the whole, while, on the other hand, it may put our general presuppositions to test and rectify our preconception of the totality. It follows, then, that the empirical and the theoretical planes cannot be kept distinct, and the positivist concept of neutral empirical material is untenable. This nevertheless does not mean that the empirical is dissolved in the theoretical. The empirical retains its relative independence and its function of justifying or refuting theories.

III

One further application of the principle of totality is for Lukács to determine the nature and possibility of historical knowledge. I should finally like to deal with that aspect of applying the totality principle.

The ultimate totality that Lukács holds to determine the place, nature, and interrelation of every partial phenomenon is history itself. To know history is to grasp it as a whole, "a unified process," with the help of "the dialectical view of totality" (p. 12).

This is the point where another, crucial question arises relating to epistemology and scientific methodology: what is to be meant by history as a totality, and how is description of a part of history related to the description of the unified historical process? What Lukács means by the totality of history is definitely not universal history as opposed to the particular histories. Thus there is only one alternative left to our interpretation: that the totality is the whole of history including both the past and the future. History including the future is known to pose grave epistemological and logical problems, for the science of history or historiography devoted to the description and explanation of history is necessarily and inevitably the science of the past. The history of the future is not available for description; it is impossible to write a narrative of the future. That is to say, the whole of history is inaccessible to science (understood as *Fachwissenschaft*). There is a fundamental difference between reflection about past history and about the totality of history. The difference appears quite clear to Lukács:

> The opposition between the description of an aspect of history and the description of history as a unified process is not just a problem of scope, as in the distinction between particular and universal history. It is rather a conflict of method, of approach. (p. 12)

What type of reflection is directed at the whole of the historical process? A plausible answer is that it is of the type characterizing philosophy of history. That is what analytical or critical philosophies have called substantive philosophy of history. It appears very likely that what Lukács had in mind, among others under Hegel's influence, was a substantive philosophy of history of some sort. Quite a few of his expressions would clearly support such a claim, for example, "It is precisely the *whole* of the historical process that constitutes the authentic historical reality" (p. 152). It is true that Lukács attempts to contain "the authentic historical reality" transcending empirical history within the world of immanence: "The totality of history is itself a real historical power . . . which is not to be separated from the reality . . . of the individual facts" (p. 152). But in any case, the phenomena of history have to be integrated into that whole encompassing the future, too. And "that integration in the totality . . . does not merely affect our judgment of individual phenomena decisively. But also, as a result, the objective structure, the actual content of the *individual phenomena* is changed fundamentally" (p. 152).

All this means, in short, that the nature and knowledge of the partial phenomena of history, the facts of the past and the present, depend on the future, without which the totality of history cannot be given. However paradoxical this conclusion may appear, it is expressive of an important aspect of the nature of historical knowledge. One necessary condition of the self-identity of a historical fact or event is the description that is given of it, and every definition must include a reference to the context, consequence, and so on of the event in question. At no point of time is it therefore possible to give a complete and final description of an individual fact. The present moment can always retroactively modify the context and thus the content and identity of any fact of the past. (The description "the 1905 revolution is a precedent to the Great October Revolution" has been valid for the 1905 revolution only since 1917.) Historical knowledge is knowledge *post festum* and, taking the above logic seriously, we are compelled to recognize that no fact will attain its final form until the end of history, that is, until the totality of history becomes actual. From the epistemological point of view, the Hegelian notion of "the end of history" designates the unique point that makes the total knowledge of history possible.

The present is therefore always in need of the future dimension in order to provide the suitable context for knowing historical facts. That is the rational core of the historical epistemology of *History and Class Consciousness*. Naturally enough, this means that the totality in which we incorporate the partial phenomena of history is always virtual, not actual. It is just the theoretical construct that puts our investigations into perspective. Again, we cannot avoid the circularity of part and whole, empirical historical research and theoretical construction. But the totality that amounts to history encompassing the future is more here than the perspective of investigation: it is also the object of will. Thus we understand partial historical phenomena seen under the angle of a future we want; however, these phenomena can only yield scientific knowledge—strictly speaking—when they have happened, when they become past.

This is also a way of pronouncing the unity of practice and theory, together with that of history and philosophy, in order to render justice to the messianism of *History and Class Consciousness* within certain limits of rationality.

Notes

1. All references by page number are to Georg Lukács, *History and Class Consciousness*, trans. Rodney Livingstone (Cambridge, MA: MIT, 1971).
2. See R. G. Collingwood, *The Idea of History* (Oxford: Oxford University Press, 1946).
3. I refer above all to Goldmann's 1967–68 lectures on Lukács (and Heidegger). See Lucien Goldmann, *Lukács and Heidegger: Towards a New Philosophy*, trans. William Q. Boelhower (London and Boston: Routledge & Kegan Paul, 1977); See also István Hermann, *Die Gedankenwelt von Georg Lukács* (Budapest: Akadémiai Kiadó, 1978).
4. Reference is made to the controversy that has raged in social scientific and philosophical circles in Germany since 1961. See Theodor W. Adorno et al., *The Positivist Dispute in German Sociology*, trans. Glyn Adey and David Frisby (New York: Harper Torchbooks, 1976). Cf. Reinhard Kreckel, "The Positivist Dispute in Retrospect," in Judith Marcus and Zoltán Tar, eds., *Foundations of the Frankfurt School of Social Research* (New Brunswick, NJ and London: Transaction, 1984), pp. 253–72.
5. Goldmann, *Lukács and Heidegger*, p. 9.

4

Georg Lukács and the Frankfurt School: A Case of Secular Messianism

By Joseph B. Maier

My remarks on Lukács and the Frankfurt School concern only a few related aspects of their work and some special problems facing the English or American reader. I propose to deal with them under two headings: (1) the difficulty of language and literature, and (2) "the most interesting sect of German Jewry."

I

There are, first of all, the linguistic obstacles in the work of Lukács, Horkheimer, Marcuse, and particularly Adorno and Walter Benjamin. It would, indeed, be difficult, if not impossible, to select sentences from their writings that are intelligible to one not trained in its vocabulary, unless the selection is accompanied by an almost word-by-word commentary. It is not merely that these writers were all at home in the German language. It is a very special German. For they all practiced the Hegelian idiom with a vengeance. Coming from someone who knows whereof he speaks, this is fair warning to anyone determined to mine the gold in their writings: "To follow the line of thought from detail to detail, you need to know Kant near-perfectly, Hegel perfectly, and Marx-Engels viscerally—not just 'by heart.'. . . Besides, you should have a working knowledge of moderns from a variety of fields, of such philosophers as Bergson, Husserl, Scheler . . . of prominent sociologists and psychiatrists, of seminal poets and composers. . . . And you should at least have heard of Karl Kraus of Vienna."[1]

The deliberate intricacy of their prose styles defies translation—especially into English. "What they all share," said another astute observer,

> is an intense seriousness and a sustained element of attention; and, with this, an explicit awareness of the intimate bond linking the substance of an argument and the mode of its presentation. For all of them language is far more than the "form" in which their "content" is transmitted. It is the constitutive medium which informs content and from which content can in no way be detached. They may sometimes be too self-conscious in their use of language; but they certainly do not mince their words. These writers therefore constitute by their existence a powerful plea for the importance of difficulty. The form is essential to the effect of their argument. Every sentence is supposed to be balanced and mediated through the totality of the piece.[2]

Horkheimer, and the same may be said of all the writers referred to here, felt uncomfortable with what he called "the treacherous lucidity of style of American philosophy." His tongue was German, not English or American. The German language, Adorno held, "has a special elective affinity (*Wahlverwandtschaft*) to philosophy, and, to be sure, to its speculative moment."[3] English is not just another code for the same message. Each language expresses a group's sense of what is important and true, each edits the universe, as it were. And "it does seem to be true," John Dewey conceded,

> that the Germans, more readily than other peoples, can withdraw themselves from the exigencies and contingencies of life into a region of *Innerlichkeit* which at least *seems* boundless, and which can rarely be successfully uttered save through music, and a frail and tender poetry, sometimes domestic, sometimes lyric, but always full of mysterious charm. But technical ideas, ideas about means and instruments, can readily be externalized because the outer world is in truth their abiding home.[4]

With Mallarmé, Maurice Blanchot, and Valéry, Herbert Marcuse shared, as he put it, "the search for an 'authentic language'—the language of negation as the Great Refusal to accept the rules of a game in which the dice are loaded. The absence must be made present because the greater part of the truth is in that which is absent."[5] The essential function of philosophy, he argued, was criticism of what exists. It was the detachment of philosophy from what is concrete and immediate that gave it power. Precisely because philosophy was concerned with concepts, with the structure of what can be thought, it confronted the world of facts, the one-dimensional world of facts, with that of possibility and of what could or ought to be. In different periods it did so in different ways.

Take the concept of essence.[6] From Plato to Hegel, philosophers used it to make the distinction between the true nature of things and the way they happen to appear at any given moment. The distinction between what is authentically real and what is mere appearance, between things as they are and as they ought to be, was not made in exactly the same way by Aristotle, St. Thomas Aquinas, and later philosophers, but it was always made. The history of philosophy, according to Marcuse, bears witness to this, as this history is situated within a more general account of the history of modern culture. The rising bourgeoisie had based its demand for a new social freedom on the universality of human reason. But reason and freedom did not extend beyond the bourgeoisie's own interests. These interests came into increasing conflict with the interests of the masses of the people. To accusing questions, the bourgeoisie responded with a decisive answer: affirmative culture, something fundamentally idealist. Says Marcuse,

> To the need of the isolated individual it responds with general humanity, to bodily misery with the beauty of the soul, the external bondage with internal freedom, to brutal egoism with the duty of the realm of virtue. Whereas during the period of the militant rise of the new society all of these ideas had a progressive character by pointing beyond the attained organization of existence, they entered increasingly into the service of the suppression of the discontented masses and of mere self-justifying exaltation, once bourgeois rule began to be stabilized.[7]

The beauty of culture may above all be an inner beauty and its realm essentially a realm of the soul, but bourgeois idealism is not merely ideology, Marcuse insists. It contains not only quiescence about what is, but also remembrance of what could be. "By making suffering and sorrow into eternal, universal forces, great bourgeois art has continually shattered in the hearts of men the facile resignation of everyday life," Marcuse states, and elaborates as follows:

> By painting in the luminous colors of this world the beauty of men and things and transmundane happiness, it has planted real longing alongside poor consolation and false consecration in the soil of bourgeois life. This art raised pain and sorrow, desperation and loneliness, to the level of metaphysical powers and set individuals against one another and the gods in the nakedness of physical immediacy, beyond all social mediations. This exaggeration contains the higher truth that such a world cannot be changed piecemeal, but only through its destruction. Classical bourgeois art put its ideal forms at such a distance from everyday occurrence that those whose suffering and hope reside in daily life could only rediscover themselves through a leap into a totally other world. In this way art nourished the belief that all previous history had been only the dark and tragic prehistory of a coming existence.[8]

Georg Lukács, it may be recalled in this context, did more than anyone to develop Engels's important distinction between realism and naturalism in literature: that is, realism as it manifested itself in the writings of Shakespeare, Goethe, and Balzac, where the objective world and the subjective imagination were creatively integrated, in contrast to Zola's work, which mechanically reported and photographed, as it were, what was out there. To Lukács, Zola was a nice guy because he sympathized with the downtrodden, but the greater artistry of the royalist Balzac enabled the writer to paint a true picture of historical reality.

The Frankfurt School writers fully shared Lukács's realism-naturalism dichotomy. However, they did go much further to welcome the artistic modernism of every kind. Lukács did not have much sympathy for Proust, Joyce, Kafka, or Nietzsche. In modern art and literature he eventually came to see, with very few exceptions, nothing but dreadful formalism, subjectivism, and irrationalism, either destined or designed to aid and abet imperialism. Coming to maturity in Wilhelmian Germany, Lukács remained convinced that the pinnacle of culture had been reached by the end of the first third of the nineteenth century—in the music of Beethoven, in the literature of Goethe, and in the philosophy of Hegel. As an art form only the novel, the work of Balzac and Thomas Mann, allowed a development beyond.

The principle that Adorno, per contrast, discovered in modern art, in Proust, in Joyce, in Kafka, and in the music of Schoenberg, was exactly what informed his own work, and that of the Frankfurt School as a whole. As he put it, "Defiance of society includes defiance of its own language."[9] He held that dialectical images "are models not of social products, but rather objective constellations in which the social condition represents itself."[10] To those who would read his writings and listen to his lectures, he would offer Hegel's advice, *die Anstrengung des Begriffs nicht zu scheuen*, not to shirk the effort of thought if they wanted to get at the truth of the world.

II

I now come to part 2 of my remarks on Lukács and the Frankfurt School. Let me state at once that I share with Zoltán Tarr the conviction that the veil surrounding what he called the "enigma" of Lukács will be lifted, when someone—for good and sufficient reasons I should like to think someone like Tarr himself, or Judith Marcus—will have made a thorough study of the life and letters of young Lukács. Quite appropriately, and not merely in jest, Gershom Scholem, the well-known author of *Major Trends in Jewish Mysticism*, has referred to Horkheimer's *Institut für Sozialforschung* as "the most interesting sect of German Jewry."[11] Lukács, too, belonged to that sect, although he would no more have openly admitted it than did any of the members of the Frankfurt School. But it is clear to me that their descent and existence as Jews, not merely their experience with anti-Semitism, were shaping conditions of their temperament, and therefore I suppose must have had an effect on their intellect. A closer examination of Lukács's *Die Seele und die Formen (Soul and Form)*, his contacts with Martin Buber, Ernst Bloch, Walter Benjamin, and others, would reveal Lukács's avid, albeit at times repressed, interest in and fascination with the revelatory, theological, mystical, and redemptive elements in Judaism. I even venture to say that Lukács, if hard pressed to reveal what was in the innermost recesses of his soul, would have admitted to what Walter Benjamin confessed about himself: "I have never been able to do research and think in a way other than, if I may so put it, in a theological sense—namely, in accordance with the Talmudic teaching of the forty-nine levels of meaning in every passage in the Torah."[12]

Within the Central European Jewish community itself, there often raged a struggle between fathers and sons over the content of Judaism and the future of the Jewish people. As Hannah Arendt has written in her essay on Walter Benjamin,

> If anything, his outlook was typical of an entire generation of German-Jewish intellectuals, although probably no one else fared so badly with it. Its basis was the mentality of the fathers, successful businessmen who did not think too highly of their own achievements and whose dream it was that their sons were destined for higher things. It was the secularized version of the ancient Jewish belief that those who "learn"—the Torah or the Talmud, that is, God's Law—were the true elite of the people and should not be bothered with so vulgar an occupation as making money or working for it. This is not to say that in this generation there were no father-son conflicts; on the contrary, the literature of the time is full of them, and if Freud had lived and carried on his inquiries in a country and language other than the German-Jewish milieu which supplied his patients, we might have never heard of an Oedipus complex. But as a rule these conflicts were resolved by the sons' laying claim to being geniuses, or, in the case of the numerous Communists from well-to-do homes, to being devoted to the welfare of mankind—in any case, to aspiring to things higher than making money—and the fathers were more than willing to grant that this was a valid excuse for not making a living.[13]

As in so many other ways, Benjamin was himself an exception to the rule, as his father refused to support him. On the other hand, few were as generous as Lukács's father, who went out of his way to assure his son in black and white, "I will make every sacrifice necessary so that you can become a great man, recognized and famous. My greatest happiness will come when I am known as the father of György Lukács."[14]

Benjamin's interest in the Kabala was undoubtedly facilitated and nourished by his lifelong friendship with Gershom Scholem. In the case of Lukács and the other writers of the Frankfurt School, the mystical and messianic strains in Jewish thought came to them, as Jürgen Habermas[15] and, more recently, my late good friend and colleague Werner J. Cahnman[16] have shown, via German idealism and especially the philosophy of Schelling. In Simmel, Habermas finds the other typically Jewish interest beside the sociological: the interest in a philosophy of nature inspired by mysticism. "In the 1920s," he says, "in David Baumgardt's 'Franz von Baader and Philosophical Romanticism,' " a Jew comes across the golden vein of those speculations on the ages of the world—so pregnant for a philosophy of nature—that lead from Jacob Böhme via Swabian Pietism to the Tübingen seminarians Schelling, Hegel, and Hölderlin. . . . However, all these Jewish scholars seem not to have attained full awareness of what force had set them on the path of this special tradition. They had forgotten what was still known at the close of the seventeenth century. At that time Johann Jacob Spaeth, a disciple of Böhmian mysticism, overcome by the consonance of this doctrine with the theosophy of Isaac Luria, went over to Judaism. A few years later, the Protestant pastor Friedrich Christoph Oetinger (whose writings Hegel and Schelling as well as Bader had read) sought out in the ghetto of Frankfurt the kabbalist Koppel Hecht in order to be initiated into Jewish mysticism. Hecht responded that "Christians have a book that speaks about the kabbalah more clearly than the Zohar's; what he meant was the work of Jacob Böhme."[17]

Habermas concludes that "it was this kind of 'theology' Walter Benjamin had in mind when he remarked that historical materialism would have been able to accept motifs of kabbalistic mysticism without further ado if only it were capable of assuming theology into its service."[18] He reminds us that this reception had happened in the case of Ernst Bloch. "In the medium of his Marxist appropriation of Jewish mysticism, Bloch combines sociology with the philosophy of nature into a system that today is borne along as is no other by the great breath of German Idealism."[19] And just as "Bloch recurs to Schelling, . . . so too it was Jewish scholars (friends of Walter Benjamin), who thought out Hegel's dialectic of the enlightenment to a point where the ongoing beginning opens up a view of the still outstanding end: Theodor Adorno, Max Horkheimer, and Herbert Marcuse, preceded by the early Georg Lukács."[20]

What Lukács shared with the Frankfurt School writers is, above all, a full-blown philosophy of history, in particular the theological concept of history as a history of fulfillment and salvation. Commenting on Lukács's *Theory of the Novel* (1920), Walter Benjamin lauded the author for a "most important elucidation" for recognizing in the novel "the form of transcendental homelessness" and "at the same time the only art form which includes time among its constitutive principles." And forthwith he proceeded to endorse the following lines from Lukács's work:

Time can become constitutive only when connection with the transcendental home has been lost. Only in the novel are meaning and life, and thus the essential and the temporal, separated; one can almost say that the whole inner action of a novel is nothing else but a struggle against the power of time. . . . And from this . . . arise the genuinely epic experiences of time: hope and memory. . . . Only in the novel . . . does there occur a creative memory which transfixes the object and transforms it. . . . The duality of inwardness and outside world can here be overcome for the subject "only" when he sees the . . . unity of his entire life . . . out of the past life-stream which is compressed in memory. . . . The insight which grasps this unity . . . becomes the divinatory-intuitive grasping of the unattained and therefore inexpressible meaning of life.[21]

In Lukács's *History and Class Consciousness* (1923), however, Benjamin as well as Horkheimer, Adorno, and Marcuse saw what thus far "no other theorist was able to provide: a Marxist analysis which stuck to the facts and yet did not renounce the Hegelian inheritance in the name of 'science.' Until the appearance of this book, these intellectuals had regarded Communism as a mere extension of the Russian Revolution: doubtless an important event, but one that did not seem to promise a solution of their own problems: a purely political movement centered on a relatively backward country. What Lukács did was to claim universal significance for it. In his interpretation of Marxism, the proletarian revolution appeared as the key to the riddle of history."[22]

Indeed, *History and Class Consciousness* provided a millenarian thrill to a whole generation of Central European intellectuals. If *Soul and Form* (1911) had aimed at a philosophy in order to pinpoint the ultimate questions of life, the later volume pointed to a reconciliation of matter and spirit, laid the foundation for the realization of the romantic dream of the healing of all contradictions and the last wholeness of nature and history. And it did so by following in the footsteps of the master himself, Karl Marx. The philosophy of the proletariat as the chosen people had already been expounded in a document, the *Communist Manifesto*, that is "scientifically relevant in its particular contents, eschatological in its framework, and prophetic in its attitude."[23] The proletariat, Hegel's and Lukács's identical subject-object of history, is the children of light engaged in a final struggle with the children of darkness. The final crisis of the bourgeois capitalist world that Marx prophesies in terms of a scientific prediction is a last judgment.

> It is only in Marx's "ideological" consciousness that all history is a history of class struggles, while the real driving force behind this conception is a transparent messianism which has its unconscious root in Marx's own being, even in his race. He was a Jew of Old Testament stature, though an emancipated Jew of the nineteenth century who felt strongly antireligious and even antisemitic. It is the old Jewish messianism and prophetism—unaltered by two thousand years of economic history from handicraft to large-scale industry—and Jewish insistence on absolute righteousness which explain the idealistic basis of Marx's materialism. Though perverted into secular prognostication, the *Communist Manifesto* still retains the basic features of a messianic faith: "the assurance of things to be hoped for."[24]

The possibility of tracing back the inspiration of the writings of both Lukács and the Frankfurt School authors to Jewish mysticism and messianism is most clearly illustrated in Walter Benjamin's last, posthumously published, essay entitled "Theses on the Philosophy of History." It contains the most unvarnished statement of the theological mode of thinking that is a hallmark of all these writers, their vision of an ultimate end, as both *finis* and *telos*, of history and a glimpse of paradise. It reads,

> "In relation to the history of organic life on earth," writes a modern biologist, "paltry fifty millennia of homo sapiens constitute something like two seconds at the close of a twenty-four-hour day. On this scale, the history of civilized mankind would fill one-fifth of the last second of the last hour." The present, which, as a model of Messianic time, comprises the entire history of mankind in an enormous abridgment, coincides exactly with the stature which the history of mankind has in the universe. . . . We know that the Jews were prohibited from investigating the future. The Torah and the prayers instruct them in remembrance, however. This stripped the future of its magic, to which all those succumb who turn to the sooth-sayers for enlightenment. This does not imply, however, that for the Jews the future turned into homogeneous, empty time. For every second of time was the strait gate through which the Messiah might enter.[25]

Notes

1. E. B. Ashton, translator's note, in T. W. Adorno, *Negative Dialectics* (New York: Seabury, 1973), p. xii.
2. Paul Connerton, *The Tragedy of Enlightenment* (Cambridge: Cambridge University, 1980), p. 11.
3. Theodor W. Adorno, *Stichworte: Kritische Modelle 2* (Frankfurt am Main: Suhrkamp, 1969), p. 110.
4. John Dewey, *German Philosophy and Politics* (New York: Putnam, 1942), p. 82.
5. Herbert Marcuse, *Reason and Revolution* (Boston: Beacon, 1968), p. x.
6. Herbert Marcuse, *Negations* (Boston: Beacon, 1969), pp. 43–87.
7. Ibid., p. 98.
8. Ibid.
9. Theodor W. Adorno, *Prisms*, trans. Samuel and Shierry Weber (London: Neville Spearman, 1967), p. 225.
10. Walter Benjamin, *Briefe*, vol. 2 (Frankfurt am Main: Suhrkamp, 1966), p. 678.
11. Gershom Scholem, *From Berlin to Jerusalem*, trans. Harry Zohn (New York: Schocken, 1980), p. 131.
12. Benjamin, *Briefe*, p. 524.
13. Hannah Arendt, introduction to Walter Benjamin, *Illuminations*, trans. Harry Zohn (New York: Schocken, 1969), p. 26.
14. Georg Lukács, *Selected Correspondence, 1902–1920: Dialogues with Weber, Simmel, Buber, Mannheim, and Others*, ed. and trans. Judith Marcus and Zoltán Tar (New York: Columbia University, 1986), p. 97.
15. Jürgen Habermas, *Philosophical-Political Profiles*, trans. Frederick G. Lawrence (Cambridge, MA: MIT, 1983), pp. 37–40.
16. Werner J. Cahnman, "Schelling and the New Thinking of Judaism," in *German Jewry: Its History and Sociology, Selected Essays by Werner J. Cahnman*, ed. and with an introduction by Joseph B. Maier, Judith Marcus, and Zoltán Tarr (New Brunswick: Transaction Book, 1988).
17. Habermas, *Philosophical-Political Profiles*, pp. 37–38.

18. Ibid., p. 38.
19. Ibid.
20. Ibid., p. 40.
21. Benjamin, *Illuminations*, p. 99.
22. George Lichtheim, *Lukács* (London: Fontana/Collins, 1970), p. 67.
23. Karl Löwith, *Meaning in History* (Chicago: University of Chicago, 1964), p. 38.
24. Ibid., p. 44.
25. Benjamin, *Illuminations*, p. 264.

5

Lukács and the Concept of Work
in German Sociology

by Harry Liebersohn

Modern German sociology originated in a perception of crisis among a handful of professors in late nineteenth- and early twentieth-century Germany. Such thinkers as Ferdinand Tönnies (1855–1936), Georg Simmel (1858–1918), and Max Weber (1864–1920) confronted a German Empire that had achieved a superficial political unity, but was rent by class, confessional, and regional differences. They viewed these problems from the perspective of Germany's Protestant *Bildungsbürgertum*—a term describing the complexity of their social and cultural habitus. They were bourgeois; each of them came from a well-to-do, middle-class family and spent some time living as a rentier or supported by family wealth. They were "educated": each of them had passed through Germany's elaborate licensing system (*Abitur, Dissertation, Habilitation*) and was a certified member of its cultural elite. They were Protestant: none was religious in a conventional sense, but each was brought up in the established Church and to some extent absorbed its culture.

This social identity conditioned their conception of work in capitalist society, which was profoundly ambivalent. On the one hand, Tönnies, Simmel, and Weber all made use of Marx's analysis of alienated labor in order to comprehend the fragmentation and impoverishment of work as they experienced it. But they also felt loyalty toward their class and its educational traditions, and discarded Marx's revolutionary philosophy of history. Instead they fell back on peculiarly German Protestant cultural assumptions: pessimism toward social change, acceptance of the existing social order, and affirmation of suffering as a source of meaning. Each of the three thinkers made his own choice of Marxist and non-Marxist elements, but whatever the mix, the resulting concept of work was fraught with structural tensions.

As a Hungarian Jew, Lukács was by birth an outsider to Germany's Protestant *Bildungsbürgertum*. Moreover (and unlike Simmel), he chose to stay outside it. Although his wealth, family upbringing, and education made him a possible candidate for assimilation, and although he felt powerfully attracted by Germany's university system, he always remained a critical observer, absorbing some aspects of its culture and rejecting others. In particular he rejected its Lutheran pessimism. In making use of the German sociological tradition, he activated its inner tensions, turning them into dynamic contradictions that pressed forward toward a utopian resolution. In the following pages we shall retrace Lukács's argument with the sociologists by focusing on one narrow aspect of it, his critique of their concept of work.

I

The founding work of German sociology, Tönnies's *Gemeinschaft und Gesellschaft* (1887), announced the general sociological schema used by his successors. The title named the conceptual dichotomy for which Tönnies is still remembered: it starkly opposed the unity of *Gemeinschaft* to the fragmentation of *Gesellschaft*. The dichotomy had two logical dimensions, objective and subjective. On the one hand, Tönnies developed a materialist theory (drawn mainly from Hobbes and Marx) of a transition from primitive community, marked by production for use and fixed personal relationships, to modern capitalist society. On the other hand, Tönnies developed a voluntarist theory (drawn mainly from Schopenhauer and Nietzsche) in which the external social transformation was only the secondary accompaniment to the primary, underlying transition from a state of organic oneness to individuation of the will.

The title page of the first edition of the book also hinted at a third stage of social evolution: socialism. Tönnies looked forward to an eventual rebirth of community and for most of his life supported social and ethical reform as a means to ease its emergence. The final lines of the book proclaimed the evolutionary necessity of socialism, too. But the book did not analyze the process by which a utopian social order might issue forth out of existing society. Its method was classificatory, listing the features of each social order with great acuity, but only superficially describing the movement from one to the other. The womblike bliss of the past confronted the total disintegration of the present. As articulated by its structure, the overwhelming message of the book was elegiac, an outpouring of grief over the death of *Gemeinschaft*.

Recently there has been some appreciation for Tönnies as an anticapitalist thinker and as a constructive influence on Lukács. This appreciation is not wholly unjustified, but can be misleading. A fundamentally different teleological orientation separated their thought. Tönnies was a nostalgic theorist, despite his progressive politics; Lukács was a utopian theorist, despite his nostalgia. It was no accident that *Gemeinschaft und Gesellschaft* enjoyed a vogue of popularity among right-wing readers in the early 1920s, the same period when Lukács created a sensation on the Left with the publication of *History and Class Consciousness*. Tönnies was dismayed by his new admirers, but the *Blut und Boden* imagery of his *Gemeinschaft* and the hysterical despair vented toward *Gesellschaft* made a reactionary reading of his book perfectly plausible.

Tönnies came from the town of Husum on the west coast of Schleswig-Holstein. His mother belonged to a distinguished family of Lutheran clergymen, and he threw off their theology only after the experience of reading *The Birth of Tragedy* in 1873 converted him to Nietzsche's secular romantic vision. His father was a businessman-farmer who speculated on the stock exchange and profited from the cattle trade with England. During his youth, Schleswig-Holstein already reverberated with the politics of German unification and the slogans of socialist organizers. Tönnies did not let these signs of change disturb his youthful myth of his homeland as a blissful *Gemeinschaft*. One of the mentors who taught him to see it this way was the writer Theodor Storm. As a boy, Tönnies sang in the choir directed by Storm and assisted him with galley proof corrections for his anthology of German poetry. Tönnies's funeral oration and reminiscences about Storm are remarkably similar, in some respects, to Lukács's essay on him in *Soul and Form*, "Bürgerlichkeit und l'art pour l'art." Both Tönnies and Lukács found Storm's way of life as significant as his work—or rather, both were impressed by a life and work that were inseparable. Storm worked in the manner of a traditional German craftsman, perfecting his work over the unhurried course of a lifetime, following the intrinsic requirements of the object, not the external demands of the marketplace. Not that Storm was a solitary genius; on the contrary, he combined the exercise of his craft with his duties as husband and father, judge and local patriot. The work of art made by Storm resulted from the same process as the work of ivory made by the craftsman. Storm's example did not permit the bourgeois distinction between spiritual and material production; he inhabited a world that was still prior to it, nurturing the writer as one among many craftsmen.

Tönnies's essays were little more than an exercise in nostalgia, using the image of the craftsman to evoke a vanishing past. Lukács, by contrast, penetrated to the thought at the heart of the image. In his interpretation, work set the fundamental rhythm underlying all other activities of the community and harmonizing them with their natural surroundings. What characterized craft work as represented by Storm was "the rule of order over mood, of the lasting over the momentary, of quiet work over genius fed by sensations. Its most profound consequence, perhaps, is that such dedication can vanquish egotistical solitude.'' Lukács thus gave his essay an analytical foundation that was lacking in Tönnies. One could go on, as he did in the rest of the essay, to inquire how a specific literary form, the novella, embodied the work rhythms of the community, and how it differed from its modern successor, the novel. One could integrate this analysis of craftsmanship into a large discussion of work in capitalism and socialism, as Lukács later did in *History and Class Consciousness*, still insisting on the holistic nature of craftsmanship but assigning it a limited place in the larger movement of history.

The aesthetics of the two thinkers further brings out the contrast between Tönnies's nostalgic and Lukács's utopian orientation. Tönnies had no higher and indeed no other notion of art than the one represented by Storm: art as imaginative synthesis of the life of the community. After initial receptiveness to the new artists and thinkers (such as Wagner and the early Nietzsche) who shared this notion, Tönnies lost touch with German culture by the late 1880s. He was completely unable to respond to the many forms of modernism that from the 1890s onward attempted to grapple with the lack of genuine community in modern Germany. Lukács for his part set limits to Storm's achievement: Storm ''marks a watershed: he is the last representative of the great German middle-class (*bürgerlich*) literary tradition. Nothing is left in him or in the world he depicts of the great old epic, such as Jeremias Gotthelf still achieved, yet the atmosphere of decay which engulfs his world is not yet strong and conscious enough to become monumental once more, as is the case with Thomas Mann's Buddenbrooks.''[1] Lukács contrasted Storm and Mann according to the same maxim he had used in his *History of Modern Drama*: great art did not represent the life of its community, but resurrected it. Lukács's profoundly spiritual point of view enabled him to carry his analysis of culture beyond the death of traditional community and to comprehend an artistic achievement that upheld communal value in modern society. In *Buddenbrooks* the values of the *Bürgertum* received artistic immortality even as it gave way to the new bourgeoisie. By arguing that the spirit of community could transcend its material existence, Lukács displayed a dialectical imagination unknown to Tönnies.

II

Simmel was Tönnies's opposite: a Berliner to the fingertips, an enthusiast for modernist culture in its impressionist and *Jugendstil* phases, a contemptuous critic of the countryside. Although he, too, made use of the schema *Gemeinschaft-Gesellschaft*, he did so to champion the dignity of *Gesellschaft*. Simmel understood, as Tönnies was constitutionally unable to do, that modern society was not tantamount to chaos, but contained its own underlying logic. Borrowing a heuristic principle from Kant, he called this the logic of interaction (*Wechselwirkung*). According to this principle, at any given instant every part of the world existed in a mutual causal relationship to every other part. Between any two social entities the sociologist presupposed such a mutual relationship. In primitive stages of social evolution—i.e., in the *Gemeinschaft* admired by Tönnies—the degree of differentiation between different parts of society was lower; in modern society, each constituent part had a relatively high degree of internal autonomy and of interaction with other parts. Hence individuals in modern society were not tending toward Hobbesian anarchy, as Tönnies imagined, but were actually gaining in interdependence.

Lukács's close relationship to Simmel is well known. The basic philosophy of the *History of Modern Drama* was, as he himself commented in 1971, Simmel's philosophy. Chronology supports the accuracy of this recollection, since he wrote the book during the period demarcated by his study with Simmel in Berlin in 1906–7 and again in 1909–10. He analyzed the fragmented relationship between stage and audience along lines laid down in Simmel's *Philosophy of Money*: the intellectualized theater-goers of the modern metropolis had trouble responding to what they saw because they were too used to abstract conceptualization of life, too far removed from the symbols that drama had traditionally relied on for its story telling. In an ironic turn worthy of Simmel, he maintained that this same intellectualization of modern life provided modern drama with the materials of its own myth. In place of the traditional dependence on other persons, modern society had created a new form of bondage, the impersonal entrapment of modern man in the abstract laws of his society. The ethical form of these laws was bourgeois convention, forming the modern fate confronting the hero of the bourgeois stage.

For Simmel, reification was inevitable and irreversible. He coped with it by finding a saving grace within it, retreating into a passive and private form of self-cultivation. The name for this, which he took from Nietzsche, was *Vornehmheit*, or aristocratic distance and inner autonomy. To be *vornehm* ("distinctive") was to find a unique individual style and make it determine every aspect of one's being. He who was *vornehm* could not divorce himself from society—that is, from interaction with other individuals and with impersonal social forces. Too extreme a withdrawal would only have the effect of drawing attention to oneself and pulling one more deeply into the web of interactions. The truly *vornehm* adopted a strategy of inconspicuous removal, neither submitting to it nor ostentatiously straining against it. At a subtle middling distance, the person of distinction found the freedom to follow this inner law, and engaged in an invisible but superhuman struggle to shape a higher self.

To be *vornehm* was a form of work. It did not result in a socially useful product; the person of distinction was so purely for his own sake, without regard to ulterior ends. It was not profitable; Simmel stressed that the person of distinction did not ask "what it cost" to be so and accepted suffering and loss when they were the price. *Vornehmheit* implied a spiritual vocation. Simmel regarded *Vornehmheit* as *the* modern vocation, the direct successor to the Christian quest for individual salvation, filling the vacuum left by the collapse of traditional faith in the nineteenth century. To be *vornehm* was an ascetic discipline, a path of secular salvation open only to those with the highest degree of self-control, who were unceasingly committed to working the material of their human nature into the pattern of personal autonomy. Some readers familiar with Simmel's biography may be surprised to see vocation, a work concept of Protestant provenance, surface in his thought. It is well known that for his society at large—especially for the anti-Semites who excluded him from the university system—Simmel was a Jew. But Simmel was a baptized, assimilated Jew who chose to ally with Germany's hegemonic Protestant culture. Social origins condition any theorist's outlook, but, as the example of Simmel reminds us, they leave room for significant choices in shaping one's cultural affinities.

Lukács demonstrates the same point. Although he came from a *grand bourgeois* assimilated Jewish milieu comparable to Simmel's, he rebelled against both the passivity and the privacy of Simmel's thinking. In the drama book, he criticized *Vornehmheit* as a form of unheroic retreat from the struggle for self-realization in the world. In Lukács's words, he who was *vornehm*, who walked by the person injuring him, who dismissed all noise with a silent gesture and kept his sorrows secret, lacked tragic pathos. The playwright whose hero was *vornehm* had not created the highest kind of art; his was an uneven contest in which the external world triumphed over its victim. Lukács accepted the accuracy of Simmel's description of modern society as a complex of interactions, but refused to imitate his attitude of resignation toward it.

This rejection of mystical and aesthetic passivity runs through "The Metaphysics of Tragedy." Bourgeois isolation had to be opposed and transcended, and this imperative catapulted the tragic hero out of this world. If modern drama lacked a genuine community to serve as an audience, then its true audience was an invisible, divine spectator—one for whom all human affairs formed a *theatrum mundi* reflected in miniature on the stage. In the absence of human community, the tragic hero sought community with God. Paul Ernst's Brunhild, the quintessential tragic hero in Lukács's essay, was surrounded by a society of conniving nitwits who understood neither honor nor destiny; she did not hesitate to confound their schemes and fulfill her calling by freely choosing suicide. Simmel and Lukács both spoke of modern society as tragic, but meant different things. For Simmel, tragedy signified entrapment in its reified interactions; for Lukács, it signified total negation of them.

III

Max Weber fashioned his interpretation of work around the conflict between two social types. One was the goal-oriented, rational, activist social actor, whose mentality made him either a shrewd entrepreneur or an efficient worker; the other was the affective traditionalist who avoided clear thinking about means and ends and preferred known comforts to the unknown risks of innovation. In *The Protestant Ethic and the Spirit of Capitalism* the arch-modernizer was the Anglo-Saxon Puritan, the arch-traditionalist the German Lutheran. According to Weber, their different religious mentalities conditioned contrasting work ethics. The Lutheran longed for an immediate, emotional *unio mystica* with Christ; he carried out his daily round of tasks as a humbly suffered burden. The Puritan had a wholly detached, intellectual relationship to the dictates of his deity; he accumulated works in the world with the conviction or anxious hope that he was one of God's elect. The Lutheran never emerged from the mists of an irrational organic community of the kind described by Tönnies; the Puritan faced society with the dignified distance bearing a familial resemblance to Simmel's *Vornehmheit*.

Weber's attitude toward the Puritan-Lutheran antimony was ambivalent. He faced the two extremes as the attracting and repelling poles of his sociological imagination. In considering them, he had a contemporary problem in mind: Germany, he feared, lacked the inner drive to compete with British and American capitalism, and he blamed Germany's supposed torpor on its Lutheran culture. Particularly worrisome to him was the neoromanticism of Germany's university students, whom he accused of preferring aesthetic withdrawal to confrontation with the struggle for existence. In addition, he blamed Lutheranism for the average German's submissiveness toward political authority, for this reason calling it a ''horror of horrors'' in a letter of 1906 to Adolf von Harnack. To some extent he clearly admired the Anglo-American work ethic as he perceived it in his 1904 visit to the United States and held up its businesslike spirit as a model for his countrymen. Yet the final pages of *The Protestant Ethic* contained a critique of the Calvinist work ethic, too. Its inner spirit had fled, and what remained was, in Weber's famous phrase, a steel-hard shell. Nietzschean note of revulsion separated Weber from the hollow men who went through the impotent gestures of modern-day work. Puritanism was the cause of modernity's spiritual impoverishment; it had shaped an empty shell from which he saw no exit.

Lukács's antithesis of *Bürger* and bourgeois in the Storm essay corresponded to Weber's antithesis of Lutheran and Calvinist. Lukács admired the craftsman-burgher's work ethic as the basis of a unified, communal way of life in the traditional German town. In Weber's interpretation this figured (with a decidedly less sympathetic variation) as *Treue im Kleinen*, the petty bourgeois Lutheran devotion to the details of daily life. Lukács was harsher toward the bourgeois than Weber; in Lukács's view, as soon as the collective rhythm of work was broken, the outward discipline of the bourgeois became a mask hiding inward disorder. Weber allowed for a heroic age of the bourgeoisie, for an early modern era of genuine Calvinist spirituality before the disappearance of religious faith. But the end result was the same: Lukács's latter-day social actors, whose mask of efficiency only hid their inward chaos, inhabited the same spiritual void as Weber's soulless specialists. For both the master sociologist and the Hungarian student who joined him in Heidelberg in 1912, modern man's isolation had become tantamount to egoism. They differed, however, in their response to it. Weber was an agnostic about the chances for a return to community and tragically affirmed modern individualism; Lukács was determined to find his way back to a collective order, even if he could not yet see his way to it.

Weber was well aware of one living source of a postbourgeois, communal ethic for modern politics. As early as 1906 he called attention to the political ethic of the radical Russian intelligentsia, which was infused with a religiously inspired disregard for the calculable consequences of its action. "Politics as a Vocation," delivered in 1919, returned to the problem of this Russian ethic, which he now called *Gesinnungsethik* and saw exemplified in the heroes of Dostoevsky. It was a model of absolute ethical righteousness and immediate community with God that Weber rejected in favor of rational calculation and individual responsibility. His ideal politician learned to think through the probable consequences of his action. At exceptional moments of crisis, the responsible politician would face a conflict between conscience and consequences, forcing him to make a deliberate choice between them. At this point, wrote Weber, he might have to say, *Hier stehe ich, ich kann nicht anders*. With these words, Weber reached back to the isolated conscience of Luther and presented his credo as a lonely and passive imperative ("hier *stehe* ich") for the alienated modern world.

As we know from his recently discovered Dostoevsky manuscript (and from his correspondence with Paul Ernst as well as *The Theory of the Novel*), Lukács reacted to the war by contrasting German individualism with the coming postbourgeois community whose home was Russia and whose prophet was Dostoevsky. If Lukács was already struggling with the antithesis of German sociology before August 1914, afterwards he radically broke with them. German culture was no longer *bürgerlich*, it was bourgeois. Wilhelm Meister, who in Lukács's prewar cosmos would have hearkened back to Germany's craft traditions, now stood condemned as a bourgeois wanderer and imposture. The wartime quest for community, the fascination with Russia, and the commitment to communism led Lukács to the discovery of a collectivist work ethic, one that, he believed, transcended the antinomies of German sociology. If sociology oscillated ineffectually between agency and reified social conditions, between the individual actor's supposed freedom and his actual inability to make more than superficial changes in his surroundings, one had to conceptualize social action from a nonbourgeois perspective. A synthesis of conviction and conditions came about when the individual ceased to act alone (in the manner of Weber's heroic politician) and merged his will with that of the revolutionary class of history. By unifying and acting collectively under the leadership of its purified consciousness, the revolutionary party, the proletariat could make the passage from domination to freedom. With this theory, Lukács did not banish all the dilemmas of bourgeois civilization, as he momentarily believed he had done. But he did break through the hypnotic spell of German sociology, with its fixation on past and present, *Gemeinschaft* and *Gesellschaft*, and its acceptance of what has been as the guide to what shall be. Conceived in the sociological tradition, *History and Class Consciousness* went beyond it and made it possible to start talking about the future again.

IV

The habits of religious culture can survive the passing of religious belief. Despite their own perception that they inhabited a fragmented world, the German sociologists inherited a culture far more cohesive than anything existing today, and their native Protestantism profoundly informed their thought, especially their pessimistic philosophy of history. This conclusion leads to a parallel question about Lukács: how did Jewish messianism affect his secular utopianism? It is easy to read Jewish themes into his work, harder to prove their presence in a thinker who refused to make them explicit. The answer would have to come from a careful examination of Lukács's family, friends, and formative social milieu. If it was in fact latent in his thought, Jewish messianism would have found powerful provocation in the Protestant ethic of German sociology. Lukács's encounter with Tönnies, Simmel, and Weber would then form part of the larger conflict between hegemonic Protestant thought and revolutionary Jewish thought in twentieth-century Germany.

Notes

1. Cited from Georg Lukács, *Soul and Form*, trans. Anna Bostock (Cambridge, MA: MIT, 1980), p. 76. Throughout the translation, Bostock translates *bürgerlich* and *bourgeois* alike as "bourgeois." I have corrected this error by substituting "middle-class" above.

Part II
LITERATURE AND AESTHETICS

6

Georg Lukács on Narrating and Describing

By Laurent Stern

We praise our teachers only if we want to forget them. Unqualified praise must yield to criticism if we want to explain what our teachers taught us and what we have learned from them. Lukács was a rather conservative thinker, yet he taught generations of rebels. We must confront an even deeper paradox. If he is judged only by what he wrote in aesthetics, philosophy, or literary criticism, he will be found wanting. According to his critics, his judgments in literature are not informed by great sensitivity and his contributions to philosophy do not illustrate penetrating insight. He did not have a good ear for music and poetry or a good eye for art. By today's standards he wasn't even a close reader of literature or philosophy. Yet generations of gifted philosophers, aestheticians, and literary critics have learned from him. Even his most severe critics have learned from him. What did they learn? An answer to this question requires that we become clear about the matters that concerned him throughout his whole literary career.

I

"Let us begin in *medias res*! A race is related to two famous, newer novels (*neuere Romane*): in Zola's *Nana* and in Tolstoy's *Anna Karenina*." These are the first two sentences of Lukács's 1936 essay "Erzählen oder Beschreiben?"[1] These novels may have been "newer novels" in 1880, but they certainly did not remain such until 1936. The newer novels during the first fifty years of Lukács's life were written by Joyce, Kafka, Musil, and Proust. Among American novelists Lukács chose to write in this essay on Dos Passos and Sinclair Lewis, rather than on Faulkner. Throughout his life he

75

ignored the unprecedented creativity displayed in works of literary art from Joyce to Beckett. Yet he found his audience primarily among the readers of those novels rather than among those who shared his judgments and preferences. Why did his informed readers ignore these judgments? What did they understand him to be saying?

Almost any paragraph selected from Lukács's early writings will answer these questions. We read at the beginning of his essay "Metaphysik der Tragödie,"[2]

> Ein Spiel ist das Drama; ein Spiel vom Menschen und vom Schicksal; ein Spiel wo Gott der Zuschauer ist. Zuschauer ist er nur und nie mischt sich sein Wort oder seine Gebärde in die Worte oder Gebärden der Spielenden. Nur seine Augen ruhen auf ihnen. "Wer Gott schaut stirbt", schrieb Ibsen einmal; aber kann der leben auf den sein Blick gefallen ist?
>
> [The drama is a play; a play of man and of destiny; a play in which God is the spectator. He is only spectator and his word or gesture never mingles with the words or gestures of the players. Only his eyes rest on them. "Who sees God dies," Ibsen once wrote; but can he live on whom God's glance has been cast?]

Early readers of this essay printed with wide margins in the 1911 edition of *Die Seele und die Formen* must have been struck by the elevated tone, compact style, and questionable word order. The essays in this book require slow and repeated readings. Against a highly developed poetic sensitivity in the foreground, native speakers are confronted by an insensitivity to idiom and word order in the background. In the 1960s Hans-Georg Gadamer found Lukács's romantic and sentimental German alien to contemporary readers. Earlier, Mihály Babits heard a German accent in his Hungarian. Yet even these failings were insignificant when compared with what his readers found in his writings.

What they found was neither literary criticism nor aesthetics nor social theory. Since they were not looking for guidance in conventional intellectual pursuits, he did not lose them even after they judged him to be severely misguided. According to Adorno, Lukács's book of 1954, *The Destruction of Reason*, reveals the destruction of his own reason.[3] Yet there is no evidence that he lost readers, even among those who did not have any sympathy for the political or philosophical views that he expressed in this book. His readers, revolutionaries in politics and modernists in art, disregarded his limitations and failings. Despite a very long and productive literary career in these fields, this conservative thinker was not interested in conventional literary criticism, aesthetics, or social theory. His search was primarily for the normative and formative principles that provide groundwork for creativity in literature and philosophy. Works of art or philosophical doctrines were not in the foreground of his interests. According to the first essay of *Die Seele und die Formen*,[4]

Jedes Bild ist aus unserer Welt und die Freude dieses Daseins leuchtet von seinem Antlitz; doch es erinnert sich und es erinnert uns an etwas, das irgendwann da war, an ein Irgendwo, an seine Heimat, an das Einzige, das im Grunde der Seele wichtig und bedeutungsvoll ist. . . . Und die, die sich am entschlossensten von den Bildern abwenden, die am heftigsten hinter der Bildern greifen, sind die Schriften der Kritiker, der Platoniker und Mystiker.

[Every image is from our world and the joy of this existence shines from its physiognomy; yet it reminds itself and it reminds us about something that was here sometime, about somewhere, about its home, about the unique that is important and significant in the soul's depth. . . . And those who most resolutely turn away from images, who reach most vehemently behind the images, are the writings of critics, Platonists, and mystics.]

There are works of art; how are they possible? There are philosophical doctrines; why are they necessary? What values inform artworks or philosophical doctrines? Lukács aimed at a glimpse behind the graven images: what made these images possible, why did they become necessary? There are no ultimate answers to these questions. There is nothing but another image behind every graven image. He admitted this, and his readers agreed. But at the same time they hoped for admission to a Promised Land behind the images in the company of those he called Platonists and mystics. Ostensibly he wrote about literary artworks and about solutions to philosophical problems. Few critics, aestheticians, or philosophers wrote more on these subjects. What he said about them does not pass critical examination, but what he implied or intimated warrants very close scrutiny. His views deserve a hearing primarily for the questions he raised concerning the formative principles that are at the foundations of literary artworks.

The epos-novel answers the question, "Wie kann das Leben wesenhaft werden?"[5] (How can life become significant?) and tragedy provides answer to the question, "Wie kann des Wesen lebendig werden?"[6] (How can what is significant become alive?). The formulation of both questions has two presuppositions. Forms of literature are forms of life, and the central concern of every literary form is an answer to the question, "How to live?" Lukács did not formulate clearly these presuppositions. They are not stated, yet they are fundamental principles in all his writings. What is implied in his writings has a greater claim upon close scrutiny than what he actually wrote. His philosophy of art was a philosophy of life, and his philosophy of life, a moral philosophy.

His readers heard Rimbaud's call, "Il faut etre absolument moderne." They came neither for guidance about literary artworks nor for instruction about political issues. Concerning both matters his judgments and preferences were embarrassments to his modernist readers, who rejected his political illusions. His Western European or North American readers did not share his enthusiasm for minor figures in twentieth-century literature or what has become known as "socialism in one country." He was deaf to the great works of art of his own time and blind to the political realities of his own period, but his conservative answers were prompted by radical questions. His readers adopted the radical questions but arrived at answers that contradicted his conservative preferences. For any period that has a style, Lukács's questions about significance will be answered differently. The question, "How to live?" leads not only to a moral quest, but also to a search for a just society that rejects past or present illusions.

II

In his essay "Narrate or Describe?" Lukács argues for the claim that in literature narration is preferable to description. In support of this claim he first discusses the distinction between narration and description. Descriptions rely on observation. The speaker or writer moves off the foreground: anyone in his position and with his knowledge could in principle offer the same description of a given state of affairs. Characters are primarily spectators rather than participants in the events described. Readers are more or less interested spectators of a series of pictures. Finally, incidents that occurred in the past often appear as if they were occurring in the present. Narrations, however, depend primarily on experiences rather than on observation. Characters participate in significant events, and readers are presented with experiences. The narrator is in the foreground, he tells us about his experiences from his viewpoint. Since what is significant among all experiences is known only by hindsight, significant experiences are narrated as past events.

Lukács introduces the distinction between narration and description to support the claim that what he calls "realism" is superior to "naturalism": the art of Scott, Balzac, or Tolstoy is preferable to the art of Flaubert or Zola. No doubt the examples of great storytellers are well chosen. But these examples will support his claim that the art of these writers is preferable to that of Flaubert and Zola, only if we are convinced on independent grounds that other concerns are of secondary importance when compared with the art of story telling. Scott certainly is a very good storyteller, but a well-told story may appeal only to what is primitive in the reader. Scott's stories should be read aloud, according to E. M. Forster:[7]

> What the story does do in this particular capacity, all it can do, is to transform us from readers into listeners, to whom "a" voice speaks, the voice of the tribal narrator, squatting in the middle of the cave, and saying one thing after another until the audience falls asleep among their offal and bones. The story is primitive, it reaches back to the origins of literature, before reading was discovered, and it appeals to what is primitive in us.

Readers may not agree with Forster's harsh or with Lukács's favorable judgment of Scott's novels. In either case Flaubert's *Madame Bovary* will remind them that Scott's stories contributed more to Emma's downfall than to her development. A major theme of this novel is that life is neither a novel nor even like a novel. Readers of *Madame Bovary* could not possibly be passive listeners as the readers of Scott's novels. Considerable work is required on their part to understand and appreciate the various aspects of this novel that make it more than a story about provincial morality. Attention to Flaubert's language rather than to character or plot is a precondition for the reader's appreciation of this novel. In this case at least, insensitivity to language cannot be replaced by a search for what is behind the graven images. Lukács's judgments about Flaubert fail to convince the reader.

Contrary to Lukács's judgment, description need not reduce the value of literary artworks. The novels of Joyce and Beckett provide evidence for this claim. In speaking about literary artworks we must remember that language is used here primarily to create fictional characters and to talk about them. In judging such artworks we must hold in view their overall purpose: to provide aesthetic delight or to entertain. Description as well as narration can achieve this purpose. Yet Lukács's distinction between narration and description survives its use in this essay. Its importance can be appreciated when we attend to writings in history.

But before examining the value of the distinction, we must remember the important role of descriptions beyond the confines of literature. Students of art history will remember St. Bernard's often quoted letter to Abbot William of Saint Thierry:[8]

> In the cloister, under the eyes of the brethren who read there, what profit is there in those ridiculous monsters, in that marvelous and deformed beauty, in that beautiful deformity? To what purpose are those unclean apes, those fierce lions, those monstrous centaurs, those half-men, those striped tigers, those fighting knights, those hunters winding their horns? Many bodies are there seen under one head, or again, many heads to a single body. Here is a four footed beast with a serpent's tail; there a fish with a beast's head. Here again the forepart of a horse trails half a goat behind it, or a horned beast bears the hindquarters of a horse. In short, so many and so marvellous are the varieties of shapes on every hand, that we are more tempted to read in the marble than in our books, and to spend the whole day wondering at these things rather than in mediating the law of God. For God's sake, if men are not ashamed of these follies, why at least do they not shrink from the expense?

Art historians are unanimous in their praise of St. Bernard's description. Meyer Schapiro[9] appreciated the vivid inventory of the subjects of these sculptures and their precise characterization. Erwin Panofsky[10] wrote about this letter, "A modern art historian would thank God on his knees for the ability to write so minute, so graphic, so truly evocatory a description of a decorative ensemble in the 'Cluniac manner'; the one phrase *deformis formositas ac formosa deformitas* tells us more about the Spirit of Romanesque sculpture than many pages of stylistic analysis."

Both Panofsky and Schapiro contrast Bernard's gift for observation and description with the complete indifference to his physical surroundings. Reminded of this contrast, we can no longer claim that Bernard was a detached observer of these sculptures. His words provide us with a precise drawing of these objects, they tell us about profound experiences. He could be indifferent to the landscape on the shores of Lake Geneva, but he was responsive to these sculptures. Because he was responsive to them, he considered them dangerous. Free of context, we could appreciate his description. But greater value is assigned to descriptions that are integrated within narrations. The interpretive comments of Panofsky and Schapiro prompt our understanding of Bernard's description as an account of his deeply felt experiences. We marvel at his gifts because they are integral parts of a story, whose elements are provided by his beliefs, desires, and biography.

Detailed descriptions integrated within narrations are highly valued. In the medical literature, the case histories of Freud or A. R. Luria[11] or Oliver Sacks[12] are good examples. The finely observed details are connected with biographical elements; together they provide descriptions that are constituent parts of a narrative. Here description plays a subordinate role to narration. However, Lukács's distinction between description and narration is fully vindicated only in the context of writings on history.

III

Texts are judged correctly by most readers as narrations or descriptions, yet it is difficult to provide criteria distinguishing between them. Narrations have a point. They not only tell us about events in history or in a story, they also tell us why they happened from the viewpoint of a historian or narrator. Two witnesses may offer different descriptions of a given event. Only the causal history of that event can serve as evidence that their different descriptions are about one and the same event. Time and space coordinates permit the identification and reidentification of objects. Causal histories warrant the identification and reidentification of events. Descriptions, on the other hand, need not have a point. They merely tell us about what a witness has observed. References to a causal history in descriptions of events are limited to what has been seen by a witness. Witnesses are often admonished in legal contexts to refrain from interpretation and speculation. The ascription of unobserved intentions, motives, reasons, causes, and effects is discouraged. Witnesses unwilling or unable to distinguish between what is observable and what is unobservable are considered incompetent witnesses.

Descriptions of events brought about by human agents can be given as if they were natural events. But if we had only such descriptions at our disposal, an important link between events and those who brought them about or made them happen would be missing. Three questions arise that cannot be answered by descriptions. How were these events seen by those who brought them about? How were they seen by contemporaries who knew about the purposes, goals, beliefs, and desires of those who made them happen? Finally—given what we know about these events, the goals of those who brought them about, and predecessors' judgment about them—how do we see these events now? Only a narrative about the agents, their contemporaries, and their surrounding world can provide answers to these questions.

In his first book,[13] written in 1909, Lukács suggested that acceptance of the Humean analysis of causality would have more untoward consequences in literary than in real-life contexts. Succeeding events in drama and tragedy would become disconnected incidents: a necessary connection between the incidents can be established only by a causal connection. Such claims cannot be defended, Samuel Beckett's plays and Robert Musil's *Der Mann ohne Eigenschaften* provide evidence that great literary artworks can be created even if the Humean analysis of causality is accepted. The acceptance of Hume's analysis is in fact at the center of Musil's great novel.

Description need not assume a subsidiary role to narration in literary texts. Also, readers of such texts need not be induced to make believe that the events described are part of a grand design or that they occur because agents or circumstances brought them about. Events may be described as they happen one after another, and they may be connected only because they occur in a given sequence. There is no difference in principle between events so described and natural events. Medieval chronicles[14] and twentieth-century insurance companies do not discriminate between earthquakes, floods, civil wars, and revolutions; they are called "acts of God." If we wish to introduce a distinction between natural disasters and public commotions, we must tell a story. The story cannot be limited to a description of observable events.

As soon as we introduce the agents' aims and contemporary judgments about them, we are telling a story about these agents. We provide a connection between the events and those who brought them about by telling that story within a historical narrative. In that narrative a causal connection is established between the agents' aims, beliefs, and desires and their actions. Evidence about such matters would not be admitted in legal contexts, for the evidence reaches beyond the limits of what can be observed. Given such a historical narrative, we can distinguish between natural disasters and civil disturbances. However, as soon as we leave the limits of what can be observed and admit a historical narrative about the agents and what they brought about, we admit speculation and interpretation.

Historical narratives become fictional narratives unless they obey constraints in interpreting. What are these constraints? It has been suggested that interpretations must be rejected if we assume that the agents could not be persuaded to agree with them. According to Quentin Skinner, "No agent can eventually be said to have meant or done something which he could never be brought to accept as a correct description of what he had meant or done."[15] Skinner's suggestion presupposes that we can always distinguish between what an agent had meant or done and what he had brought about. But from a historical perspective, what had been meant or done is always seen in the light of what had been brought about. Historians believe Kaiser Wilhelm's protest that he did not mean to bring about the suffering and carnage of his soldiers in World War I, yet they blame him for the suffering. Also, it is up to us to decide whether our ancestors could be brought to accept our story of what they brought about. Since we ascribe to them the beliefs, purposes, and desires that brought about the events that happened, an additional claim that they would agree to our speculations and interpretations is an empty gesture.

There are only two candidates for providing the required constraint for historical narratives. Obviously, the narrative must be compatible with the available evidence. Also, wherever no evidence is available, the narrative must establish a probable connection between the related events. The narrative will serve as an explanation of these events only if the probable connection is a causal connection. There are no theoretically satisfactory constraints on the beginning or ending of historical narratives. A narrative's beginning, the conceptual framework that provides for a causal connection between related events, and a narrative's end depend on a given historian's viewpoint and perspective. What happened becomes a historical event only if it plays a role within a narrative. Its place in the historical narrative provides an explanation for that event. In ordinary contexts the connection between the agents' aims and what they did or brought about is provided by a story about the agents. Historical narratives offer causal explanations of events by assigning a role to agents, facts, accidents, and other events within narratives.

The agents' purposes, beliefs, and desires in doing what they did may have been known by their contemporaries. But the agents and their contemporaries were ignorant about what they brought about. Later historians know more about what was brought about, but they may be ignorant about their ancestors' aims, beliefs, and desires in doing what they did. The ages in the narrative are filled by claims about the causal role of events that are only partially supported by the available evidence. Accordingly, the causal connection suggested between events reported in historical narratives serves three different purposes. It permits the identification and reidentification of a given event under different descriptions. It offers an explanation for the occurrence of a given event. Finally, in case there is doubt about the occurrence of a given event, it supports claims about that event by indicating its causal role for later events. Historical narratives permit the "retrodiction"[16] of events.

Lukács wrote in "Erzählen oder Beschreiben?":[17]

Man kann ohne Weltanschauung nicht richtig erzählen, keine richtige, gegliederte, abwechslungsreiche und vollständige epische Komposition aufbauen. Die Beobachtung, das Beschreiben ist aber gerade ein Ersatzmittel für die fehlende bewegte Ordnung des Lebens im Kopfe des Schriftstellers.

[Without a worldview one cannot narrate well, one cannot construct a well-articulated, complete epic composition that is rich in reversal of circumstances. Observation and description are means of replacement for the missing dynamic organization of life in the writer's head.]

Long before Lukács wrote these lines, great twentieth-century novelists had turned away from writing narratives that bring out the causal connection between events imagined. However, even if causal connections between imagined events in a given novel are not shown, the episodes in that novel need not appear disconnected. They can be connected in many other ways. Examples are the stream-of-consciousness technique, a correspondence to related episodes in Homer, or reliance on speculative philosophical views about memory. Critics, historians, or theoreticians of literature engage in a futile exercise if they offer suggestions about methods of connecting incidents in an epic composition. Novelists will disregard these suggestions as empty legislation.

In historical narratives there are no substitutes for the causal connection between the events related. In addition to a narrative, historians may offer descriptions and even suggest moral or political lessons to be learned from their narratives, but these tasks are quite secondary to their major task of showing the causal connection between the events related. What Lukács had to say about narration applies more to historiography than to literature. "Without a worldview, one cannot narrate well"—for historians must select those events from the available evidence that can be fitted within their narrative. Whether an event is fitted to the *Haupt- und Staatsaktion* (high politics and great events) dear to German historians or to the *histoire des mentalités* of French historians, the principles of selection among events depends primarily on the historians writing about them. Geographical features, climatic conditions, and demographic changes are described in a given historical narrative only if a historian assigns them to causal role in that narrative. Even the search for documentary evidence is guided by the questions historians ask. These questions depend on their own worldview, conceptual framework, and what Lukács called "the dynamic organization of life in the writer's head." Medieval chroniclers may have written about the death of kings, miracles, and the plague. These writings provide twentieth-century historians with evidence about class struggle, social mobility, conspicuous consumption, or lifestyle.[18]

The new questions historians ask in every generation prompt not only the rewriting of history, but also the discovery of new evidence. But that very evidence depends on contemporaries understanding events that they witnessed, on other historians including them in their narrative, and on the preservation of the record of these events by archives and institutions. According to Paul Veyne, matters of fact are known to historians only within an interpretation. Also, the history of sequence of events is available only through the construction and understanding of a narrative.[19] This does not imply freedom from the constraints of the available evidence. But there are additional constraints. Historians must decide on both matters of fact and matters of interpretation. Since they are not confronted with bare facts independent of interpretations, they must decide simultaneously about two different questions: What happened? How is it understood? Answers to both questions are given within historical narratives. For an event is a historical event only if a historian assigns a causal role to that event within his narrative; but he assigns a causal role to that event only within a given conceptual framework. His narrative relies on what witnesses recorded about these events, how other historians understood and interpreted them, and on his own understanding and interpretation of witnesses and historians.

Historical narratives are subject to constraints, but they are underdetermined by the available evidence. Any account of events that ventures beyond the limits set to eyewitness testimony in legal contexts can be claimed to rely on "retrodiction," interpretation, and speculation. We may wish to substitute for the historian's work the Ideal Chronicler's eyewitness report, but as Arthur Danto[20] has demonstrated, the Ideal Chronicler is merely an incomplete and rather ignorant historian. He is ignorant of the later significance of events, and he cannot appreciate the difference between what agents did and what they brought about. But the underdetermination of a narrative by the available evidence need not discredit the narrative. Of course, it may be replaced by better supported narratives or by narratives that offer better explanations of the events related from the viewpoint of our purposes, beliefs, and desires.

IV

Much of what has been said here about historical narratives would have been acceptable to Lukács in 1914, when he wrote part 1 of *Die Theorie des Romans*, but it was certainly unacceptable twenty years later, when he wrote "Kunst und objektive Wahrheit." In the opening paragraph of this essay he wrote what became a guiding principle for all his later writings.[21]

> Jede Auffassung der Aussenwelt ist nichts anderes als eine Widerspiegelung der unabhängig vom Bewusstsein existierenden Welt durch das menschliche Bewusstsein. Diese grundlegende Tatsache der Beziehung vom Bewusstsein zum Sein gilt selbstverständlich auch für die künstlerische Widerspiegelung der Wirklichkeit.

[Every conception of the external world is nothing but a reflection of the world that exists independently of consciousness by human consciousness. This fundamental fact of the relation between consciousness and being applies also for the artistic reflection of reality.]

Lukács credits Lenin's epistemology for this insight. But the credit belongs neither to Lenin nor to Marx, Engels, and Stalin, who are also mentioned in this context. This insight originates in an older view that regarded the mind as a passive mirror of the world. By the end of the nineteenth century this view was discredited in science as well as in art. The claim that science and art are reflections of reality implies a further claim that reality can have only one adequate reflection. In the sciences this claim has been discredited at least since the publication of Heinrich Hertz's *Die Prinzipien der Mechanik* in 1894. Hertz found that even in the best understood science of his time there were three different ways of representing the available knowledge of the motion of bodies. In 1906, when Pierre Duhem published *La théorie physique, son objet et sa structure*, philosophers of science understood that there may be several incompatible yet adequate representations of the motion of bodies. The development of twentieth-century science becomes incomprehensible unless we accept the view that scientists make choices among different representations of reality and that scientific theories are underdetermined by the available evidence.

The great achievements of modern art, music, and literature since the late nineteenth century become incomprehensible if we accept as a guiding principle that art is a reflection of reality. Other aestheticians, historians, or critics of art, music, and literature judged past art in the light of these new developments. But when Lukács compared impressionist or cubist masters with their great realist predecessors, he found them wanting. His preference for the realism of a bygone age was a consequence of his acceptance of a discredited view in the philosophy of science and the philosophy of art.

Marx's eleventh thesis on Feuerbach—"The philosophers have only *interpreted* the world in various ways; the point is to *change* it"—contains a firmer guiding principle for the philosophy of science or the philosophy of art than any reflection theory. Conceptions of reality are not reflections of the external world. But as Ian Hacking wrote, "Our notions of reality are formed from our abilities to change the world."[22] Our conceptions of reality are dependent on what we use in bringing about a change in our world and what can be used in bringing about a change in us. We become convinced about the reality of entities conjectured in physics when we bring about a change in nature by using the causal properties of these entities. Only if we reject the view that art is a reflection of reality can we appreciate the profound changes brought about in us and our world of modern art, music, and literature. Modern art has shaped at least a part of our world and illuminated our experience of that world.

V

Theories of literature need not prejudice practical literary criticism. The young Lukács taught his readers about principles of literary forms. These principles guided them in interpreting these modern and classical literary works that the later Lukács excluded from the canon. The notion of reflection of reality plays a predominant role in his later work, and it provides limits to what he admitted to the canon, but it does not facilitate practical criticism. However, once he admitted a literary work to the canon, was his practical criticism informed by his theory of literature? Wherever he provided successful models in interpreting, his results were not influenced by theory, and conversely, wherever his results were influenced by theory, he did not provide successful models in interpreting. His readers have inherited the task of providing application in practical criticism for his successful theories and theories for his successful critical interpretations.

Notes

1. Georg Lukács, *Probleme des Realismus* (Berlin: Aufbau, 1955), p. 103.
2. Georg von Lukács, *Die Seele und die Formen* (Berlin: Egon Fleischel, 1911), p. 325.
3. Theodor Wiesengrund Adorno, *Noten zur Literatur 2* (Frankfurt am Main: Suhrkamp, 1961), p. 153.
4. Lukács, *Die Seele*, pp. 12–13.
5. Georg Lukács, *Die Theorie des Romans* (1st ed. 1920; quoted from 2d ed., Neuwied and Berlin: Luchterhand, 1963), p. 23.
6. Lukács, *Die Seele*, p. 335.
7. E. M. Forster, *Aspects of the Novel* (1st ed. 1927; quoted from 1954 rpt., New York: Harcourt, Brace & World, 1954), p. 40.
8. See Meyer Schapiro, "On the Aesthetic Attitude in Romanesque Art" (1947; rpt. in *Romanesque Art*, New York: George Brazillier, 1977), p. 6.
9. Ibid., p. 8.
10. Erwin Panofsky, *Abbot Suger, on the Abbey Church of St. Denis and Its Art Treasures* (1st ed. 1946; quoted from 2d ed., Princeton: Princeton University, 1979), p. 25.
11. See, for example, A. R. Luria, *The Man with a Shattered World* (New York: Basic Books, 1972), and *The Mind of a Mnemonist* (New York: Basic Books, 1968).
12. Oliver Sacks, *Awakenings* (1st ed. 1973; rev. ed. New York: E. P. Dutton, 1983). See also an account of his own accident and recovery in *A Leg to Stand On* (New York: Summit, 1984).
13. Lukács, *A modern dráma fejlödésének története* (Budapest: Franklin Társulat, 1911), p. 23 and passim.
14. See, for example, Hayden White, "The Value of Narrativity in the Presentation of Reality," *Critical Inquiry* 7(1980): 11.
15. Quentin Skinner, "Meaning and Understanding in the History of Ideas," *History and Theory* 8(1969): 28.

16. Paul Ricoeur, *Temps et récit*, 2 vols. (Paris: Editions du Seuil, 1983), 1:191.
17. Lukács, *Probleme des Realismus*, p. 134.
18. Paul Veyne, "L'histoire conceptualisant," in *Faire de l'histoire*, ed. Jacques Le Goff and Pierre Nora, 3 vols. (Paris: Gallimard, 1974), 1:67.
19. Paul Veyne, *Les Grecs ont-ils cru à leurs mythes?* (Paris: Editions du Seuil, 1983), p. 117.
20. Arthur Danto, *Analytical Philosophy of History* (Cambridge, MA: Harvard University, 1965), ch. 8, "Narrative Sentences," pp. 143–81.
21. Lukács, *Probleme des Realismus*, p. 5.
22. Ian Hacking, *Representing and Intervening* (Cambridge: Cambridge University, 1983), p. 146.

7

Georg Lukács's "Goetheanism": Its Relevance for His Literary Theory

By Ehrhard Bahr

Visitors to Lukács's apartment in Budapest reported that he had only two pictures in his large study lined with books: one of Balzac and one of Goethe. No Lukács scholar would be surprised at this choice for interior decoration. Lukács esteemed Balzac above all other nineteenth-century novelists, because Balzac reflected historical developments objectively in his novels, even when he was opposed to them ideologically. Friedrich Engels was the first to recognize this phenomenon in his famous "realism letter" to Miss Margaret Harkness of 1888. This letter is not only one of the most important documents of Marxist aesthetics, but it also exercises a profound influence on Lukács's theory of literature.

The "realism letter" by Engels became known to Marxist critics as late as 1932, when it was first published in German in *Die Linkskurve*. This letter constituted a point of departure for Lukács's principle of great literature, the so-called triumph of realism, implying that despite their own political affiliations and preferences, great realist writers cannot help but reflect faithfully the social realities of their times. Although Balzac was politically a legitimist and a follower of the royalist party, he wrote, according to Engels and Lukács, with great objectivity about the republicans, his political enemies.[1] The "triumph of realism" constituted for Lukács not only the essence of great literature, but also a strategy for including his favorite bourgeois authors in the canon of socialist literature. Balzac and Goethe represented the cultural heritage of the past, which Lukács tried to save as a model for socialist literature. No wonder that Lukács chose their portraits to hang in his study.

From the Dramabook to the Goethe Prize:
Goethe's Place in Lukács's Lifework

Lukács's preference for Goethe dated back to his pre-Marxist period. Even in his first major work, *Entwicklungsgeschichte des modernen Dramas*,[2] published in Hungarian in 1909, considerable space was devoted to Goethe, although upon closer examination the book shows that Goethe's inclusion was inevitable, because Lukács had chosen German classical drama as one of his points of departure for modern drama. He could not very well have left out the author of *Iphigenie* and *Tasso* when discussing classical German drama. In comparison with Schiller, however, Goethe's name is quoted less frequently, yet Schiller never achieved the same prominence in Lukács's later works as Goethe did. Whether Lukács wrote on Shakespeare, Cervantes, Sir Walter Scott, Pushkin, Tolstoy, or Ibsen, Goethe was to become his constant point of reference and his standard for literary excellence.

Lukács himself dated his preference for Goethe to *Die Seele und die Formen* (*Soul and Form*), published in German in 1911.[3] Although there is not a single essay on Goethe in this volume, it is in the essay on Novalis and the romantic philosophy of life that Goethe comes to the fore as a counterpart to romanticism. Although Novalis is the topic of the essay, Goethe is its central subject throughout. On the occasion of the award of the Frankfurt Goethe prize in 1970, Lukács declared that he considered Goethe a standard for human excellence.[4] The book also contained "A Dialogue concerning Lawrence Sterne," in which two young philologists, a dogmatic one and an enthusiastic one, discuss the merits of the great English novelist. Again Goethe serves as a foil, when the dogmatist declares, "It is impossible to love Goethe and Sterne at the same time. The man to whom Sterne's writings mean a great deal doesn't love the real Goethe."[5] The proposition is absurd, as Lukács shows—one can indeed love Goethe and Sterne at the same time, if one has an understanding of irony—yet the dogmatist wins the debate, an allegorical battle that is fought like a medieval joust in front of a young woman. The enthusiast, however, wins the favor of the young woman. Because he does love the real Goethe, Sterne's writings mean a great deal to him.

Lukács's next book, *Die Theorie des Romans* of 1920 (originally published as an essay in 1916),[6] also has Goethe at its center. The connecting link between *Die Seele und die Formen* and *Die Theorie des Romans* is irony as a formative element of the novel. Lukács conceived Goethe's *Lehrjahre*[7] as an attempt at synthesizing reality and transcendence. Goethe's creative irony provided reality with sufficient substance that any transcendent tendencies were counterbalanced by form, although Lukács had to admit that no formal element could completely camouflage this generic dichotomy of the novel.

Between 1918 and 1929, Lukács devoted his life to active participation in politics, first within the short-lived Soviet Republic of Hungary, then, after its defeat, within the exile politics of the Hungarian Communist party. After a short stay in Moscow, where he worked on the edition of the collected works of Marx and Engels at the Marx-Engels-Lenin Institute, Lukács returned to literature and literary criticism in 1931, when he relocated to Berlin from 1931 to 1933 as member of the Communist party of Germany. Here he emerged as the leading spokesman of Marxist literary theory in the controversy about realism in *Die Linkskurve*, the monthly journal of the League of Proletarian Revolutionary Writers (*Bund Proletarisch-Revolutionärer Schriftsteller*).

His return to literary criticism was also a return to Goethe. During the Goethe Year of 1932 Lukács participated, together with Ernst Bloch, Friedrich Burschell, Erich Mühsam, and Herbert Ihering, in the Goethe conference of the oppositional faction of the Association of German Writers (*Schutzverband Deutscher Schriftsteller*) in Berlin, where they raised the question, "What does Goethe mean to us today?" In a special Goethe issue of *Die Linkskurve*, Lukács published an article on "The Fascisized Goethe" ("Der faschisierte Goethe"),[8] in which he demonstrated on the basis of quotations from leading German newspapers that Fascist ideology with its irrationalism had penetrated even the democratic liberal press when it celebrated Goethe as a representative of the modern irrational philosophy of life (*Lebensphilosophie*) and a spiritual forefather of Schopenhauer and Nietzsche.

When Hitler came to power in 1933, Lukács went into exile again, in the Soviet Union, where he devoted himself exclusively to literary criticism and became involved in the second major debate of Marxist aesthetics, the so-called expressionism debate of 1937–38. At the end of the 1930s Lukács wrote major articles that show a new image of Goethe emerging from the previous debates about literary theory. They are "Der Briefwechsel zwischen Schiller and Goethe" of 1937 ("The Correspondence between Schiller and Goethe"), and "Die Leiden des jungen Werther" ("The Sorrows of Young Werther") and "Wilhelm Meisters Lehrjahre" ("Wilhelm Meister's Apprenticeship"), both of 1939. Only the "Fauststudien" ("Faust Studies") were completed in 1941. The manuscript of a special monograph on "Goethes Lebensführung" ("Goethe's Conduct of Life") composed during the late 1930s was lost, when he was arrested and held in custody by the NKVD in 1941. Under the title *Goethe und seine Zeit* (*Goethe and His Time*), his collected Goethe articles of the 1930s and 1940s were published after World War II, in 1947. Lukács's professed goal in these articles was a critical review of German culture, past and present, designed "to influence the democratic renovation of contemporary culture'"[9] Lukács wanted to mobilize the traditions of the Enlightenment and humanism against the heritage of fascism.

This is not the place to present a descriptive account of Lukács's Goethe studies. I have done so in the chapter "World Literature" of my Lukács monograph.[10] The most important feature of Lukács's Goethe studies is his grounding of Goethe in the Enlightenment tradition. With the exception of Ferenc Fehér's article "Lukács in Weimar," which deals with the implications of Lukács's classicism for his postulate of ethical democracy, an analytical assessment of Lukács's Goethe studies is still lacking. The term "Goetheanism," coined by Hans Mayer, is another brilliant attempt at coming to terms with Lukács's Goethe studies, implying that Lukács's image of Goethe was more Goethean (that is, classicist) than the historical Goethe himself. Without doubt, Mayer is right in his assessment. Lukács concentrated on the Weimar Goethe after his return from Italy at the expense of the young Goethe and especially also the old Goethe. He neglected Goethe's *West-östlichen Divan* as well as his *Wanderjahre* (*Wilhelm Meister's Journeyman Years*), and he did not recognize the allegorical mode of Goethe's *Faust, Part II*, although he read it as such. Mayer, however, criticized Lukács's approach mainly by juxtaposing his Goethe studies with Adorno's *Iphigenie* essay of 1967 and by reviving the critical strategy employed against Lukács during the expressionism debate, namely, that Lukács concentrated on literary theory rather than literary practice.[11]

Goethe, or the Option for an Alternative in Art

It is my thesis that Lukács's option for Goethe was basically an aesthetic one, that is, an option for one of the two alternatives in art, namely, the "closed" work of art (*geschlossenes Kunstwerk*) versus the "open" work of art (*offenes Kunstwerk*). Lukács's decision for this option can be traced back to his Heidelberg philosophy of art (*Heidelberger Philosophie de Kunst*) of 1912–14, which was finally published in 1974.[12] The two alternatives constituted for Lukács the two fundamental possibilities in art. By implication Lukács identified these alternatives with the historical typological opposition of the classical versus the romantic concept of art. On the basis of the adequacy of form and content as the principal standards for art, Lukács opted for the closed work of art or classicism and identified the open work of art with modernism or avant-garde art.

My second thesis is that Lukács's Goetheanism is behind the positions he took in the major debates of Marxist aesthetics during the 1930s, during the *Linkskurve* debate as well as the expressionism debate. Behind his articles against Willi Bredel and Ernst Ottwalt in *Die Linkskurve* in 1932–33, behind his articles against Ernst Bloch and Hanns Eisler in *Das Wort* in 1938, and behind his controversy with Bertolt Brecht which was not fully recognized until the 1960s, there is an attempt at providing historical and philosophical foundations for closed forms in literature. In this context, his postulate of closed forms constituted a postulate of realism. Socialist literature was to reflect "the driving forces of processes in their totality."[13] One of the prime examples of such an approach among bourgeois writers is Goethe, as he was perceived by Lukács. In a footnote he referred by implication to Goethe's "naive materialism" as well as his "intuitive dialectics."[14] As a "great realist writer of the revolutionary phase of the bourgeois class," Goethe is claimed as the literary heritage of socialist literature.[15] Bredel and Ottwalt, on the other hand, were attacked by Lukács as proponents of the concept of open forms in literature.[16]

At this stage of Lukács's reception, it appears to me more important to recognize the Goethean foundation of his literary criticism than to denounce it from the Brechtean perspective as conservative, old-fashioned, abstract, dogmatic, or idealistic.[17] The controversy between Brecht and Lukács was based not on personal conflicts or party politics, but on two fundamentally different and irreconcilable definitions of art, definitions that form the bases of legitimate forms of art and may coexist even within Marxist aesthetics. In other words, it was a conflict about the merits of an Aristotelian concept of art versus a non-Aristotelian concept.[18]

My final and last thesis concerns the continuity of Goetheanism in Lukács's literary theory. Goethe continued to be present in Lukács's writings as an indisputable standard of life and art through his late works of the 1960s and early 1970s. His projected ethics was based on a maxim by Goethe that the common man, too, could be perfect and that, therefore, "the ethical perfection of man does not depend on his mental faculties or on his talents."[19] Likewise, Lukács's *Ästhetik* of 1963 has Goetheanism at its center. Goethe functions as a discoverer of *Besonderheit* (specificity) as an aesthetic category, and his distinction between symbol and allegory becomes crucial to Lukács's definition of art. Although he realized that Goethe's distinction was a historical one, Lukács did not hesitate to follow Goethe's lead in evaluating symbol as more characteristic of art than allegory, even though he was fully acquainted with Walter Benjamin's theory of allegory in his book *Ursprung des deutschen Trauerspiels* (*Origin of German Tragedy*). Lukács justified his option for Goethe as an option for realism. For Lukács, Goethe's concept of symbol constituted the essence of realist art.[20]

Lukács's goal at the end of World War II was to influence contemporary culture in the direction toward ethical democracy. This is an old idea of his, expressed as early as his chapter on *Wilhelm Meister's Lehrjahre* with its emphasis on social community and its form in literature.[21] For this reason, Lukács turned to Goethe as a "mentor of *modern* times."[22] In Goethe's maxim from the *Lehrjahre* that all men constitute humanity, Lukács found a literary equivalent of Marx's concept of man as *Gattungswesen* (species being). It was postulated by a Goethe who was more Goethean than the historical Goethe himself. But this form of Goetheanism provided Lukács with a theory of literature that is, in principle, available to all and was to offer alienated individuals an opportunity to experience themselves as integrated "species beings."

Notes

1. See Georg Lukács, *Studies in European Realism*, introd. Alfred Kazin (New York: Grosset & Dunlap, 1964), p. 11.
2. Georg Lukács, *Entwicklungsgeschichte des modernen Dramas*, ed. Frank Benseler, trans. from the Hungarian by Dénes Zalán (Darmstad and Neuwied: Luchterhand, 1981). Not yet translated into any other language.
3. See Georg Lukács, *Soul and Form*, trans. Anna Bostock (Cambridge, MA: MIT, 1974).
4. See Georg Lukács, "Zur Verleihung des Goethepreises," in *Georg Lukács zum 13. April 1970: Goethepreis '70*, ed. Frank Benseler et al. (Neuwied and Berlin: Luchterhand, 1970), pp. 121–31.
5. See Lukács, *Soul and Form*, p. 127.
6. See Georg Lukács, *The Theory of the Novel*, trans. Anna Bostock (Cambridge, MA: MIT, 1971).
7. Reference is to Goethe's *Wilhelm Meisters Lehrjahre*.
8. Georg Lukács, "Der faschisierte Goethe," *Die Linkskurve* 4(1932), "Goethe Sonderheft," pp. 33–40.
9. Georg Lukács, *Goethe and His Age*, trans. Robert Anchor (New York: Grosset & Dunlap, 1969), p. 7.
10. See Ehrhard Bahr and Ruth Goldschmidt-Kunzer, *Georg Lukács* (New York: Frederick Ungar, 1972), pp. 78–81.
11. See Hans Mayer, *Goethe: Ein Versuch über den Erfolg* (Frankfurt am Main: Suhrkamp, 1973), pp. 69–74.
12. See Georg Lukács, *Heidelberger Philosophie der Kunst (1912–1914)*, ed. György Márkus and Frank Benseler (Darmstadt and Neuwied: Luchterhand, 1974).
13. Georg Lukács, "Reportage or Portrayal?" in *Essays in Realism*, ed. Rodney Livingstone, trans. David Fernbach (Cambridge, MA: MIT, 1981), p. 52.
14. Ibid., p. 240.
15. Ibid.
16. For an account of the controversy, see Helga Gallas, *Marxistische Literaturtheorie: Kontroversen im Bund proletarisch revolutionärer Schriftsteller* (Neuwied and Berlin: Luchterhand, 1971), p. 157.
17. See Lothar Baier, "Streit um den Schwarzen Kasten: Zur sogenannten Brecht-Lukács Debatte," in *Lehrstück Lukács*, ed. Jutta Matzner (Frankfurt am Main: Suhrkamp, 1974), p. 245.
18. Werner Mittenzwei, "Der Streit zwischen nichtaristotelischer und aristotelischer Kunstauffassung: Die Brecht-Lukács Debatte," in *Dialog und Kontroverse mit*

Georg Lukács: Der Methodenstreit deutscher sozialistischer Schriftsteller, ed. Werner Mittenzwei (Leipzig: Reclam, 1975), pp. 192–203.

19. *Gespräche mit Georg Lukács*, ed. Theo Pinkus (Reinbek bei Hamburg: Rowohlt, 1967), p. 109.

20. Georg Lukács, *Die Eigenart des Ästhetischen*, vol. 2 (Neuwied and Berlin: Luchterhand, 1963), pp. 197 and 727–66.

21. See Lukács, *Theory of the Novel*, pp. 136–39.

22. See Ferenc Fehér, "Lukács in Weimar," in *Lukács Revalued*, ed. Agnes Heller (New York: Columbia University, 1983), pp. 75–106.

8

Music and Society in the Twentieth Century: Georg Lukács, Ernst Bloch, and Theodor W. Adorno

By Robert Lilienfeld

Introduction: The New Sociology of Music

The sociology of music, neglected until recently, has begun to attract the labors of many scholars. One chapter in this musical sociology will belong to the writings of Georg Lukács, Ernst Bloch, and Theodor W. Adorno. Their writings are interrelated; each was influenced by, and opposed to, the others in complex ways. None of them was a musicologist or sociologist in a conventional academic sense; rather, each was an odd mixture of aesthetician, social philosopher, ideologue, and critic.[1]

The writings of Lukács, Bloch, and Adorno on music span the period from about 1915 to about 1975; Western music has undergone revolutionary changes to which these authors attempted to respond by developing their own interpretations of the meaning of those changes. Characteristic of their interpretations is an attempt to establish relationships between the meaning of music as a cultural form and the social and political structures of Western society. For them, working from Marxist perspectives, the major issues of the music of their time—the struggles over program music and absolute music; the growing crisis of tonality that overshadowed the second half of the nineteenth century; and the changing social support of music and musicians—were less important than the political and philosophical issues. In this essay, I will examine the limits and constraints that these three imposed upon themselves by their political and ideological rigidity as well as their genuine perceptions and insights.

The Transition to the Twentieth Century

Lukács and Bloch were born in 1885, Adorno in 1903; thus, they began their studies and their lifework within the cultural atmosphere of the nineteenth century. The cultural order of that century did not end until the war of 1914–18, and in some areas it lingered on well into the 1930s; the 1920s was a decade that saw a decisive departure from the culture of the nineteenth century. I can mention only such developments as the break that the poetry of T. S. Eliot and Ezra Pound represented, and the formulation, in 1924, of the twelve-tone system of composition by Arnold Schoenberg. This was intended to be the decisive break with the music of the nineteenth century.

Thus, Lukács and Bloch came to awareness in a time of transition, but nevertheless a time that remained within the nineteenth-century cultural atmosphere; in retrospect, this resembles a Golden Age before the descent into cultural emptiness that has been the gift of the twentieth century to the world. Adorno's writings, begun somewhat later than those of Lukács and Bloch, reflect the difference. Still based within a rich musical heritage, Adorno was, even more than Lukács and Bloch, willing to do violence to his own experience by the rigid enforcement of dialectical fantasies. Yet in all three are to be found brilliant observations and theoretical formulations that are valid and fruitful.

The musical world into which these men entered offered three features that form the salient background to their writings:

1. The struggle between "program music," so-called, and "absolute music."
2. The growing exhaustion of the language of music, which can be called the crisis of tonality. This began with the chromaticism of Chopin-Liszt-Wagner, continued through the experiments of Debussy-Mahler-Richard Strauss, and later with those of Scriabin, Reger, and Schoenberg, culminating in Stravinsky, Alban Berg, and Anton von Webern. (Adorno studied composition with Alban Berg.) Thus, what began as a common musical language ended in a multiplicity of aesthetic experiments, each in a private or cultic vocabulary.
3. Changes in the social condition of music and musicians, and, with this, change in the character of composers and composing. The rise of avant-gardism, as an aesthetic attitude, influenced not only musical practice, but even more, the ways in which these matters were written about. Lukács, Bloch, and Adorno were each partly influenced by avant-gardism, and in part were uncomfortable with the avant-garde—an ambivalence they did not resolve.

Changing Conceptions of Music in Society

Ancient music had never stood by itself; it was always inseparable from ritual, legend, dance, and poetry; its "meaning" was given to it from outside of music. But a distinctive feature of Western music has been its long struggle to create a music separated from exterior meanings—to develop its own autonomy. A first step in this direction was the late medieval and Renaissance development of polyphony and of choral harmony, the historically unique features of Western music. But these developments occurred when the music was still primarily vocal and choral; instrumental music remained rudimentary. A second major step was taken with the emergence of perfected keyboard instruments, systems of tuning, and perfected families of instrumental design such as the string family—violin, viola, violoncello, and contrabass—and of choirs of wind and brass instruments as well. Now instrumental music could become autonomous.

And now there could evolve an art of abstract instrumental music. This long development culminated in the sonata form brought to early perfection by the "first Vienna school"—Haydn, Mozart, and Beethoven. The sonata form was a genus of which the various species included the piano sonata, the string quartet, and other genres of chamber music, the concerto, and the symphony, the latter being a "sonata" for orchestra.

A new language also emerged; or rather, music had developed its own language. Musical meanings were now conceived entirely in musical terms; there were forms of musical motion (phrase systems); goals of motion (various keys); delaying devices (sequences, modulations); and tonal regions within which musical themes and dramas could unfold, changes of scenery involving departures, wanderings, and returns.

Now the instrumental sonata undoubtedly began as a dance suite, that is, as something related to extramusical meanings; but the dances quickly became more and more abstract and stylized. The minuet survived for a time, but only for a time; it was replaced by the scherzo, which quickly evolved into an abstract instrumental form. But while this rich language of absolute or abstract music was being developed, another musical trend of thought, that of program music, was preparing to attack absolute music and to appropriate its language for other purposes.

Musicians have always imitated natural events: bird songs, battles, storms, animal cries. They have composed music for rejoicing and for lamentation. One trend of musical aesthetics had always claimed that music not only expressed emotions but could evoke them. Fearful soldiers could be made brave by appropriate music, and the same music could strike fear in the hearts of the enemy. The sick could be healed by music, as was King Saul by David's playing of the harp.

This musical tradition was linked to the musical conceptions of antiquity, which equated musical harmonic ratios with the "music of the spheres"; specific musical scales were associated with gods and goddesses, or with seasons of the year, or with planets. Ancient literature is full of stories concerning the ability of a great musician to create effects "out of season," by performing music in the scales associated with winter or summer, or to heal the sick, or to make audiences laugh or cry. Music was linked to magic. Thus, the older conception of music would not surrender easily to absolute music.

The doctrines of the musical Baroque—the *Affektenlehre*—taught that specific musical motives represented specific "affects"—hope, guilt, despair, anger, and the like. It was not clear whether these motives were expressions of these affects, or were symbols of them, or could evoke them, or perhaps all at once. But by the late eighteenth century the *Affektenlehre* had retreated—as had tone painting in general—in the face of the triumphs of abstract instrumental music. Composers certainly would continue to write program pieces, or, as they were sometimes called, "character pieces," but these were regarded somewhat as a trick or a joke. Thus, we listen quite seriously to a Beethoven sonata or symphony, but his "Wellington Victory" or "The Rage Over a Lost Penny" are considered to be trifles. Increasingly separated from practicality and from the need to legitimate itself by creating emotional moods, music could claim an intrinsic value in its own right.

The breadth and depth of the triumph of absolute music can be seen in the usages of concert life. Music is performed today with a complete disregard for practical occasions; one may hear at the same concert a cantata or motet, a serenade, excerpts from an opera, and even dances. Such mixtures suggest that the value of the music transcends its intended function, and is best comprehended in a purely musical occasion. Often, a church will advertise that a Bach cantata will be performed at a Sunday service; and one must wonder—as clerics have worried for generations—whether the church service is being overshadowed by the musical experience.

But the sovereignty of absolute music was seriously contested. The romantic movement reawakened program music in all sorts of ways. The principal early representatives of the new program music included Hector Berlioz, Karl Maria von Weber, and Franz Liszt. Liszt especially claimed that music could tell a story—not only this, but that in telling the story of a hero's life, the composer could depart from rigid formal procedures in music; the expressive program was more important than the formal program of symmetry, recapitulation, and resolution. The later representatives of this approach, such as Richard Wagner, Richard Strauss, and Claude Debussy, were to carry the expressive and programmatic features of music to the forefront. Richard Strauss even boasted that program music had made such strong progress that if a composer wished to portray a dinner party in music, the audience would be able to tell the difference between knife, fork, and spoon by the music alone. (Some romantic composers, like Schumann and Mendelssohn, not only produced program or character pieces with literary or poetic titles, but were also masters of the intricacies of absolute forms such as the string quartet and the symphony.)

Program music as a movement was attacked in the year 1854, when Eduard Hanslick published his remarkable treatise *On the Beautiful in Music*.[2] Hanslick, the Viennese contemporary of Bruckner, Wagner, Brahms, and Mahler, was a formidable figure: the world's first professor of musicology and a powerful critic whose writings are of lasting interest. He was satirized without mercy by Richard Wagner in his opera *Die Meistersinger von Nürnberg* as Beckmesser, a sterile, carping critic. In an early version of the libretto, he had been named ''Hans Lich.'' A critic, of course, is someone who tells others how their work might be better but does no work of his own. Yet Hanslick's essay remains a powerful and brilliant work to this day, though an angry and ill-tempered one.

Hanslick pointed out that any piece of music played into a roomful of listeners could evoke as many different responses as there are listeners. Some would ''see'' in the music a storm at sea; others, a quarrelsome dialogue between lovers; others still might evoke the lamentation of Dido for her lost lover Aeneas; and so on. Hanslick called attention to the fact that many composers—Bach and Handel among them—had used the same music in different operas, or once for an opera and later for a cantata, and the music served equally well for both occasions. He selected a phrase from Gluck's *Orpheus*, set to the words, ''I have lost my Eurydice; nothing can equal my grief,'' and showed that the music could just as easily be sung as, ''I have found my Eurydice; nothing can equal my joy.'' Hanslick's point is powerful, for I can remember first hearing Josquin des Prez's marvelous composition set to words from the Gospel, in which the angel at the tomb of Jesus announced that He was risen; later, I learned that Josquin had used the same music for the words of King David lamenting the death of his son Absalom. In both settings the effect was equally powerful. How could the same music serve so well for such different texts? Noting this point, Hanslick argued that ''program notes'' were a kind of libretto without actors, which an uneducated audience needed or demanded in order to supply the response desired by the composer. Music by itself could not do this, since it was an autonomous language, a self-referring one, separated from specific associations with explicitly defined emotive responses or images.

The struggle between the opposed points of view—program and absolute music—was artificially polarized by musical journalists such as Hanslick,

Hugo Wolf, and George Bernard Shaw. Wagner was established as the great representative of program music, and Brahms as the exemplar of absolute music, though each admired the other's work. It was this kind of question, at the center of debate in the late nineteenth century, that Georg Lukács strove to answer in his writings on musical aesthetics.

Lukács on Musical Aesthetics

Georg Lukács always insisted that he was musically untrained, and he approached musical matters with great caution. His ambitious work on aesthetics, written late in his career, offers seventy pages about music out of many hundreds devoted to literature and the other arts.[3] And in 1970 he wrote a brief article on Bartók for the twenty-fifth anniversary of Bartók's death in 1945.[4] Despite this caution, or perhaps because of it, his writings on the aesthetics of music show an impressive grasp of the philosophical problems, accurate musical judgments, and some genuine innovations.

Lukács rejected the point of view of absolute music, the idea that music could generate a world of meanings all its own. That approach could lead to a sterile mathematicization of music. At the same time, he rejected the musical aesthetics of Wagner and Schopenhauer. Wagner had been inspired by Schopenhauer, the first serious philosopher of music. Schopenhauer regarded music as the expression not of human feelings but of the will to life that permeates all creatures and drives them forward, a blind striving that can be overcome by very few, among them philosophers and great artists. Lukács rejected this view also.

Instead, he argued that music expresses feelings. The composer learns how to mimic feelings and, therefore, how to evoke them in others. Yet he need not feel these emotions himself. "We have seen," stated Lukács,

> that music originates from this social and human need, and creates its own unique medium, in order to fulfill this need. . . . We see this in the once universal custom of professional mourners (*Klageweiber*, that is, women hired to weep and wail at funerals. . . . Their mimesis of grief could not only evoke grief in those attending the funeral, but could express their grief by breaking through their inhibitions.[5]

Beyond that, they stand as an objectification of these feelings, which are experienced in a richer and intensified form. This of course refers not only to grief; the composer must learn how to express through mimesis the full range of emotions. The composer objectivates human emotions in all their subjective purity and genuineness, which remain sterile if they are not objectified and expressed.

Lukács thought to refute the positions both of Hanslick on the one side and of Schopenhauer-Wagner on the other, by an ingenious argument. Music is a form of knowledge but not a science; it does not generalize as do the sciences—thus it does not express "universal" or "cosmic" emotions as per Schopenhauer. Neither does it express the purely personal and individual; rather, music expresses the logic of the emotions—which do have a logic of their own, and this can be described independently of either a scientific approach or an individual, biographical approach.[6] For Lukács, not only does music express the logic of the emotions; beyond this, the emotions of a people are governed by their social condition, and this in turn is expressed by their music. It should be remarked that Lukács never developed anything like a formal sociology of music, unlike Adorno, but it is found in his aesthetic writings as part of his general philosophy.

In this connection, Lukács saw a link between musical expression and the emotions of a people in the debates over the growing crisis of tonality in Western music. To this we must turn briefly.

The Growing Crisis of Tonality

By the second half of the nineteenth century, the harmonic language of classicism had been thoroughly explored; the harmonic experimentation of the romantic composers led to an increase of expressive power but not to an increase of constructive power. Without this power, the architecture of large structures, which Beethoven carried to such great heights, began to disappear. Compared to Beethoven's work in its spaciousness, a romantic composer like Chopin or Grieg could produce beautiful miniatures, but not extended structures. This very expressiveness would not only focus attention on the immediate horizon of the music, and away from its long-term architecture; it would also produce a habituation to the new expressive effects—after which a search for even newer expressive effects would be undertaken. Eventually every possibility of dissonant harmonic combination was explored, with the paradoxical result that increased expressiveness resulted ultimately in fatigue and indifference.

Several generations of composers had to confront this growing problem: first were three born in the 1860s, Gustav Mahler, Claude Debussy, and Richard Strauss. As they came of age in the 1880s and 1890s, each responded in a different way to the exhaustion of the old harmonic language. Mahler developed highly original explorations of modal music and of melodic development, and in his short life evolved toward a new tonal language, "pantonality." Debussy experimented with the whole-tone scale, and with the creation of harmonic textures based on the overtone series. Richard Strauss, experimenting in new and original ways, may have been the first composer ever to experiment with tone-rows at a time when Arnold Schoenberg was still writing music in imitation of Wagner and Brahms; but

Strauss lost his nerve and abandoned his experiments. He did not wish to sacrifice his popularity and returned to the tonal language of romanticism.

The next generation, Alexander Scriabin, Max Reger, and Arnold Schoenberg, all born in the early 1870s, were confronted by the crisis of tonality in a much more intense form. All three were highly gifted and engaged in original experiments. Unfortunately, both Reger and Scriabin died young—in their early forties—and so their experiments did not crystallize in any usable way. But Arnold Schoenberg, who lived to more than 70 (1874–1951), created the twelve-tone system, which, however, was slow to become accepted.

A third generation emerged: Béla Bartók, Igor Stravinsky, Alban Berg, Anton von Webern. For this group, the problem of a viable musical idiom was the central problem of their art, and the work of each shows a striking series of stylistic inconsistencies and discontinuities. What we witness here is the breakup of the tonal language from a common language into a multiplicity of aesthetic experiments, with each composer trying to develop a musical idiom in a variety of ways. Berg and Webern were associated with Schoenberg's twelve-tone system almost from the beginning of their careers. Stravinsky, starting from the influence of Rimsky-Korsakov in early works like the *Firebird*, moved toward an experimental neoprimitivism in the *Sacre du Printemps*; he attempted a neoclassicism in other works such as *L'Histoire du Soldat*, and finally adopted Schoenberg's twelve-tone style.

Only Béla Bartók held aloof from these tendencies. He too engaged in stylistic experiments of all kinds. But along with these went his researches into Hungarian folk music, followed by explorations of the folk music of other peoples. His explorations of the tonal idioms that he found in these folk musics found their way into his own composing with fruitful results. It is here that musical and sociological considerations converge.

Lukács and Adorno did not deal with the crisis in tonality in any specific detail; rather, they equated it rather loosely with what they saw as the decline of capitalism. Adorno for a long time dismissed all folkloristic experiments as politically "reactionary" and therefore musically worthless, and treated Bartók with a scorn that he was forced to retract later in his career.[7] Lukács, however, praised Bartók's work with folk idioms. Here, he offered some interesting ideas on the relation between folk music and a general tonal language.

Lukács on Bartók's Music

Writing in 1970, Lukács offered a retrospective view of musical and sociological developments.[8] Briefly, his argument runs as follows. The failed revolutions of 1848 placed Central European nations in a stagnant condition. In Hungary, the feudal landowners, in alliance with the newly developing capitalism, jointly exploited the Hungarian workers and peasants. Both artistic development and personal development were deformed. Poets and musicians could not express themselves openly; the same was true in Germany. Wagner, who had been a revolutionary in 1848, made his peace with the ruling powers; others, who did not, gave themselves up either to a deep melancholy (Brahms) or to a humor and irony of self-mockery (Fontane). Thomas Mann coined a phrase to describe the prevailing attitude among artists: "Inwardness protected by power," or "power-protected inwardness" (*machtgeschützte Innerlichkeit*). Artists were reluctant to grumble or show discontent, and emphasized in their subject matter the personal, the intimate, as a way to avoid social, political, and economic conditions.

Expressions of discontent did emerge and took a new form. In Russian literature, the Count Leo Tolstoy produced the first portraits of the Russian peasants. But in music, it was Bartók who first explored Hungarian folk music and then went on to explore the folk music of the Czechs, Slovaks, Arabs, and Portuguese—indeed, "all folk music." Thus, the growing exhaustion of the tonal language based upon the triad and on the cadential progression led to a search for new resources that might be found in folk music, with its archaic and preharmonic traits. Lukács related this to social developments: the peasant was to represent the next turning point in history, just as at an earlier time the bourgeois, as portrayed by Rembrandt, had emerged as a turning point.

"Bartók himself considered the peasants a natural force, and this is why he could . . . artistically transcend the artificial alienated human type created by . . . capitalist development."[9] Lukács relates Bartók's later compositions to this same sociological process, and thus creates a theoretical category for the understanding of this process. He calls it "undetermined objectivization." When social conditions create obstacles to the possibility of expression, these obstacles—insurmountable obstacles—actually operate to broaden and deepen the possibilities of artistic expressions. There then will emerge what Lukács calls "deep and poignant human emotions through which the beginning of a new era can mean a memorable turning point in the development of the human race." Lukács evokes the names of Tintoretto, Monteverdi, Rembrandt, Goethe, and, finally, Bartók.[10]

By this concept of undetermined objectivization Lukács appears to mean the appearance of a point of genuine originality and authentic creation. These critical points emerge when social conditions weigh upon human emotions sufficiently to evoke new forms of expression. Lukács's sociology of music is broadly aesthetic, historical, and philosophic, as we can see; it is not at all empirical or research oriented. He, like Ernst Bloch and Adorno, often proclaims the social conditioning of music in broad programmatic terms.

Ernst Bloch on Music and Society

Ernst Bloch carried this view even further by arguing that not only musical forms, but specific composers reflected social conditions. Bloch writes,

> The dominance of the melody-carrying upper part and the mobility of the other parts correspond to the rise of the entrepreneur just as the central *cantus firmus* and terraced polyphony corresponded to the hierarchical society. Haydn and Mozart, Handel and Bach, Beethoven and Brahms all had a social mission which was very specific. . . . Handel's oratorios reflect, in their proud solemnity, the rise of Imperialist England and her claim to be the chosen people. There would have been no Brahms without the middle class concert society and no musical *neue Sachlichkeit*, no expressionless music, without the enormous increase in alienation, objectification, and reification of late capitalism. It is always the consumer sector and its requirements, the feelings and aims of the ruling class, which are expressed in music. [11]

The reader who is not musically trained may find the first sentence a bit obscure. When instrumental music and chordal harmony came to the fore in the seventeenth and eighteenth centuries, the musical texture came to be for the most part a two-part texture of melody and supporting bass, with inner parts that would fill in the harmony. This texture more or less was dominant from the late Baroque era onward (Bach's polyphonic music, which his contemporaries regarded as archaic, was an exception). This texture had been preceded by the medieval-renaissance polyphonic musical texture in which melodic action was dispersed among all the voices, and in which one voice carried a preexistent melody, the *cantus firmus* (the "given melody"); the *cantus firmus* was, originally, based on plain chant, but early along, secular melodies were also used.

Bloch here draws a too facile parallel between features of society and musical textures. And Bloch's reduction of great artists like Handel or Brahms to mouthpieces of a specific social time and place raises some obvious objections. If Handel's oratorios reflect only the rise of imperialist England, or Brahms's works reflect only the rise of a German middle class addicted to concert going, why do their works continue to arouse the admiration and emotions of peoples who are not English, not imperialist, not German, and so on? The experience of these works is not an antiquarian one, but rather of something living. Clearly there are great artists whose works appeal to nations and cultures far different from their points of origin. (Why is the Viennese waltz now conquering Japan? Why just at this time?) And Lukács's notion that the artist expresses the emotions of the folk may be out of date. The working classes and peasantries of the world have proven to be much more conservative in a social and artistic sense than most avant-garde intellectuals have ever imagined; I have not seen many workers or peasants at avant-garde music recitals, either listening to or pretending to enjoy those works. Neither do they seem to respond any more to the political dreams of these avant-garde intellectuals. In this respect, the views of Bloch and Lukács—that music both is determined by social conditions and at the same time "outstrips" and transcends "a given age and ideology," both is the captive of the ruling class and yet expresses the forces that will overthrow the social system—seem based more on their political ideologies than upon any observation of musical history.

Bloch has for long been regarded primarily as a Marxist philosopher of a controversial sort; those sympathetic to his work regard it as an attempt to prevent Marxism from petrifying into an orthodoxy. Those opposed see him as a pseudo-Marxist, a romantic, and a mystic, as a symbol of the decomposition of Marxism.[12] His musical writings were completely overlooked until recently. Of the Adorno-Bloch-Lukács group, his writings are the most voluminous and the best, full of brilliant observations on specific composers and on the history and aesthetics of music. His writings on music deserve close study, but that study will be difficult, because his essays are not systematic or logical but poetic and profound: they are a kind of mood music that cannot be reduced to a logical system of propositions. But scattered among them are to be found a series of observations on the relation of music to society that, while suggesting his close intellectual kinship with both Lukács and Adorno, adds an original perspective of his own.

Ernst Bloch was the philosopher of utopia and of hope. He saw utopian dreams and hopes as unrealities that could transform or destroy reality. Utopia was the hint of the future that would invade the present despite all resistance, and would transform it in the process. And when that happened, there would be a retroactive transformation of many things. A central idea of Bloch's was that of *what has not yet happened*. And once that happens, everything will be transformed. Musical expression is a kind of foretaste of this.

> Musical expression as a whole is the viceroy for an articulate utterance which goes much further than is currently understood. . . . Should visionary hearing of that kind be attained . . . then all music we already know will later sound and give forth other expressive contents beside those it has had so far, then the musical expression perceived up to now could seem like a child's stammering toy by comparison. . . . Nobody as yet heard Mozart, Beethoven or Bach as they are really calling . . . this will only happen much later.[13]

For Bloch, music is thus *the* utopian art.

I do not know which came first: Bloch's political philosophy or his musical aesthetics. Perhaps they were one and the same. But there is no doubt that Bloch saw something in the musical developments of the late nineteenth century that he formulated with great precision: that absolute music was changing from an art that could be described as past-oriented to one that was future-oriented. What I mean is that what happened in a Bach fugue or an early classical sonata was the unfolding of a theme that had already been stated at the beginning. All that came later was the unfolding of the potentialities of the opening thematic materials. But slowly this changed, so that what came early had the quality of an anticipation of, a reaching out for, something that was to arrive later. Themes were presented that were fragmentary, nebulous, incomplete, not so much a ''being'' as a ''becoming.''

In the early classical symphony or sonata, the first movement was always deeper, heavier, more profound than the following movements; the later movements were lighter, more relaxed, with the finale most often being light or playful. Mozart and Haydn deepened the second movement—the slow movement, the more ambitious scherzo. And in his Ninth Symphony, Beethoven tried but failed to make the finale as profound as what had gone before. The finale even of his Fifth Symphony is a letdown, a disappointment, especially after the thrilling transition from the scherzo.[14]

It was, then, Schubert, Bruckner, and Mahler who struggled to shift the symphony's center of gravity from the first movement to the last. Bruckner never succeeded in doing this; the marvelous adagio of his Ninth Symphony exhausted his energies, and he never wrote the finale. He bequeathed this problem to his young disciple, Gustav Mahler, who dealt with this problem successfully (as did Brahms in his Fourth Symphony). From now on the symphony was controlled by its future, not its past. Bloch seems to have been among the first theoreticians of this musical change, and this accords with the keen perceptiveness of his musical writings. Bloch, like Lukács, paints a sociology of music in very broad strokes:

> Human needs, socially changing tasks, have been behind it ever since the days of the syrinx. It is clear that the means and techniques of so companionable an art are largely determined by the given social conditions, and that society will extend far into the sound-material, which is in no sense self-active or Nature-given. . . . Sonata form . . . presupposes a capitalist dynamics; the multi-layered and totally undramatic fugue, a static hierarchical society. So-called atonal music would not have been possible in any other era than that of the late bourgeois decline to which it responded in the form of a bold perplexity. The twelve-tone technique . . . would have been inconceivable in the age of free enterprise. . . . Hence each musical form itself and not just its expression depends on the given relationship of men to other men and is a reflex of this.[15]

The difficulty here is the leap from one sphere of meanings to another. Lukács, Bloch, and Adorno see the problem of tonality not in its own terms but only as a symptom of a deeper malaise in the civilization beyond music. They do not grant to composers the authenticity of the musical problem per se, which may reflect an entirely different kind of experience and attempt at world ordering than that of *litterateurs*. Of the three, it was only Adorno who had some sense of the autonomy or authenticity of musical problems as expressible and resolvable only in musical, not sociopolitical, terms. But this sense, in Adorno, was more often than not overshadowed by his ideological and philosophical rigidities.

Adorno: The Musician as Intellectual

Theodor W. Adorno (1903–69) studied music, sociology, and philosophy and was active in all three fields. With Max Horkheimer, he was a principal founder of what is called the Frankfurt School and, as such, a spiritual father of the New Left. He composed music and performed as a jazz pianist; he served as close musical adviser to Thomas Mann when Mann was writing his novel about a composer, *Doctor Faustus*.

Of the three, Adorno was the most highly trained musically (Bloch was reportedly a competent pianist and at one time considered musical composition; Lukács appears to have been musically untrained). Adorno also was the only one to attempt a systematic sociology of music.[16] The sociological and historical features of music that were most salient to Adorno were two: first, the changing social position of music and musicians; and second, the crisis of musical language of his time.

Composer, Performer, Audience

The separation of composer, performer, and audience that we now take for granted would have seemed strange to the ancients. Music was something improvised by a community, by embellishing and decorating preexistent melodies and scales that had no "composers," or only mythical ones like Apollo or Orpheus.

But in medieval Europe, something new emerged: a polyphonic music, a music of multiple melodies unfolding at once. In order to record these complexities, an entirely new form of musical notation was evolved, which could capture not only the spatial relations of these melodies, but the temporal durations of their tones; time was not captured in a new symbolism. Only now could there emerge the composer of music, who had to master not only the art of combining these multiple melodies, but even more the art of writing them in the new notation system. Even then, compositions began as decorations and elaborations of preexistent materials, the Gregorian chants; only slowly did the idea of a composition that was original emerge: the *res facta*, a thing that had had been made, rather than improvised.

The composer emerged as master of this new technique; but he was for long seen as a craftsman. Composers never were only composers: they were performers, choirmasters, and instrument makers. Johann Sebastian Bach not only composed music, he was also a superb performer on keyboard instruments; he built organs; he engraved and printed music; he showed great interest in the emergence of the rudimentary pianoforte and made suggestions for its improvement to its pioneers. But this older social role of the musician as craftsman began to be eclipsed, replaced by the composer as intellectual.

Beethoven was, in this respect, an unfortunate influence; this great performer was forced by his deafness to give up piano recitals and conducting, and to live by composing alone. Because of his stature as a creative artist, he succeeded. But he unintentionally created an unhealthy model: younger men began to think of the composer as a lonely, isolated spiritual giant who did not have to bother with performing before audiences. The romantic movement, which made high claims for art as a source and expression of a wisdom as profound as that offered by science or philosophy, assisted in this development. Now composers emerged who were not performers on the professional level, or who could not even play an instrument at all; in our time there are some who depend on others to orchestrate their compositions.

In many respects, Lukács, Bloch, and Adorno were romantics, and they are inheritors of that claim for art as wisdom first made by romantic philosophers like Schelling and Schopenhauer. Certainly, their writings assume that the arts, and music especially, are somehow integral to the whole of society.

By the late nineteenth century, the aristocratic and churchly support of musicians was fading, increasingly supplanted by a new concert industry based upon mass audiences. The newer composers dismissed as "philistines"—those who welcome only what is familiar and poses no problems for understanding—these new mass audiences. Composers increasingly began to write music not for audiences but for one another. And between composers and audiences a new factor entered the picture: the journalist and critic who acted as mediator between the audience and the creative artist. Increasingly deprived of the older forms of sponsorship—courts, churches, and municipalities—the composer had to relate himself to the new concert and recording industries, and to the new cultural and state bureaucracies that undertook to sponsor—and control—the arts. With the recent emergence of bureaucratic colleges and universities as sponsors of the arts, the separatist tendencies of composers have increased.[17]

As a consequence, we witness the metamorphosis of the composer from a craftsman responsible to a community into an intellectual who adopts the stance of avant-gardism, engaging in experiments deliberately intended to be incomprehensible or repellent (all the while proclaiming his compassion for the oppressed; of course music must be ugly, he will say: how else to express the ugliness of this age?).

This is the background against which Adorno developed his sociology and aesthetics of music. For Adorno, the central fact of his world was the era of the Nazi death camps. From this horror and from despair over the postwar world that had failed to deliver the redemption of humankind, he developed an aesthetic and a philosophy of supreme pessimism; it appears that this total pessimism was intended as a direct challenge to Ernst Bloch and his philosophy of hope; and his glorification of Schoenberg's twelve-tone system was aimed against the folkloristic and popular explorations of composers like Mahler, Janáček, and Bartók, which were supported by Lukács. Thus, Adorno also opposed Lukács's musical aesthetic. (The personal and intellectual relations among Adorno, Bloch, and Lukács are very complicated indeed, and scholars are only now beginning to examine them. Often, it appears, a slighting allusion to a composer may well be aimed by one of this trio toward any other).[18]

Briefly, Adorno's musical sociology shows the following major features:

(1) Adorno rejected the dominance of the culture industry. This had transformed music into a commodity. People walking down the street might be heard whistling a theme of Mozart or Beethoven; but their experience of this music would be completely passive. They would make no effort to understand the formal transitions and relations between the various parts of the musical forms—its architecture—but would only greet the recurring good tunes. Thus, the culture industry had captured the great works of the past and reduced them to the level of a commodity, a best-seller, admired but not really understood.

(2) Accordingly, Adorno also rejected a sociology of music that took the form of market research comparable to studies of the popularity of soap or cigarettes.

(3) To counter the capture of music by the culture industry, Adorno demanded that modern music forcibly eclipse the masterworks of the past by destroying their musical language. The weapon for this destruction was the twelve-tone system of Schoenberg, which would obliterate harmonies, scales, keys, cadences, and the intelligible presentation of musical themes. Especially to be obliterated was the old distinction between consonance and dissonance. In this respect, Adorno seemed completely opposed to the use by composers of "identification patterns," and for this reason completely rejected all popular music. Here Adorno aligns himself totally with certain forms of avant-gardism.

(4) Adorno recognized the significance of the critic. A new mass audience, eager for music but uncertain of its tastes, wanting authoritative guidance, relied on the critic, who in his reviews exercised a power of life or death over composers and performers. This had led, of course, to the contemporary con-

dition of the arts, dominated by the creation of artificially inflated reputations (and the eclipse of genuine artists) through a falsifying publicity. (Claude Debussy, in his musical journalism, contributed to this development. His way of writing criticism has been imitated by countless journalists: the tone and language of his writing are those of the languid young *décadent* who is bored by everything, especially the masterworks. And criticism itself has become a pseudo-art, full of pretentious aesthetic jargons of all kinds—sociological, aesthetic, psychoanalytic—to which Adorno himself made major contributions.)

(5) The gulf between popular art and high art was something managed by the "system" and had to be rejected. Composers like Haydn and Mozart had the popular touch, as did Johann Strauss. But popular music as a commodity was "depraved," said Adorno, and he added that "mindlessness defending the existing evil system" reigned, the defining traits being banality and vulgarity. Composers of operettas produced a kind of musical "ready-to-wear," and Adorno traced a connection between such an attitude toward musical substance and such American shows as *Pins and Needles* and *The Pajama Game*.[19] Especially exasperating to Adorno seems to have been the condition that popular art relies upon standardized patterns of identification (as if the classical music of high art did not do so: What did he consider to be the function of recognizable themes and thematic developments, of cadential patterns and modulating chords?). Adorno's rather contemptuous rejection of popular music and of jazz has received much critical attention recently, and he has been reproached for his mandarin contempt for popular art, all of which he dismissed as kitsch.[20] And yet he was of two minds about it; he conceded, in a grudging way, that popular song, especially in America, could often exhibit "beautifully arched melodies" and pregnant turns of phrase and of harmony, and that some popular songs seemed to retain their charm and their appeal for many years. Adorno called these songs "the evergreens"; why they existed was unclear and needed study. But, he hastily added, popular music was "objectively untrue" and therefore harmful.[21]

(6) Adorno's musical aesthetics was governed entirely by his political views, and he saw everything in simplistic terms: what he chose to call "fascism" was struggling against what he called "socialism"; he never considered that history might render this opposition obsolete, and that all sorts of other political and social forms might exist. In accordance with this politicized way of seeing music, Adorno identified Schoenberg's twelve-tone system with the forces of progress and revolution, and Stravinsky's style of composing with fascism and reaction. Adorno misjudged the efforts of Bartók to reconcile folklorism with certain features of Stravinsky's style, especially the neoclassic elements. Such a simplistic opposition exposed itself to serious embarrassments. First, the adoption by Stravinsky himself of the twelve-tone

technique proved a major difficulty. Second, as the value of Bartók's work became undeniable with the passage of time, Adorno tried to cover his footprints surreptitiously. Lukács launched a scathing attack on Adorno for his earlier misreading:

> It was no accident that Adorno, whose musical theory postulated Schoenberg's standpoint as the only one leading to salvation, saw something suspicious in Bartók's folkloristic approach. Such persons would quite naturally shrink from the truly great innovator whose truly revolutionary attitude blew up the human foundations underlying the merely formal innovations.[22]

Despite the somewhat overblown language used here (did Bartók, merely by writing music, really "blow up" human foundations? And how?), Lukács's judgment of Bartók's significance is more accurate than Adorno's contemptuous dismissal, which he later modified.

Because music was seen almost wholly as a political problem, Wagner posed an insoluble difficulty for Adorno. On the one hand, Wagner was seen as a forerunner of Nazism—a theorist of racism and anti-Semitism, a crude and vulgar thinker—yet nevertheless a powerful and original musical personality and above all a precursor of Schoenberg: without Wagner, no Schoenberg.

Adorno, in his book *In Search of Wagner*,[23] written in 1937–38, chose to dissect Wagner using the polemical weapons of both psychoanalysis and Marxism. In his Marxist sociology, Wagner's music was an expression of social forces: "Wagner was an impressionist *malgré lui*, as is only to be expected in view of the backward state of the technical and human forces of production and hence too of aesthetic doctrine in Germany in the middle of the 19th century." Wagner, without being aware of it, expresses "the unity of the productive forces of the age"; his treatment of musical themes is analogous to labor on an industrial assembly line:

> Wagner's work comes close to the consumer goods of the 19th century which knew no greater ambition than to conceal any sign of the work that went into them, perhaps because any such traces reminded people too vehemently of the appropriation of the labour of others, of an injustice that could still be felt.[24]

In this kind of polemical writing, there is not much reasoned argument; rather, the cloudy imagery works to dissolve individuals into the scenery of social forces. Thus, it is the forces of production that generate Wagner's musical aesthetic *and* his librettos *and* his music, and even those musical innovations that, without Wagner's knowing or intending it, would lead to Schoenberg. Wagner, in effect, is banished from his own lifework; and Adorno attributes to him all sorts of motives, impulses, and hidden instincts that are clear to

Adorno but would make Wagner unrecognizable to himself.

Adorno's polemic against Wagner appears also to have been part of his quarrel with Lukács and Bloch, and designed as an attack on Bloch's much more favorable and sympathetic writings on Wagner. Where Adorno gave himself over to destructive "explanations" that sought to destroy Wagner, Bloch approached his work by way of poetic descriptions, a much more difficult task.[25] A detailed comparison of the two men's views of Wagner will interest aestheticians and sociologists of music.

The Avant-Garde Intellectuals

These three gifted men created a sociology of music out of their political and Marxian styles of thought. Their writings on music in society offer a series of keen aesthetic judgments on specific artists, plus accurate perceptions of the relation between music and society, mixed paradoxically with cloudy programmatic declarations of the ways in which the relations of production somehow generate musical styles and genres. One often has the feeling that these writers get over their heads in deep waters. All three want to have it both ways: music is integral to society, a social product; and music is revolutionary, can blow up the foundations of the existing order (Lukács), is a "kind of analogue to . . . social theory" (Adorno), and is created in advance for another kind of society, thereby helping bring about that new society (Bloch). All three foreshadowed the cultural politics that we appear to have inherited from the New Left, or that perhaps only appears after the collapse of the New Left; the idea of cultural salvation had a brief run after the post-1960s hangover.

In addition, all three exhibited the dialectical hocus-pocus that uses paradox in place of either thought or research. Adorno is the most self-indulgent of the three in this respect. His writing is laden with paradox on every page. A few examples:

> Art aids enlightenment only by opposing obscurity to false clarity; then it shows its own darkness.[26]

> The inhumanity of art must triumph over the inhumanity of the word for the sake of the humane.[27]

> Music is doomed, but this historical process in turn restores it to a position of justice and paradoxically grants it a chance to continue its existence. The decline of art in a false order is itself false.[28]

> Art would perhaps be authentic only when it had totally rid itself of the idea of authenticity.[29]

On and on goes this sort of thing. I have attempted a parody of this idiom:

For Adorno to write doublethink both before and after Orwell invented doublethink—which not Orwell but the paradox of the age created through Orwell—is an achievement that barely manages to hide its own lack of achievement.

The Theory of the Avant-Garde: this was the title of a remarkable work by Renato Poggioli.[30] The author traced the changing historical meanings of avant-gardism. This began with an "alliance between political and artistic radicalism," but then evolved into a kind of dialectic of opposition to whatever styles happen to prevail at a given time. Poggioli labels this "antagonism," not only to tradition but also to the public. The artistic sect and movement becomes a caste. Precisely because of this, the modern artist becomes declassed and can alternate between two postures, "now plebeian and now aristocratic, now 'dandy' and now 'bohemian,' " with both being "equal and opposite manifestations of an identical state of mind and social situation." It was precisely this bohemian spirit, Poggioli pointed out, that provoked all the external manifestations of avant-garde antagonism toward the public.

From this, avant-garde art moved to other views: "down-with-the-past" (in Italian, *antipassatismo*), which quickly became futurism and the glorification of the machine; nihilism, which took many forms, dadaism and other forms of obscurantism foremost; agonism, a kind of hoping and striving for catastrophe; experimentalism; and, of course, alienation.

It seems clear that Lukács, Bloch, and Adorno all were, in one way or another, influenced by avant-gardism and hoped to enlist it for their political purposes. But although they trained the powerful weapons of sociological and cultural criticism against others, they did not sufficiently examine their own roots in the avant-garde movement. Adorno especially appears to have tried to make these avant-garde traits into a permanent feature of his aesthetic. Poggioli himself remarks that Georg Lukács "never directly faced the particular problem of the avant-garde"; he treated it only in passing:

> He is in fact inclined to attribute an exclusively negative value to the concept of the avant-garde. The only form of modern art which seems to him to anticipate the future, or to be, as he himself would put it, progressive, remains the surviving—and sometimes the outlived—realistic tradition, always the primary object of his inquiries. Lukács himself assigns the task of judging the seeds of the future in today's art not to contemporary criticism but to future history. . . .

> Surely there is an element of truth in the claim that the avant-gardistic quality of a given work of art . . . can only be perceived by some future consciousness. We might say that no ambitious critic can make do without yielding to the appeal of a futuristic utopia. But it is neither fair nor precise to limit the progressiveness of art to a single type of content (Marxist sociology) and to a single style (realistic narrative).[31]

Thus we see that Lukács stands in a peculiar half-relationship to avant-gardism, being in some sense future-oriented but also too closely tied to the tradition of realistic narrative. It is perhaps this relationship that made him so cautious in his approach to the least realistic of the arts, music.

Adorno stands much closer to the avant-garde; there is a sentence in his *Philosophy of Modern Music* that suggests a possible clarification:

> Music is inextricably bound up with what Clement Greenberg called the division of all art into kitsch and the avant-garde, which is cut off from official culture. The philosophy of music is today possible only as the philosophy of modern music. The only hope is that this culture will herald its own demise: it only contributes to the advancement of barbarism.[32]

Despite the element of truth in Adorno's words, he missed some important things here. First, the two attitudes—the production of kitsch and the production of avant-garde complexities—can coexist in the same artist's mind (consider Schoenberg's *Verklärte Nacht*, a monument of kitsch; and much the same can be said of Prokofiev's dissonant complexities in his Third Piano Concerto alongside his "Classical" Symphony). Second, Adorno disregards the genuine elements in popular music, the fact that American popular song from about 1900 to about 1950 was something unique, the only music to have had a worldwide response. Third, if we drop the unpleasant word kitsch, and refer instead to popular or populist or folkish elements in art, we can see that many artists show, in their work, an uncomfortable mixture of two disparate elements: the folk element on the one side, and avant-garde experimentation on the other. We find this in Mahler, in Bartók, in Chagall, and in countless others. The struggle to reconcile these elements, not always successful, appears to be an important element in the arts of the last 100 years at least. Artists resorted to these two very different resources in their struggle to escape from the styles and themes of "mainstream" art, "bourgeois' art, "academic" art—it is hard to find a precise term to cover what is intended here. Perhaps the best way of describing what these artists have opposed is to say that works of art that have proved to be of enduring merit have come to be regarded as forming a tradition, and it is to this that the avant-garde has been opposed rather than to any specific artistic school or style. More than this, the avant-garde has seen a body of critics and academics emerge who have become the self-appointed guardians of "tradition," as though they were curators of a great but invisible museum of culture. Finally, the avant-garde has defined itself not only by what it has opposed; it has come to show a specific content and character best shown in Poggioli's remarkable portrait. Lukács, Bloch, and Adorno stood in a complex but unclarified relation to the avant-garde; their failure to clarify this relation constitutes a limitation on the fruitfulness of their sociology of music.

Conclusion

The musical sociology offered by this gifted trio contains many valuable elements. However, the overall picture is marred by the political and ideological blinders they wore, which led them often into large, vague, cloudy statements on the links between musical developments and social developments. One wishes here for a Max Weber to put their broad statements to some kind of historical test. The very condition of music today calls for a different kind of sociology from their approach: the fragmentation of music into a multiplicity of styles and audiences, the cornucopia of choices that make available almost all musics from all eras throughout the world, the specialization and fragmentation of audiences for the classics, for avant-garde experiments, for folk music, for rock, punk, and whatever else, the coexistence of more than one style of composition—all mean that a sociology of music today cannot be encompassed by any unified philosophical approach.

Notes

1. This is a revised version of a paper read at the Universidad Autonoma Metropolitana, Xochimilco, in Mexico City, on November 19, 1985.
2. Eduard Hanslick, *On the Beautiful in Music*, trans. Gustav Cohen, ed. and introd. Morris Weitz (New York: Liberal Arts Press, 1957).
3. Georg Lukács, *Die Eigenart des Aesthetischen*. 2. Halbband (Darmstadt: Luchterhand, 1963), pp. 330–401.
4. Georg Lukács, "Béla Bartók—On the 25th Anniversary of His Death," *New Hungarian Quarterly* 41(1970): 42–55.
5. Lukács, *Die Eigenart des Aesthetischen*, pp. 363–64.
6. A recent article by Jacques Barzun offers support for Lukács's position (it does not appear that Barzun has read Lukács). Barzun argues that the formal order of music and its expressive order need not be artificially separated, as they are in the quarrel between the advocates of "absolute" versus "program" music. The musician actually follows "a double program, constrained and also helped to create order by two preexisting patterns that intersect only at certain points. Part of his merit consists of the deftness with which he reconciles the independent demands of the two schemes. The tension between them is a spur to his artistry and technical skill, just as it is a source of the listener's admiration and pleasure." Barzun in effect elucidates the logic of the emotions mentioned by Lukács: "Haydn's 'C major brilliance' would go as well with 'relief after anxiety' or 'indications of innocence after being under a cloud.' This last phrase is chosen on purpose to show how words themselves play upon likenesses that defy analysis. . . . The proof of this is the practice of self-borrowing among the great composers . . . just in the proportion that music is not literal, denotative, it can connote the essence of diverse experiences." See Jacques Barzun, "The Meaning of Meaning in Music: Berlioz Once More," *Musical Quarterly* 66, 1 (January 1980): 1–20. Further, see pp. 5–6 and 16–17, respectively, for the quoted passages.
7. See Georg Lukács, *Die Eigenart des Aesthetischen*, p. 393. See also the interesting essay by Ferenc Fehér, "Negative Philosophy of Music: Positive Results," in

Foundations of the Frankfurt School of Social Research, ed. Judith Marcus and Zoltán Tar (New Brunswick, NJ, and London: Transaction, 1984), pp. 193–205, specifically pp. 204–5.

8. Lukács, "Béla Bartók," pp. 51 and 55.
9. Ibid., p. 51.
10. Ibid.
11. Ernst Bloch, *Essays on the Philosophy of Music*, trans. Peter Palmer, introd. David Drew (Cambridge and New York: Cambridge University, 1984), pp. 200–201. Publication of this work in a generally excellent translation and with a valuable introduction by Drew is an important event. But I must report one error of translation on p. 106: there are no such things as "major" fifths or "minor" fourths; the correct translation is "upper fifths" or "lower fourths." See p. 127 of the German edition. Also, *Neue Sachlichkeit* refers to the deliberately cold, affectless music of the 1920s.
12. Ibid., pp. xvi ff., offers a helpful discussion by David Drew of some of the principal attackers (Leszek Kolakowski) and defenders of Bloch.
13. Ibid., p. 207.
14. Ibid., pp. 40–41, offers a partial discussion.
15. Ibid., p. 209.
16. See Adorno's *Introduction to the Sociology of Music*, trans. from the German E. B. Ashton (New York: Seabury-Continuum, 1976). His *Philosophy of Modern Music*, trans. Anne G. Mitchell and Wesley V. Blomster (New York: Seabury-Continuum, 1973), though more aesthetics than anything else, offers sociological observations throughout. Other writings such as *Dissonanzen* (1972) and various scattered essays are untranslated.
17. Adorno, in his *Introduction to the Sociology of Music*, p. 146; "there really are no more musical partisans in public opinion, like the ones of Gluck and Piccinni or of Wagner and Brahms. They have been succeeded by schools squabbling in the cenacle."
18. David Drew's introduction to Bloch's *Essays*, pp. xxx, xxxiv–xxxv, and xxxviii ff., offers illustrative material.
19. See Adorno, *Introduction to the Sociology of Music*, which is the primary source for these observations. The fact that this book was an outgrowth of a lecture series broadcast in Germany may account for its unusual (for Adorno, that is) clarity.
20. Ibid., pp. 21ff.
21. Ibid., pp. 37–38.
22. Lukács, "Béla Bartók," p. 54. This may reflect the generational differences between the two men.
23. Theodor W. Adorno, *In Search of Wagner*, trans. Rodney Livingstone (Thetford, England: NLB Verso Reprint, 1984). First published as *Versuch über Wagner* in 1952.
24. Ibid., p. 83.
25. Bloch, *Essays*, III, "Paradoxes and the Pastorale in Wagner Music."
26. Adorno, *Philosophy of Modern Music*, p. 15.
27. Ibid., p. 132.
28. Ibid., p. 113.
29. Ibid., p. 217.
30. Renato Poggioli, *The Theory of the Avant-Garde*, trans. Gerald Fitzgerald (Cambridge, MA: Harvard University, 1968; Harper and Row rpt., 1971).
31. Ibid., pp. 170–71.
32. See Adorno, *Philosophy of Modern Music*, p. 10.

9

Georg Lukács and Thomas Mann: Reflections on a Relationship

By Judith Marcus

> *Nicht das Richtige oder Falsche an . . . Ideen ist es, was uns hier in erster Linie interessiert, sondern das Charakteristische daran.*
> Thomas Mann

> *I was expected to feel myself inferior and an alien because I was a Jew. [Thus] I was made familiar with the fate of being in the Opposition. . . . The foundations were thus laid for a certain degree of independence of judgment.*
> Sigmund Freud

> *The stranger is . . . being discussed here . . . as the person who comes today and stays tomorrow. . . . [To] be a stranger is naturally a very positive relation; it is a specific form of interaction.*
> Georg Simmel

Introduction

In 1925, Walter Benjamin informed his friend Gershom Scholem that he had just finished reading two books, both of which were extraordinary and

119

made for exciting reading.[1] The two books, singled out as the best products of the time, were Thomas Mann's novel *The Magic Mountain* and Georg Lukács's *History and Class Consciousness*. To the best of my knowledge, this was the first time that a perceptive reader established a connection of sorts between the works of two towering figures of twentieth-century European cultural life. It was not to be the last. For a number of reasons, however, among which figure prominently the political and social upheavals on the Continent that eventually landed Mann in sunny California and Lukács in Stalin's Moscow, it took almost four decades for anybody to take a second and closer look at the possibility of a certain connection between the two men and their work. In the meantime, there has grown up an immense literature around Mann (who died in 1955) and Lukács (who died in 1971). Even though a number of critics and scholars have begun to pay attention to the relation between the two men, they have seldom gone beyond the "fact" that Lukács's physique and revolutionary career inspired Thomas Mann's portrait of Leo Naphta, the Jewish-Jesuit-Communist character of *The Magic Mountain*.[2] (To which Lukács responded with good-humor, "So what if I lent him my nose? He gave so much to me—I am happy I could do that little for him in return!") This is not to imply that the focus on that one aspect would need justification: even if it only could be proven that Lukács served as the model for one of the most interesting, the strangest, and the most complex figures in Mann's oeuvre, this alone would be worth a separate study. I myself felt the fascinating ambivalence emanating from this fictional character; moreover, my previous acquaintance with Lukács's work (and with Lukács himself) made me wary of accounting in toto the (mostly Marxist) interpretation of those— among them, Hans Mayer and Lukács himself—who saw in the character the prototype of the Fascist intellectual.[3]

Be it as it may, there was in the past widespread skepticism even among literary scholars that Thomas Mann and Georg Lukács may have had anything in common, that a case could be made for interaction, influence, and congruence, for a relationship. The fact that the focus on some selected problematic of such a relationship has a lot to do with both the sociology of literature and the exploration of interaction of two men who are representative polar opposites in a common time provides sufficient rationale to explore this specific relationship. The linkage could be proven in more ways than one—as I found out in the course of my investigation.

Here and now, I wish to limit myself to the summary discussion of one aspect of this relationship: Thomas Mann's perception of Georg Lukács in juxtaposition with his narrative method, the *Anlehnung* (borrowing), and Mann's conception of the modern novel as "that stage of 'criticism' that immediately follows the 'poetic' one,"[4] or as Harry Levin put it, "an act of evocation, peculiarly saturated with reminiscences.'"[5] Even within the limitations of this short paper, some important points will be highlighted, because we are dealing here with the constellation of two eminent cultural representatives of twentieth-century Europe, a constellation that has come to be recognized by now as one of the most remarkable critic-author relationships in recent times.[6] For one, both the literary and ideological issues involved here go a long way toward explaining some central characteristics of the modern novel; second, the analysis of this constellation is bound to illuminate part of the inner history of an epoch.

The Artist and the Philosopher-Critic

The definition of a correct stratagem for the sociological approach to literature was at one time offered by Harry Levin; it was addressed to Lucien Goldmann and was meant as a corrective for Goldmann's interpretation of André Malraux's work in 1963. Levin wrote,

> Rigor must be achieved empirically, through a substantive acquaintance with the relevant texts . . . and with the exact relations between imaginative fiction and the socio-cultural facts—not by the imposition of vague absolutes from on high or the importation of categorical sanctions from the east.[7]

By substituting an imaginative recreation of perception, feelings, attitudes, and thoughts for ''imaginative fiction,'' the stratagem recommends itself for an investigation of the relationship between the great twentieth-century German novelist, Thomas Mann, and the Hungarian Marxist philosopher and literary critic, Georg Lukács. (The irony of the matter is that Lukács was made responsible by scholars for most of the import of ''categorical sanctions'' that had come ''from the east.'') However, a substantial degree of incompatibility has to be assumed between these two men, one a thoroughly bourgeois man and artist and the other just as thoroughly a Communist philosopher, whose representativeness as polar opposites in a common time is recognized by all. Common sense would suggest sharp distinctions that are biographically grounded and should summarily be outlined.

Thomas Mann (1875–1955), one of the greatest European novelists of the twentieth century, is also considered to have been the most representative of German writers and as such, in the words of Georg Lukács, symbolized ''all that is best in the German bourgeoisie.''[8] Through his work, Mann succeeded in giving a complete picture of the *bürgerliche* life and its predicament in a certain stage of development. Although the emerging picture was of a critical nature, he treated the spiritual and moral problems of the *Bürger* as his own, stressing the significance of his social and cultural inheritance. His philosophical foundations were in Nietzsche, Schopenhauer, and Wagner, as was the case for a large segment of the German intelligentsia of his time.

This is not the sole reason for his being called a thoroughly German writer and a very conservative one. It is not even the reason that he passionately pleaded for the just cause of Wilhelminian Germany's going to war in 1914 (especially in his early work *Reflections of a Non-Political Man*) for imperialistic and expansionistic purposes. After all, many liberal Germans, Max Weber and Georg Simmel among them, were equally enthusiastic, if only for a time.[9] Nor was it the young Mann's slightly anti-Semitic inclinations, clearly traceable in his early writings and private utterances. It is partly because, among the German writers of his generation, few have been as conscious of tradition and have stressed so insistently their relations to tradition. "I am a man of the nineteenth century," Mann said on many occasions, thinking more likely to Goethe and of the romantic school (especially of Novalis) than of then-industrializing Germany. But then again, there was too in Thomas Mann an almost Faustian urge to experiment, to explore, as Henry Hatfield put it, "The cautious bourgeois is an explorer, as bourgeois often are."[10] Mann also possessed the conscious thoroughness of the bourgeois (he did "research" for his artistic task at hand in the strict meaning of the word), a trait attributed to the Germans in general. For him, only the thorough was truly interesting, as he remarked in the introduction to *The Magic Mountain*.[11]

Finally, and more important, a consistency runs through Mann's literary career. Students of Mann's artistry often emphasize the break in his lifework; it is pointed out time and again that although in his early writings he confined himself almost exclusively to ingenious variations on the theme of the artist, there was later a move away to novels of ideas on a grand scale. An argument for such a case can be made if we put on the scale works like the novelette *Tonio Kröger, Death in Venice*, the story *Tristan*—or even the novel *Buddenbrooks*, in which the solid bourgeois degenerates into an artistic one—and then weigh them against the series of grand novels of ideas starting with *The Magic Mountain*. However, there appears a continuity to the discerning eye: these variations on the artistic theme are played out against the sociopolitical, cultural, or intellectual background of their times. Whether we think again of *Buddenbrooks*, written at the turn of the century, of the short story "Mario and the Magician," placed in Mussolini's Italy, or of *Doctor Faustus*, written in the 1940s and depicting Germany's slide into Nazism, the need for "much full-blooded reality" was always there, supplied in part by "concrete observation."[12] On the other hand, the artistic variation is played out as late as the *Joseph* tetralogy, *Doctor Faustus*, and *Felix Krull, the Confidence Man*, as the other aspect of that consistency. Last but not least, there was the very element of the German *bürgerliche* artistry, the transferring of the "ethical characteristics of the burgherly way of life: order, sequence, rest, 'diligence' . . . in the sense . . . of faithful workmanship—to the exercise of art," in Mann's apt summation.[13] This "primacy of ethics over *esthetics*," says Mann, was the main characteristic first recognized by Lukács.[14]

At the opposite pole is Georg Lukács (1885–1971), born in Budapest as György Bernát Löwinger into an assimilated, wealthy Jewish family. His father was a self-made millionaire banker who changed his name to Lukács in 1891 and became ennobled in 1901; after this, the "von" was attached to the name. Lukács received his education, including his two doctoral degrees, in Hungary; thus he seems to be situated in an entirely different social, cultural, and intellectual context from that of Mann. But again, Lukács not only grew up bilingual (his Viennese mother, Adele Wertheimer, never quite mastered the Hungarian language); he also received a cosmopolitan education. At the age of 86, Lukács still fondly recalled his Gymnasium graduation present from his father: a trip to Norway to visit the ailing Ibsen, the admired artist of his childhood.

Lukács chose German at an early age as a medium for his public discourse and often for his private one. He pursued his postdoctural studies in Germany in the same Wilhelminian era that was the background for Mann's early works, including *The Magic Mountain*. He came under the influence first of Wilhelm Dilthey and Georg Simmel and then, more important, of the neo-Kantian Emil Lask and the sociologist Max Weber, both in Heidelberg. This meant a change in general orientation from pure aestheticism to philosophy and social science, followed by a change in philosophical orientation from Kant to Hegel and, finally, to Marx. But the definitive change in Lukács's life and intellectual career came with his change in political orientation, his embracing of Marxism and communism, moving, as George Steiner put it, "into the Marxist promise of social justice or rather, into the Marxist promise of method."[15] Thus, Lukács became less and less compatible with everything that Thomas Mann stood for; after all, he is thought of today as the most original and important Marxist thinker of the twentieth century, and as one of the in most controversial figures in its cultural history. These twists and turns in Lukács's career gave rise to the notion of the "enigmatic Lukács"[16] and the search for the "real" one that seems to go on unabated. (A 1975 article tried to sum up the "real" Lukács with the somewhat sensational title, "Orthodox Heretic, Stalinist Romantic.")[17]

It is true that many of Lukács's studies on realism and his pursuit of dogmatic Marxist doctrine of the social relevance of art, not to mention his treatment of the development of modern philosophy in his book *The Destruction of Reason* (1954), provoked derision (cf. T. W. Adorno, G. Lichtheim, S. Sontag, et al.). It is equally true that the influence of his first major Marxist treatise, *History and Class Consciousness* (1923), stretches from the Frankfurt theorists to Sartre and the New Left. The interest in the young Lukács, that is, in his pre-Marxist writings, is of more recent vintage; since the late 1960s, the notion has been widely held that the "real" Lukács would not emerge until his early phase was explored. My first attempt to explore the Lukács-Naphta linkage dates back to 1968; it was based on the conviction that despite the apparent discontinuity—meaning a turning from bourgeois aestheticism to Bolshevism in 1918–Lukács's lifework shows a certain unity and continuity. As Lukács himself said, "Each and every thought and action of my life grew out of one another; they are organically related."[18] This notion of organic development and the interrelatedness of everything that follows is, by the way, a central one for Thomas Mann and can be a good starting point in the pursuit of a possible linkage of the two men. Just as Thomas Mann's solid anchorage in German cultural tradition and high-bourgeois values is stressed, so is Lukács's "homelessness," the fact that "exile was his natural habitat" in several respects. This is not so clear-cut an issue, though. George Steiner, one of the most insightful critics of Lukács, perceives certain factors that went unnoticed by others or are dismissed as irrelevant:

> Yet, in another sense, Lukács was deep-rooted. He was curtly dismissive in reference to his own Judaism, but a Jew to the tip of his fingers. Unhoused, peregrine, he is one of the tragic constellation (Ernst Bloch, Walter Benjamin, Adorno, Herbert Marcuse) of Jewish abstractionists, possessed by a messianic rage for logic, for systematic order in the social condition of man. Lukács's Marxism is, in essence, a refusal of the world's incoherence. . . . Like the other Jewish self-exiles whose radicalism out of Central Europe has so incisively marked the century, Lukács is an heir in immanence to the transcendent absolute of Spinoza.[19]

This statement contains some truth and can be considered important in the sense that, as will be shown, Thomas Mann's perception of Lukács partly corresponds to the description offered by Steiner.

Personal and Literary Interaction

When I visited Georg Lukács on May 7, 1971, four weeks before his death, I carried with me my findings from the Thomas Mann Archiv at Zurich, including some transcribed notes of Mann to his work. My research had uncovered the existence of extensive cross-fertilization of ideas, and even the use of the same language and certain terms in the early work of both Mann and Lukács.[20] That both of them spoke of the problem of the artist and art in a quasi-religious tone, evoking Ibsen's dictum that "to write means to pass the last judgment upon oneself," might have meant only that both of them reacted on their heightened awareness of the crisis of culture, and that there was a dominant ethical element in their lives and work. But there was the additional evidence of direct influence in that Thomas Mann verbally transposed some of Lukács's reflections in his youthful essay collection *Die Seele und die Formen* (1911) and incorporated them structurally, thematically, and even verbally into his story-in-the-making *Der Tod in Venedig*. I venture to say that without Lukács's special sensibility displayed in his essays of that time, Mann's story would be a vastly different work. Gustav von Aschenbach's problematic in transcending his love for a beautiful boy into art at the end of the novella, in particular, and the problematic of the modern artist, in general, were based on Lukács's musings on the Socratian love, namely, that "it will always be denied to men and poets to soar as high as [Socrates]. . . . Their soaring is always tragic, and in tragedy hero and destiny must become form. . . . In life, longing must remain love: that is its happiness and its tragedy."[21] Lukács accepted these revelations as a "great gift," and stated that his relationship to Thomas Mann remains the one mystery in his life to which he truly desires an explanation before his death. What are the reasons, he wanted to know, for Thomas Mann's lifelong distance, his refusal to even answer Lukács's letters and his personal aloofness in spite of the intellectual compatibility that amounted to a *geistige Symbiose* (spiritual affinity)? Even today, only a tentative answer can be offered. I could convey to Lukács only my (at that time vague) notion that it was not the Marxist Lukács specifically and primarily but the "young Lukács" endowed with specific personal and intellectual characteristics that effected Mann's aloofness—and rubbed off on the financial character of Leo Naphta in *The Magic Mountain*.

This last aspect was the first one to which scholars and critics had begun to pay attention when contemplating the possibility of real-life models for the fictional figure of Leo Naphta, the Jewish Communist Jesuit of *The Magic Mountain*. Most of them commented on the "fact" that Lukács's physique or revolutionary career inspired Mann's portrayal of this "enigmatic" fictional character. Pierre Paul Sagave, the French literary historian, was among the first who "established" the identity by comparing photos of Lukács he thought were from the 1920s. To complicate matters, two Marxist critics of Mann, Hans Mayer and Lukács himself, chose to emphasize the Fascist—not the Communist—prototype in Naphta. The view also surfaced that the "great patrician author" and the "social revolutionary were life-long friends."[22] It was time to take a second look at these literary rumors and theses and either prove or disprove them. It is fairly obvious to the discerning eye that there are traces of the Marxist Lukács in Naphta, that is, in the fictional character's argumentation and in his "intellectual duels": Lukács's Hegelianism, his damnation of the capitalist system, the concept of totality, and, of course, the belief in the redemptive role of the dictatorship of the proletariat. But there are other equally important characteristic traits to consider that set them apart: the rejection of the Enlightenment, of faith in humanity, and of progress, and adherence to romanticism and irrationalism. Further exploration was therefore called for, which could be done only by a Lukácsian analysis, if you will, meaning the category of totality, exploring all facets of the question in their sociohistorical anchorage.

Leo Naphta, as a Jewish-Jesuit-Communist combination, is certainly one of the most intriguing, most complex, and strangest figures in Mann's oeuvre. The following two points have to be made, somewhat forestalling the conclusion: first, Lukács is not Naphta, but he contributed to Mann's portrayal of Naphta to a large extent; second, as stated by the author himself unequivocally, Mann had "not read anything by Lukács of a political nature, not in the 1920s or ever, just his literary criticism," and consequently "*Geschichte und Klassenbewusstsein* was and remained unfamiliar" to him.[23] Thus, his assessment of Lukács is based on Lukács's early writings, that is, his pre-Marxist period, and on a one-time meeting that lasted about two hours.

Thomas Mann's novel *The Magic Mountain* marks the end of his early period: he started writing the novel in 1915, abandoned the project until after World War I, and had it published in 1924. Mann spoke of the genesis and nature of his novel at a Princeton lecture in 1939 and characterized it as a "document of the European state of mind and spiritual problematic in the first quarter of the twentieth century." Its setting in the enclosed and self-sufficient world of illness does not detract from its validity and potency. On the contrary! The tuberculosis sanatorium of Davos itself is conceived as a symbol for certain social institutions of that time, which "represented a typical phenomenon of the pre-WWI era that are conceivable only in the case of a still-intact capitalistic economic formation." Indeed, as Mann said, *The Magic Mountain* "has become the swan-song of that existence."[24] It neither could have been written at any other time nor would it have found as receptive an audience as it did. It is not only a *Zeitroman*, though. It is also a *Bildungsroman* (novel of development and education), in which all elements, action, character, and environment act primarily to form the hero's character. Any such novel also records its author's growth in understanding life; it tells about his personal history linked with its time. As Mann stated, "A man lives not only his personal life as an individual, but also, consciously or unconsciously, the life of his epoch and his contemporaries."[25] (This is one of the reasons why Mann's novels lend themselves so well to a sociological approach.) Space does not permit me to elaborate here on the epoch that forms the background; it is one familiar to students of European history and culture. A good way to summarize it is to mention the works that come out of it, such as Oswald Spengler's *Untergang des Abendlandes*, Ernst Bloch's *Geist der Utopie*, Lukács's *Geschichte und Klassenbewusstsein*, Karl Mannheim's *Ideologie und Utopie*—and I might add Julien Benda's *The Treason of the Intellectuals* and José Ortega y Gasset's *Revolt of the Masses*.

As to what would explain the strangeness and complexity of the Naphta combination, Mann's only clue was his favorite remark, *Es lag einfach in der Luft* (it was all in the air), meaning that he was alert to the undercurrents, ideas, and events around him and captured them; while he was doing so, he, of course, transformed and transcended them. Beside the textual analysis, it is thus prudent to investigate in Mann's case what *lag in der Luft* and also how his method made use of it.

Apart from his imaginative and combinatory skills, Mann was also a thorough researcher of the facts he needed for a solid foundation. He studied and used physical environment, customs, and manners carefully and never denied his reliance on real-life models. He emphasized that the writer "never creates *ex nihilo*." In complete accord with an important tendency in aesthetics around 1910, Mann mentions the term "construction," which was the password in painting and music. He praised those who found the "constructive element" in his *Königliche Hoheit*, which "comprises the new aspiration of the novel."[26] Mann used the realistic details in a special way that partly explains the Naphta combination. He himself stated that although he might have the idea of a figure and its setting in composition, he needed "to see, to hear and to comprehend" such a real person before the fictional character could be born.

Mann spoke of his "daemonic urge to observe, to notice small details that in a literary sense were *typical*, characteristic and showed perspectives and/or significant *racial*, social and psychological traits."[27] Since his figures often stood for certain spiritual and intellectual spheres, principles, and a specific Weltanschauung, all the elements that made up a (fictional) character had to complement each other: the biography, the physique, and the intellectual personality had to typify what the character represented. Equally important is the organic nature of Mann's creative process, the relatedness of everything to everything else that follows, just as in Lukács's case. It means that motives, concepts, and characters do not just appear and disappear in Mann's lifework; they may surface in other variations, may be refined or changed in certain respects, indicating an abundance of *Möglichkeiten* (possibilities), as he called it. Nothing gets lost in the process, everything is used prudently, redefined, or expanded. Thus, to say that Naphta came out of nowhere, was an entirely new fictional character on the basis of acquaintance with Georg Lukács, is to misunderstand the nature of Mann's creative process.

In this connection, mention should be made of an important trait of Mann that Hans Mayer first noted as he spoke of the "idealtypical" manifestations of currents and movements through the fictional characters. Mann, of course, was unaware of Max Weber's conception of the "idealtype." He did, however, come close to Weber's formulations when he spoke of his own literary approach (as in the case of Lukács, there are even similarities in the use of terms). In the essay *Betrachtungen eines Unpolitischen* Mann stated that his *Königliche Hoheit* is a book thoroughly formed, guided by an idea, an intellectual formula, that comes alive by a one-sided accentuation of details the synthesis of which resembles—but is not—the real. It is only the "illusion" of it. (Weber calls it "utopia.") Here one has to think of Mann's boasting about having done a better job than some sociologists when portraying the bourgeoisie in *Buddenbrooks*, well before Werner Sombart wrote his book entitled *The Bourgeois*.

Leo Naphta can be considered the idealtypical representation of one way out of the historical malaise. He also stands in for the concept and role of the "Stranger" (Simmel), a potential wanderer whose position "within a spatial group" is determined "by the fact that he has not belonged to it from the beginning, that he imports qualities into it, which do not and cannot stem from the group itself"; consequently, he acquires an objectivity, but any relation to him has to be of "an abstract nature."[28] Thus, all the details of Naphta's makeup, such as his biography, physique, and personality, should add up to a conceptual construct (*Gedankenbild*)—and it does. Naphta appears late in the novel, at that point when Settembrini has exhausted his repertoire of ideas and the novel's hero, Hans Castorp, feels that he can learn nothing more from him. What strikes one first in the introduction of the character (in the subchapter "Noch Jemand") is that "everything about him was sharp." The sharpness of the physical appearance presages the story of his life and culminates in the sharpness of his intellectual makeup, his mind, and his argumentation, and then, finally, the extreme nature of the solutions he offers both for the redemption of the world and for his own fate. At the same time, in each of Naphta's aspects, I first eliminated those elements that could not have come from Lukács or were recurring traits or attributes in a redefined form.

As to the life story of Leo Naphta, two facts stand out: first, both Lukács and Naphta are *aus dem Osten*—of the Eastern European sphere; second, both are of Jewish origin. Otherwise, as Sagave noted, there is not much similarity between the son of a banker in Budapest and a Galician kosher butcher's son, whose father became the victim of a pogrom and who was first the student of a rabbi and later a respected novice at a Jesuit institute. The main idea about Naphta is that his biographical data must match Mann's concept of what kind of life an outsider must have. Mann's fictional prototype of the "exceptional case of life" (*Sonderfall*) was one of the most persistent and varied in his oeuvre. These *Sonderfälle des Lebens* must have had a certain fate assigned to them: illness, deformation, artistic or intellectual exceptionality, and so on. Those traits were present in order to separate them from the "ordinary burgher." Whether it is exceptionality in a positive or a negative sense was always of secondary importance. Thus, Naphta has his forerunners, that is, characters sharing the kind of life Naphta had to have. For example, as early as the novel *Königliche Hoheit*, we have the life story of a Dr. Raoul Überbein: no father, origins unknown, starving, but determined to overcome such tremendous handicaps, a self-educated intellectual. In most cases such characters belong to a specific racial group: they are Jewish.

I cannot go into here how I developed and illustrated the necessary ingredients in the biography of an outsider in Mann's lifework. Suffice it to say that this prototype does not disappear with Naphta: it reappears in the figure of Dr. Chaim Breisacher, for example, in *Doctor Faustus*. As far as I can ascertain, Ernst Bloch's work *Thomas Münzer als der Theologe der Revolution* contributed a few direct biographical snippets to Naphta's life story. Thus, the conclusion can be reached that without having met Lukács, Mann could have set up Naphta in the same way.

Mann may have "smuggled" in Lukács's father as Elia, Naphta's father, and the relationship of respect and understanding between father and son. Similarly, the description of the relationship between mother and son has some resemblance to the situation in the Lukács household: Mann knew the parents of Lukács, as he was guest several times in the house of the banker, Joseph von Lukács, and must have been attuned to the family dynamics. It is now a well-publicized fact that Lukács once remarked that if there could be a psychological explanation for his rejection of the old world order, it would be in his relationship to his mother—one of unmitigated contempt. Lukács himself related the following story: when he wrote a friendly letter to his mother, she concluded that she must be gravely ill—which she was—otherwise her son could not have been persuaded to be so attentive and nice to her.[29]

Concerning the physical appearance and attributes of Leo Naphta, Sagave made the most of the "nose" issue, the sharpness of the features, even the eyeglasses. To be sure, both Naphta and Lukács could be called small and frail-looking; the young Lukács certainly was not "extremely ugly," as Naphta is. Moreover, the typical outsider—and the Jewish outsider to boot— was there in some form or another in Mann's early works, starting with the Hagenström children in *Buddenbrooks* (e.g., the nose, the small body, ugliness, reddish blond hair, and so on). If Lukács's personal appearance contributed to Naphta's physiognomy, it was only in the sense that the image Mann had was finally "seen, heard, and comprehended; it was also in tune with Mann's ideas about the intellectual personality of that specific type. Interestingly, Thomas Mann did not write to anybody about his meeting with Lukács and his impressions during those two hours in the Viennese hotel in January 1922. He reported to Ernst Bertram in June 1922 that "Leo Naphta is found; as a half-Jewish pupil of the Jesuits, he has an ongoing sharp debate with Settembrini."[30] The discovery of the so-called symbolic physique was first mentioned by Arthur Eloesser, first and only authorized biographer of Thomas Mann. Eloesser made the remark in 1925 that Naphta was supplied by the "geniality of real life" in the form of a "little ugly Jew, who was a rabiat theoretician with a steely logic, defending during a discussion all forms of absolutism and anti-individualism, from counterreformation and Jesuitism up to the Communistic revolution and Leninism."[31]

And, thus, we have arrived at the most significant aspect of Naphta in relation to Lukács, his intellectual personality. I cannot go into the discussion of Mann's preoccupation and fascination with the problem of personality formation here and now. One only has to go to his essays on "personalities at the end of a cultural era," ranging from Dante to Dostoevsky and Karl Kraus. Mann was very much in tune with the reigning currents of his time: he was an avid reader of Nietzsche, Kretschmer, Lombroso, Klages, and so on. Physical attributes are everywhere a clue to personality. Thus, when Hans Castorp and Joachim first meet Naphta, they immediately notice his being a "stranger." Joachim does not go further than noticing the figure and nose; he is distrustful. Hans Castorp sees the perspectives this stranger can reveal for him by becoming his next "teacher": Naphta, after all, comes from a sphere that Castorp never explored and can offer him new insights.

Admittedly, it is impossible to describe Naphta's personality in a few words, but a summary can be provided here. First of all, he has a sharp mind, and he is logical to the point of becoming inhuman in his argumentation; he is a fanatic when it comes to ideas and ideologies; he has the intellectual courage to go to the bottom of problems and then suffer the consequences; he is deeply apodictical and thoroughly ascetic. In short, Naphta represents the radical repudiation of the whole liberal tradition. There is some irony involved here in that Thomas Mann took many of his reflections from the pages of his *Betrachtungen eines Unpolitischen*, meaning that he incorporated his own earlier views into Naphta's position. Much is made of Naphta's instincts, which were "revolutionary and aristocratic at the same time, as is the case with many Jewish intellectuals";[32] equally emphasized is Naphta's elitist inclinations and his achievement-oriented characteristics. And again, we find traces of the concept of the compatibility of the religious and the ideological in one person, which may have been suggested in part by Bloch's *Münzer* book. In addition, we have Jesuits with many of the above-mentioned traits. There is ample evidence that Mann studied biographies and interpretations of Loyola and of Jesuitism. Jesuit-Jew as a combination was not as uniquely his own as Mann liked to believe: Harry Graf Kessler's diaries, for example, describe Hugo Haase, famed politician of the Weimar Republic, as "a small man, a somewhat Jesuitic Jew."[33] It was one of those things "in the air."

That Lukács represented the "stranger" for Thomas Mann is a fact; many ideas presented by Naphta can be found in the conclusions of some of Lukács's early writings, mainly in the essays of *Die Seele und die Formen*. Just as important is another little-known work by Lukács, published in German in 1912 in the journal *Neue Blätter*: the work, entitled, "Von der Armut am Geiste" ("On Poverty of Spirit"), was both confessional and autobiographical. One can perceive the line of argumentation that is woven into Naphta's discourses in such works as Lukács's Kierkegaard essay, with its partiality for dogmatism, and his Theodor Storm essay, for the statement on manifestations of asceticism when work—even artistic work—is called "forced labor" against which our instincts might rebel and have to be restrained by the cruelest means possible. The Lukácsian dialogue "Von der Armut" contains several statements that I explored in my book in relation to Naphta: first, the cement that binds the work is "fashioned out of human blood"; second, "I believe in the quality of remaining pure [meaning ethically pure] through sin, deception and horror," a statement that is echoed in the 1918 "Bolshevism as a Moral Problem"; and, finally, Christ said after all, "He who comes to me . . . and hates not his father, . . . cannot be my disciple." This represents only a sample. The dialogue also contains a defense of the Middle Ages and, as the final act, the hero's suicide: just like Naphta in *The Magic Mountain*, the hero shoots himself in the head. Thomas Mann was acquainted with this work, as well as with the essay collection *Die Seele und die Formen*. Several of the passages mentioned here were underlined and noted in Mann's own copies, which are to be found in the Thomas Mann Archiv.

So far we have discussed asceticism, achievement through violence, and the necessity for inhumanity in certain cases. We can also find examples of "things that do not rhyme," as Naphta is wont to say. It is interesting to note in this connection that Lukács wrote an essay in 1913 entitled "Aesthetic Culture," in which he explicitly brings together "things that do not rhyme": he writes, for example, that "form is a judgment that forces salvation on everything by a holy terror."[34] This Hungarian work has never been translated into any other language, and the creator of Leo Naphta was unaware of these connections drawn by the young Lukács. Yet Thomas Mann uncannily perceived the radicalism of Lukács's position on ethical and aesthetic questions, a position that not only pointed to Lukács's later decision to embrace the cause of revolution, in which ends justify all means, but also adapted very well to the strange and often contradictory ideological disputations of the stranger in the novel, Leo Naphta. That Lukács, in Thomas Mann's eyes the quintessential Jewish intellectual, cites Christ, Meister Eckhart, or Francis of Assisi and finally depicts Abraham's willingness to perform the ultimate sacrifice, rounds out the picture.

Conclusion

Just as the fictional figure Leo Naphta is the prototype of the irregular, the other, because he is irregular as a Jew, as a Jesuit, and as a Communist, so

was Lukács perceived by Mann as irregular on account of his bourgeois asceticism, which permitted the use of terms such as "violence and dogma" and
"holy terror," and on account of his religiosity and concept of terror. The
tendencies presumably perceived in Lukács—the tendencies toward "extremes," for being "absolute," for "fanaticism" and "asceticism"—not
only helped to shape the totalitarian personality of Naphta but also deterred
the establishment of a meaningful personal relationship between Thomas
Mann and Lukács. Not only did Lukács possess characteristics that Mann dis-
liked, despised, or simply was afraid of, but first and foremost he came from
the "non-German sphere," that of a Dostoevsky, of the Jewish literati—in
sum, from the "East." The Eastern sphere had the well-documented fascination for the type of artist Thomas Mann was, but with which he could never be
on intimate terms. Thus, the *Distanz* could not be bridged.

Notes

1. See Theodor W. Adorno and Gershom Scholem, eds., *Walter Benjamin. Briefe*,
   vol. 2 (Frankfurt am Main: Suhrkamp, 1966).
2. For one of the best and most extensive treatments of the Lukács-Naphta problem,
   see Ehrhard Bahr, *Georg Lukács* (Berlin: Colloquium Verlag Otto H. Hess,
   1970); Pierre-Paul Sagave, *Réalité sociale et idéologie religieuse dans les romans
   de Thomas Mann*, Publications de la Faculté des lettres de l'universite de
   Strasbourg, fasc. 124 (Paris, 1954).
3. See Hans Mayer, *Thomas Mann. Werk und Entwicklung* (Berlin: Volk und Welt,
   1950).
4. Mann's reflections on the state and nature of the modern novel appear in his
   unfinished—and unpublished—notes to a planned large-scale essay with the title
   "Geist und Kunst" ("Intellect and Art"). See ch. 1 in my book *Georg Lukács
   and Thomas Mann: A Study in the Sociology of Literature* (Amherst: University of
   Massachusetts, 1987).
5. Harry Levin, "Toward a Sociology of the Novel," in *Refractions: Essays in
   Comparative Literature* (London, Oxford and New York: Oxford University,
   1966), p. 248.
6. See Hans Vaget, "Georg Lukács und Thomas Mann," *Die Neue Rundschau* 88,
   4(1977): 656–63.
7. Levin, *Refractions*.
8. Georg Lukács, "In Search of Bourgeois Man," in *Essays on Thomas Mann*
   (London: Merlin, 1964), p. 45.
9. For an account of differing views concerning this "great and wonderful war" as
   Max Weber put it, see Zoltán Tar and Judith Marcus, "The Weber-Lukács Encounter," in R. M. Glassman and V. Murvar, eds., *Max Weber's Political Sociology: A Pessimistic Vision of a Rationalized World* (Westport, CT: Greenwood,
   1984), pp. 125–26. See also Marianne Weber, *Max Weber: A Biography*, ed. and
   trans. Harry Zohn (New York: Wiley Interscience, 1975). Both the Webers and
   Georg Simmel discussed Lukács's "inability" to understand the "just cause." In
   response, Lukács had started to write an essay on "The German Intellectuals and
   the War," which was never completed.
10. Henry Hatfield, *Thomas Mann*, rev. ed. (New York: New Directions, 1962).

11. Thomas Mann, foreword to *The Magic Mountain*, trans. H. T. Lowe-Porter (New York: Modern Library, 1955), p. x.

12. Thomas Mann, *The Story of a Novel: The Genesis of Doctor Faustus*, trans. Richard and Clara Winston (New York: Knopf, 1961), p 25.

13. Mann's remarks follow his reflections on the critical sensibilities of the "young" Lukács. In *Reflections of a Nonpolitical Man*, trans. W. D. Morris (New York: Frederick Ungar, 1983), p. 73.

14. Ibid.

15. See Georg Steiner's review of Lukács's *Gelebtes Denken*, "Making a Homeland for the Mind," *Times Literary Supplement* (January 22, 1982), p. 67.

16. The definition used by several Lukács critics and reviewers.

17. See Henry Pachter, "Lukács Revisited: Orthodox Heretic, Stalinist Romantic," *Dissent* (Spring 1975), pp. 177ff.

18. Georg Lukács, *Record of a Life: An Autobiographical Sketch*, ed. István Eörsi, trans. Rodney Livingstone (London: Verso, 1983), p. 81.

19. See Steiner, "Homeland," p. 67.

20. For the report on the visit with Lukács, see Judith Tar, "Georg Lukács, Thomas Mann und 'Der Tod in Venedig,' " *Die Weltwoche* (July 2, 1971), p. 31.

21. Passage is from Lukács's essay "Longing and Form: Charles Louis Philippe," in *Soul and Form*, trans. Anna Bostock (Cambridge, MA: MIT, 1974), p. 94. For discussion and transcription of Mann's original note, see Marcus, *Georg Lukács and Thomas Mann*, ch. 1.

22. The statement appears on the jacket of Ehrhard Bahr's book, *Georg Lukács*.

23. Unpublished letter to Pierre-Paul Sagave of February 18, 1952, which is at the Thomas Mann Archiv, Zurich. My translation.

24. See Mann, *Magic Mountain*, pp. 328–29.

25. Ibid.

26. Mann's letter to Hugo von Hofmannsthal, in *Thomas Mann. Briefe 1889–1936*, ed. Erika Mann (Frankfurt am Main: S. Fischer, 1962), p. 76. My translation.

27. Thomas Mann, "Goethe and Tolstoy," in *Three Essays*, trans. H. T. Lowe-Porter (New York: Knopf, 1929), p. 90.

28. See the essay by Georg Simmel, "The Stranger," in *The Sociology of Georg Simmel*, ed. Kurt H. Wolff (New York: Free Press, 1950), pp. 402ff.

29. Georg Lukács's own recollections in *Record of a Life*, p. 35.

30. See *Thomas Mann an Ernst Bertram. Briefe aus den Jahren 1910–1955*, ed. Inge Jens (Pfullingen: Günther Neske, 1960), p. 109.

31. See Arthur Eloesser, *Thomas Mann: Sein Leben und seine Werke* (Berlin: S. Fischer, 1925), p. 193.

32. See the chapter "Operationes Spirituales," in *Magic Mountain*, p. 443.

33. See Harry (Count) Kessler, *In the Twenties: The Diaries of Harry Kessler*, trans. Charles Kessler (New York: Holt, Rinehart and Winston, 1971), p. 36.

34. See György Lukács, *Esztétikai kultúra. Tanulmányok (Aesthetic Culture: Studies)* (Budapest: Athenaeum, 1913), p. 27.

Part III
CULTURE AND POLITICS

10

Georg Lukács's Cosmic Chutzpah

By Marshall Berman

Georg Lukács, one of the remarkable men of the twentieth century, began life in the age of Disraeli and Nietzsche and carried on into the age of the Beatles and the moon shots. He is the author of two world-class masterpieces, *History and Class Consciousness* and *Theory of the Novel*, and of dozens of other books and thousands of articles, pamphlets, manifestos, and other writings of nearly every genre on nearly every subject we can imagine. His ideas are central to the history of both Marxism and existentialism. He spent the last half-century of his life as a committed Communist, participating in the revolutions of 1918–19, living through the horrors of Stalinism, emerging into political life again in the Hungarian revolution of 1956, suffering imprisonment by a wide assortment of jailers, surviving to protest the bombs over Hanoi and the tanks in Prague.

Record of a Life[1] is a series of sketches and interviews that Lukács hastily put together shortly before his death in 1971, when he realized that he would never live to write his autobiography. There is a wonderful grandeur about Lukács as he emerges here. He is physically frail but intellectually powerful and spiritually intense, striving to grasp the meaning of his life and work. He radiates the aura of those old men of Greek mythology, Philoctetes with his wound and his bow, Oedipus at Colonus, the androgynous prophet Tiresias who has foresuffered all. These comparisons are meant only to show what a problematical figure he was: his intellectual and visionary powers were always intertwined with blindness, wounds, and guilt.

I

I first encountered Lukács in Washington Square Park, in the spring of 1958. I was a freshman at Columbia, out of the Bronx for the first time in my life, enthralled by the sights and sounds of Manhattan and the books and ideas of the world. As I wandered through the park one lovely afternoon, I saw, among the singers and players and hustlers and kibitzers, a fellow I had known in high school, standing under the arch, declaiming and handing out leaflets to the crowd. He had been a Communist party stalwart all through school, but the events of 1956 had hit him hard, and after Budapest he seemed to drop out of sight. Now here he was again, testifying that capitalism was on its last legs, and that the international working class and its vanguard party were alive and well. I greeted him and got him to take a break; we walked around the park, gossiped about old school friends, looked longingly at the girls, and started to worry about the world.

He remarked on the books I was carrying—Kierkegaard, Dostoevsky, Martin Buber—and wondered if I was becoming a junkie on that old opium of the people. I in turn wondered if he was still recruiting people to join the Red Army and see the world. Suddenly he turned dead serious: "Are you asking if I'm still a Communist?" All right, I said: was he, could he be, even now? He replied that he was more of a Communist than ever. I must have looked dubious, or maybe just disgusted. He reached into his briefcase and pulled out a text, poorly mimeographed and heavily underlined: it was called "What Is Orthodox Marxism?" by a Georg Lukács. "Here," he ordered, "read this!" The text began with the proclamation that even if every single one of Marx's theses about the world were to be proved wrong, an orthodox Marxist could simply discard them "without having to renounce his orthodoxy for a single moment." I was instantly stunned: who was this guy and what was he saying? I fell back on a reality I was sure of: "And those tanks in Budapest? Don't they prove something?" My friend hesitated for a moment, then drew himself up and answered decisively. "They prove," he said, "that the USSR is not orthodox."

I can still remember the way that first page of Lukács made my head spin. The cosmic chutzpah of the man was staggering. I'd known plenty of Marxists who were willing to admit that Marx might be wrong about many things; in spite of this, they said, he was right about the essential things, and that was why they were Marxists. Now here was a Marxist saying that Marx might be wrong about everything, and he couldn't care less; that the truth of Marxism was independent of anything that Marx said about the world, and hence that nothing in the world could ever refute it; and that this was the essence not merely of Marxist truth, but of Marxist orthodoxy—even if it was the orthodoxy of a single believer, shut out from the communion of the ecclesiastic party, keeping the faith alone in the park. When I thought about it later, it struck me that the Marxism of "What Is Orthodox Marxism?" had more in common with the existential flights of the religious writers whose books I was carrying that day—Kierkegaard, Dostoevsky, Buber—than with the Stalinist dogmatics on which my friend had grown up. As I thought of Lukács in their company, it flashed on me that what I had just read was a Marxist *credo quia absurdum*. Could it be that communism had found its St. Augustine at last?

I asked my teachers about Lukács and found out all I could. No one knew too much in those years, but everyone found him fascinating. He was a Hungarian Jew, son of a banker, born in Budapest in 1885. He had studied in Heidelberg with Max Weber and in Berlin with Georg Simmel, who considered him, though still in his twenties, one of the most brilliant and original minds of the age. He had begun his career as a writer on art and culture, a founder of magazines and a theater—he brought Ibsen and Strindberg to Budapest—but then, radicalized by the experience of World War I, became a member of the Hungarian Communist party and a militant activist. He had emerged as a leader, and served as Commissar of Education and Culture, in the short-lived Soviet Republic of Hungary in 1919. After its overthrow, he escaped to Vienna and then to Berlin, where he became active in the Communist International through the 1920s. When Hitler came to power he found himself a refugee again, this time in Moscow, where he helped to discover, excavate, and publish the buried writings of the young Marx. At the end of World War II he returned to Budapest, where he wrote and taught philosophy for the rest of his life.

Lukács's reputation rested on a work of philosophy, politics, and social theory that he brought out in German in 1923, *History and Class Consciousness*.[2] This book had been long out of print and was virtually impossible to obtain, and therein lies a tale. It began with the essay I had read that day in the park, "What Is Orthodox Marxism?" Ironically, although Lukács had been constantly preoccupied with establishing a Marxist orthodoxy, he became a prime victim once the Communist movement began to persecute internal heresy. In the Comintern in 1924 and 1928, in Moscow in 1934, in Budapest in 1949, he was subjected to campaigns of the crudest abuse and vilification;[3] three generations of Stalinist hacks had stigmatized him as a symbol of all the dangers of "deviation." In all these cases (Morris Watnick chronicled them in *Soviet Survey* in 1958, the first discussion of Lukács in English),[4] he had submitted to his persecutors, repudiated his ideas, and begged forgiveness, rather than be isolated from the world Communist movement. In 1928 he was condemned by the Comintern for premature antifascism (he was vindicated later, but too late for him). He then withdrew from political activity and hoped for a quieter life, writing literary and cultural history. But is was not to be.

In 1934, when *History and Class Consciousness* was condemned for the heresy of philosophical idealism, Lukács seemed to enlist actively in the fight against his life and thought. He confessed "not only the theoretical falsity of my book, but its practical danger." The diatribes against him "all the more strengthened by conviction that, in the intellectual sphere, the front of Idealism is the front of Fascist counter-revolution.'' He ended by praising Comrade Stalin and his henchmen for their ''iron implacability and refusal to compromise with all deviations from Marxism-Leninism.'' He did not offer to burn *History and Class Consciousness* (or himself) in Red Square, but he did swear to do everything in his power to ensure that his masterpiece would never be reprinted anywhere again.

When I read this, I felt confirmed in my sense of Lukács as a religious figure. His capacity for abjection and repentance, his drive to punish and mortify himself for the sake of sanctity, had more in common with the inner world of Augustine's *Confessions* than with the sensibility of Karl Marx. But this was a very modern Augustine, as he might have been imagined by Dostoevsky or Freud: endlessly reinventing himself, hoping to obliterate his past once and for all, only to trip over it—or maybe dig it up—again and again; persecuting and purging himself in a quest for pure orthodoxy, only to find himself inventing new modes of heresy, leading to new orgies of guilt, confession, and self-recrimination.

In 1956, Lukács went through a stunning metamorphosis. That year, as the Stalinist system shook and crumbled, the Hungarian people rose up against their Soviet masters. Lukács participated enthusiastically in this revolution, and once again, after thirty-seven years, served as minister of education and culture in a Hungarian revolutionary government. When the USSR moved in, Lukács, as a member of Prime Minister Imre Nagy's cabinet, was one of the first to be arrested. Imprisoned in Count Dracula's old Transylvanian castle, he was interrogated by the Soviet secret police and put under pressure to submit, confess, recant, inform, denounce. Lukács had gone through these motions many times before over the past thirty years. This time, however, he refused to betray his comrades, his people, or himself. Pressed to denounce Imre Nagy, Lukács said that he would be glad to air his opinions about Nagy once the two of them were free men in the streets of Budapest, but he would never break solidarity with a fellow prisoner. After six months in prison, Lukács was released and allowed to return to Budapest. It was understood that he would not agitate actively against the new government; neither, however, would he endorse it. At the age of 70, this lifelong seeker after orthodoxy found himself an authentic heretical hero.

II

History and Class Consciousness appeared in French translation in 1960. Lukács protested its publication, but his objections only made the book more notorious and intriguing. My friends and I, and many intellectuals like us—members of the generation that would soon be called the New Left—opened the book with breathless anticipation, and found that it lived up to its advance notices. Whatever we might think about its many theories and arguments, *History and Class Consciousness* convinced us that socialist thought in our time could be carried on at the highest pitch of intellectual power, fused with the most passionate feeling, transformed into an inspired vision. Lukács gave us both a standard that challenges and a specter that haunts any radical who sits down to write today.

The heart of *History and Class Consciousness*, and the primary source of its power, is a 140-page essay, situated at the book's center, entitled ''Reification and the Consciousness of the Proletariat.'' ''Reification'' is a poor Latinized equivalent for *Verdinglichung*, a German word that means ''thingification,'' the process by which a person is transformed into a thing. The basic trouble with capitalism, Lukács argues, is that it treats people as if they were things, and treats human relationships as if they were between things. The particular sort of thing that people in modern capitalist societies get turned into is the commodity. Lukács takes Marx's idea of the ''Fetishism of Commodities'' (*Capital*, vol. 1, ch. 1), and extends it into a total vision of what capitalism does to human life.

He begins with an exploration of work, carrying Marx's discussion of nineteenth-century industrial labor into the age of immense bureaucracies (private and public), efficiency experts, system analysis, and long-range planning. The process of labor is ''progressively broken down into abstract, rational, specialized operations.'' Workers lose contact not only with the products or services they create, but with their own thoughts and feelings and actions. ''Even the worker's psychological attributes are separated from his total personality, and placed in opposition to it, so as to facilitate their integration into specialized rational systems and their reduction to statistical units.'' This fragmentation of activity tends to generate a ''fragmentation of the subject,'' so that a worker's personal qualities, talents, or idiosyncrasies ''appear as sources of error.''

The worker is meant to be ''a mechanical part incorporated into a mechanical system. He finds it already pre-existing and self-sufficient, it functions independently of him, and he has to conform to its laws whether he likes it or not. . . . Here, too, the personality can do no more than look on helplessly while its own existence is reduced to an isolated particle and fed into an alien system.'' In such a system we feel passive and contemplative; we experience ourselves as spectators in processes that happen to us, rather than active participants shaping our lives.

Most of Marx's successors focused almost exclusively on the miseries of industrial workers. Lukács shows how the force of Marx's analysis and indictment goes far beyond the oppression of this class. In fact, capitalism treats all men and women as interchangeable parts, as commodities exchangeable for other commodities. Administrators, soldiers, scientists, even entrepreneurs—

everybody in modern society—is forced into the Procrustean bed of reification and systematically deprived of the freedom that everyone is supposed to enjoy. Even the modern capitalist "experiences the same doubling of personality, the same splitting up of man into an element of the movement of commodities and an objective and impotent observer of that movement." Capitalists are rewarded for their inner passivity and lack of integration; but it is urgent to see the human costs of this system, even to its ruling class. Lukács deepens the case against capitalism by showing us how, even in its mansions on the hill, no one is at home.

He puts much of his energy into a critique of early twentieth-century forms of discourse that passed for social science. He attacks the attempt to formulate laws of human behavior that will have the static, timeless quality of physical laws about the behavior of matter and energy. Such an aim assumes that human realities and social relationships are immutable, unchangeable, inexorable as gravitational force, impervious to human will, beyond any kind of social or political control. This paradigm masks the enormous diversity of human relationships in different times and places—indeed, even within the same time and place—and the capacity of human beings, acting collectively, to change the world. Something is fundamentally wrong with modes of thought—whether they are called philosophy, history, or science—whose main force is to convince people that there is no alternative to the way they live now. One of the most insidious powers of modern capitalism, Lukács believes, is its capacity to mobilize the energy of our intellects—and of our intellectuals—to blur our minds and paralyze our will, to reduce us to passive spectators of whatever fate the market inflicts on us.

In such a world, revolution is a categorical imperative. It is the only way to seize control of our fate, to assert ourselves as subjects, as people, against a social structure that treats us as things. Lukács insists on the crucial importance of consciousness, or self-knowledge and self-awareness, in political life. Capitalism may be breaking down, but there is no reason to think that it will give way to something better, unless the workers are conscious that things can be better, that they have the power to transform and renew the world. If the workers can come to know themselves—to grasp the sources of their present weakness and self-alienation, of their potential freedom and power—then capitalism is doomed. Lukács connects the Marxist ideal of "revolutionary class-consciousness" with the ancient Socratic demand for communal self-knowledge. But this project means an arduous process of education and self-education, of struggle (in practice as well as theory), of continual self-criticism and self-overcoming. One of the main reasons for having a Communist party, Lukács argues, is to focus and organize this work of self-knowledge. Equally important is the development of a vibrant, dynamic, self-critical, and self-renewing radical culture. Without culture and consciousness, the workers will not be able to grow in awareness and autonomy, to develop their will and their sense of power. If they don't grow and develop this way, the reification-machine will go on running, and its victims won't ever know what's hit them or why they feel like hollow men.

If they do learn and grow, the soviet or worker's council will be the ideal expression of their new life. Government and politics won't be obscure processes enacted on behalf of remote or invisible interests, but activities that men and women do, on their own, in their everyday lives. The economy won't be a machine running on its own momentum toward its own goals, but a structure of concrete decisions that men and women freely make about how they want to live and fulfill their needs. Culture, instead of being a veil of mystification thrown over everyday life, will be created by ordinary people out of their real desires and needs and hopes. In a workers' democracy, the constraints of the exploitive economy, of the repressive state, of the culture of mystification, will all wither away. Then "the life of man as man in relation to himself, to his fellow men and to nature, can now become the authentic content of human life. Socially, man is now born as man."

History and Class Consciousness appeared at an ideal moment for an emerging generation of radical intellectuals. It helped us in the West to see how, even where capitalism was highly successful in economic terms (the 1960s, remember, was the climax of the greatest capitalist boom in history), it could still be humanly disastrous, inflicting insult and injury on the people in it by treating them as nothing more than commodities. Simultaneously, Lukács's book enabled intellectuals in the Soviet bloc to understand how the so-called Workers' States had developed their own distinctive forms of reification. The 1960s spawned an amazing variety of eruptions and rebellions by people who were sick and tired of being treated as things, who fought to end reification and to assert themselves as subjects, as active participants in their everyday lives. For those of us who were trying to think about what was going on, *History and Class Consciousness* was a rich source of ideas, of energy and inspiration. Moreover, for a generation accustomed to a Marxism of sterile formulas and rigid dogmas enforced by party hacks, this book brought Marxism back to its deepest sources as a vision and a theory of human liberation.

One of the most striking things about *History and Class Consciousness* was the pervasiveness of religious language in it. First there was the theme of "orthodoxy" with which the book began; then the goal of socialism was said to be "the redemption of man"; the transition from capitalism to socialism would be "a leap into the realm of freedom," after which "man is now born as man." No one knew enough about Lukács, back in the 1960s, to sort out these ideas and drives. But it was clear that one of his most important achievements was to bring together the body of Marxist theory and practice with the stream of spiritual yearning, which, more than any economic analysis or attachment to the working class, has led countless men and women to "prove their ideas by action, by living and dying for the revolution."

This fusion was the primary source of Lukács's power and originality. But it had its dark side as well. One of the most disturbing of his religious ideas—an idea that has been deeply problematical whenever it has occurred in the history of religion—is the idea of *incarnation*. Thus, in the course of expounding on the Leninist idea of a "vanguard" Communist party, Lukács gives it a twist that would have been unimaginable to a pragmatic and materialist mind like Lenin's: "The Party," he says, "is the historical embodiment and active incarnation of [revolutionary] class consciousness" and, again, "the incarnation of the ethics of the fighting proletariat."

Lukács's doctrine of incarnation is as profound a mystery as anything ever proclaimed by any Christian church. But it poses special dangers all its own. If the Communist party, in some mysterious way, "is" the revolutionary working class, then it becomes impossible to imagine that, say, the party might be betraying the working class; it even becomes impossible to ask whether the party is serving the working class as well as it should be: the party stands not only beyond doubt, but beyond question or scrutiny.

Similar problems arise around Lukács's notion of Marxist orthodoxy, equally impervious to any facts or events that might cast doubt on its truth. Finally, there is the idea of *totality*, according to which the question of freedom becomes "purely tactical," because "freedom cannot represent a value in itself": the only real issue is whether the Communist party, incarnation of the working class, holds the "totality of power." If these ideas were brought together—the trinity of totality, orthodoxy, incarnation—they could generate a theology of total submission, a metaphysical undertow that might well be strong enough to drown all Lukács's dreams of liberation.

III

The radical contradictions that animate this book, and the strength and depth with which its contradictory ideas are expressed, mark *History and Class Consciousness* as one of the great modernist works of the century. To young readers who discovered Lukács in the 1960s, he seemed to belong in the company of great modern thinkers at war with themselves—Rousseau, Dostoevsky, Nietzsche—theorists and exponents both of liberation and of domination. (Although Lukács was a Marxist, his kindred spirits were all a lot weirder than Marx.) We were just getting used to seeing Lukács as a great modernist when he came out with a scurrilous, hysterical attack on modernism.

"The Ideology of Modernism"[5] reads like an indictment at a Stalinist trial. It puts together an amalgam in the defendant's box, consisting of great twentieth-century writers (Kafka, Proust, Joyce, Faulkner, Musil, Freud), utterly mediocre writers (Steinbeck, Thomas Wolfe), and assorted Nazi ideologues and hacks. It then assaults these "modernist" subjects. In "their" writings, the personality is dissolved, the objective world is inexplicable, there is no past and no history, perversity and idiocy are the essence of the human condition. Modernism has no perspectives, furthers the dissolution of the personality, destroys the complex tissue of humanity's relations with the environment. Kierkegaard says that the self is opaque to itself, and this furnishes a convenient alibi for Nazi murderers. Kafka "substitutes his *Angst*-ridden view of the world for objective reality." Freud is "obsessed with pathology" and sickens an otherwise healthy audience; he lacks the sane wisdom of Pavlov, "who takes the Hippocratic view that mental abnormality is a deviation from a norm." So it goes.

"The Ideology of Modernism" is colossally, willfully ignorant. Or maybe it is not exactly ignorance, but rather what Veblen called "trained incapacity" to see what is there. This learning disability is a special embarrassment for those who like to think of themselves as Marxists. Marxists are supposed to be able to understand art in relation to historical and material reality. Instead, Lukács speaks as if it were writers who autonomously create reality: as if Freud had created the twentieth century's pathologies and Kafka its police states. (After his imprisonment in Dracula's castle, Lukács was reported to have said, "I was wrong, Kafka was a realist after all." But he never put this into print or thought it through.)

Lukács says that he is fighting in the name of "realism," whose basic idea is that "reality can be known." But his real argument, we see as we read on, is that reality *is* known, and he knows it—indeed, reality has been known since Goethe's and Balzac's and Marx's time—and he doesn't want to read any writing that doesn't tell him what he knows already. But the worst thing about "The Ideology of Modernism" is the way Lukács has identified with the aggressor, assaulting Kafka and Joyce and Freud in exactly the language that the hacks and thugs of the Kremlin used to assault him, hoping to destroy a whole generation of masterworks in just the way that his Soviet masters destroyed his own. The one great modernist who was within Lukács's reach, and whom he violated and degraded most brutally, was himself.

I remembered hearing that in *The Magic Mountain* Thomas Mann had used Lukács as a model for Leo Naphta, one of his most luminous characters, a Jewish-Jesuit-Communist who kills himself on the verge of World War I.[6] I was glad that Lukács was living on (and on). But Mann was surely right about his need to inflict dreadful wounds upon himself. In works like "The Ideology of Modernism," Lukács seemed to be killing himself again and again. What was he atoning for, and how long would his trial by ordeal last?

By the early 1970s, you could find people in American universities who had actually worked with Lukács, or with younger members of his circle. I remember asking them how one of the best minds of the century could sink so low. They said that I had to understand the political context. Surely I must have noticed, they said, that even as he assaulted modernism, Lukács also denounced socialist realism, the one form of literature that Stalin condoned. In fact, Lukács was the only writer in the Soviet bloc who had ever been able to get away with this. Did I think it had been easy, or without risks? By attacking the "Western orthodoxy" of modernism, Lukács was clearing space in which he would be free to attack the "Eastern orthodoxy" of socialist realism. Couldn't I see how, within the immense constraints of life in the Soviet bloc, Lukács had created space for literary and cultural freedom? Yes, I could see it. Still, I feared that the force of Lukács's cultural politics might well be to open the door for the freethinkers and writers of the 1860s, while keeping those of the 1960s locked out.

More of Lukács writings were reissued and translated in the course of the 1960s. There were the works of literary criticism and cultural history written in the 1930s and 1940s: *Studies in European Realism, Goethe and His Age, The Historical Novel, The Young Hegel.* These books lacked the brilliance and originality of *History and Class Consciousness* but moved on a level far above the antimodernist diatribes of the 1950s. The books were full of marvelous connections and insights, and full of nostalgia for the sweetness of life before World War I. They showed Lukács as a conservative thinker; conservative in the best sense, striving to embrace, nourish, and protect the heritage of bourgeois humanistic culture, even as the twin menaces of Nazism and Stalinism were closing in. Lukács's comrades in this preservationist enterprise were a generation of gifted Jewish scholars, scattered to the four winds by Nazism—among them, Ernst Cassirer, Erich Auerbach, Karl Loewith, Arnold Hauser, and Erwin Panofsky. In these works, Lukács's Marxism and communism often faded into the background. But he was absolutely right in arguing, as he did, that any socialist movement that abandoned this heritage, or let it die, would be surrendering its soul.

As Lukács's historical works were being reissued, a number of his post-Stalin political essays were coming out, hot off the presses. (The *New Left Review* played a crucial role in getting this material to British and American readers.) These articles made it clear how thrilled Lukács was to see Stalinism unmasked, and how eagerly he embraced Khrushchev's promises of domestic liberalization and international détente. Some of this writing showed an unprecedented emotional openness, and readers could not help sharing the old man's unmediated joy that he had come through, outlived his jailers.

But even here shadows of ambiguity begin to close on the pure daylight. Lukács's invectives against Stalin cite many disastrous flaws but make only the briefest, most cryptic reference to his mass murders. And it is disturbing that, in his essays on Stalin, Lukács spends so much time and energy denouncing Trotsky—as if, just as in his attacks on modernism, he needs to prove his own orthodoxy, lest the force of his criticism place his loyalty in doubt. Often in this period, Lukács seems to be going out of his way to protest too much, to suggest inexhaustible ironic depths, to force us to question what he says and means. This systematic ambiguity pervades the process of the republication of Lukács's early works, complete with recantations, official bans, and underground printing. The wheels within wheels seemed to be turning more frantically than ever in a 1967 preface to a new edition of *History and Class Consciousness*, an edition that Lukács had apparently fought to suppress: he testified that it was a mistake to write the book, and advised readers not to read it—but in a language of enticement that ensured his advice would fail.

IV

Lukács's death in 1971 was far from the end of his story. In the years since, an amazing array of his early writings has come to light, including much that Lukács himself believed lost; some of his most brilliant and original writing is just beginning to appear in print. We are still in the process of discovering Lukács, running the movie backwards, and getting the first things last. In fact, we are discovering parts of the movie that Lukács clearly hoped to censor, faces he left on the cutting room floor, the return of the repressed.

The most fascinating of Lukács's early works is *Theory of the Novel*,[7] written in the midst of the horrors of World War I, long suppressed by the author, finally republished (with another of those famous seductively self-denying prefaces) shortly before his death. *Theory of the Novel* argues that every literary form expresses a particular "metaphysical dissonance," which springs from the inner contradictions of its historical and social milieu. It goes on to evoke, with great lyrical brilliance, the dissonances that were tearing the modern world apart in 1915. It tries to imagine, and indeed to call into being, a true modernist art in which "all the fissures and rents inherent in the historical situation [will] be drawn into the form-giving process." *Theory of the Novel* is one of the great works of romantic criticism, in the class of Schiller's "Letters on the Aesthetic Education of Man" and Shelley's "Defence of Poetry." At the same time, although it was written before Lukács thought of himself as a Marxist, it is one of the most exciting Marxist works of our century. It concludes with a ringing declaration that the inner dialectic of the modern novel leads beyond the novel and, indeed, beyond the wretched and alienated world whose spirit the novel expresses. The emergence of Tolstoy and Dostoevsky are distinctive "signs of the world to come." Their interpretations of the modern world mark the start of a great wave of change in this world, a "breakthrough into a new epoch," the dawn of a "new unity" of soul and social institutions. Moreover, even before the Russian Revolution and Lukács's conversion to communism, he insisted that backward Russia was destined to be the salvation of the corrupt and decadent West.

Theory of the Novel is also fascinating in its religious anguish and longing. Lukács describes the modern novel as "an expression of transcendental homelessness"; the novel's typical environment as "a universe abandoned by God"; the epoch in which he writes as "an age of absolute sinfulness"; the modern hero's predicament as "the torment of a creature condemned to solitude and devoured by a longing for communion." Here, and throughout the book, Lukács makes clear the sort of inner needs that his commitment to communism would soon—for a time, at least—fulfill.

Recent scholarship has unearthed the way in which Lukács became a Communist. In fact, it was a religious conversion, an upheaval of the mind and heart, a second birth. It seems to have happened very suddenly, in the last days of 1918. According to one of his intimate friends, it happened "between one Sunday and the next, like Saul turning into Paul."[8]

Even as he was turning, Lukács wrote two remarkable brief essays, perhaps the clearest and most candid things he ever wrote: "Bolshevism as a Moral Problem,"[9] a few days before his conversion, and "Tactics and Ethics,"[10] a few days after. The "Bolshevism" essay, which was long believed lost and was rediscovered shortly before Lukács's death, makes it clear that he saw himself as making an existential "leap of faith" into Bolshevism, and moreover considered this revolutionary faith to be utterly absurd. The question at hand was whether the Bolshevik revolution would really "mean the end of *all* class domination" or "simply entail the reshuffling of classes" in which "the previous oppressors will become the new oppressed class"; whether the emerging socialist regime would really "bring about the salvation of humanity" or merely create "an ideological shell for class interests." Anywhere a Bolshevik regime comes to power, "the existing class oppression will . . . be replaced by that of the proletariat." The Bolshevik regime will aim "to drive out Satan, so to speak, with the help of Beelzebub—in the hope that this last and therefore most open and cruel of class oppression will finally destroy itself, and in so doing put an end to class oppression forever." In order to become a Bolshevik,

> We have to believe—this being the true *credo quia absurdum est*—that no new class struggle will emerge out of this class struggle (resulting in the quest for a new oppression), which would provide continuance to the old sequence of meaningless and aimless struggles—but that oppression will effect the elements of its own destruction.
>
> It is, therefore, a question of belief—as it is in the case of any ethical question—of what the choice will be. . . . Let me emphasize again: Bolshevism rests on the metaphysical assumption that the bad can engender the good, or, as Razumikhin says

in Dostoevsky's *Crime and Punishment*, that it is possible to lie our way through to the truth.

This author is unable to share this belief.[11]

And yet, within a few days of this essay, Lukács had decided to make the leap. What changed his mind? It's hard to say for sure. "Tactics and Ethics" offers a pragmatic argument that in East Central Europe in 1919, the likely political alternatives are either a Communist revolution or a Fascist dictatorship; at this time, in this place, liberal democracy is simply not in the cards. This argument is plausible but has a limited force. It justifies participating in a Communist movement, on the grounds that it is the lesser of two available evils. But Lukács invests far more emotion in communism, and expects far more from it, than his pragmatic argumentation could ever comprehend. We need to look between the lines of his text and search out the emotional subtext. The most intense emotion in the inner world of "Tactics and Ethics" is Lukács's sense of guilt. The ethical rhetoric he speaks in at first sounds Kantian: we should act as if we were universal legislators, ethically responsible for the whole world. But if we listen for the feeling, it is less Kant than Dostoevsky, or Kant as he might have been remembered by Raskolnikov.

Thus, for Lukács, we really are responsible for all the oppression, violence, and murder in the world. If we become Communists, we are guilty of all the murders committed in the name of communism, not only now but in the indefinite future, "just as if we had killed them all." If we refuse to commit ourselves to communism, and fascism triumphs instead, we are guilty of all Fascist murders, now and to come. No matter what happens, whatever we do or don't do, we are all murderers; there is no way to escape the blood on our hands. What can a murderer do? Is there any way to atone? These were the sorts of questions that were tormenting Lukács at the end of 1918. He seems to have concluded that if the criminal were to lean to the Left, his crimes might actually accomplish something, his murders might help to end murders, his lies might open the way to truth.

Lukács, in his later years, disparaged the thinking that led to his conversion as "utopian," "messianic," "sectarian." It wasn't till later on, he said, that he became a "realist" and "materialist" and learned true Marxism. After digging deep into his early work, I would argue the exact opposite: that at the high tide of his messianic hopes, Lukács's moral and political thinking was clear, honest, and deeply attuned to material realities, in the finest Marxist tradition. He said repeatedly, in 1919, that it was impossible to know how history was going to turn out, that all political choices would have to be continually reappraised, that the ethical subject would have to weigh the violence and evil he helped to perpetrate against the actual freedom and happiness that he was helping to create.

It was only afterward, when it became clear that his hopes were not being fulfilled in the real world, that his leap of faith froze into a form of bad faith. We can see this happening even in the last sections of *History and Class Consciousness*, where Lukács's religious and moral hopes are gradually reified into a theological system of beliefs. His concept of incarnation, orthodoxy, and totality become a trinity in a secular political theology. Lukács's *credo quia absurdum est*, and his real bad faith, lay not in his 1919 hope that oppression today might help to end oppression tomorrow, but in his post-1921 doctrine that through the party's fullness of power, oppression had ended already. He clung to this doctrine all through the Stalin era, even as it undermined and slowly poisoned his thought and his life.

There is one more crucial clue to Lukács's life that came to light after his death. In 1973 a Heidelberg bank released a safe deposit box full of long-lost Lukács letters, diaries, and manuscripts.[12] This material uncovered the story of his first love. Late in 1907, Lukács and Irma Seidler, and a young Hungarian Jewish painter, met and fell in love. She wanted marriage and a normal life with him. He seems to have genuinely loved her from the first but, like many men before and since, feared commitment. "What I wish to accomplish," he wrote her, "only an unattached man can accomplish." For three years, even as he idealized and mythicized her ("Irma is Life," etc.), he fought her off. In the spring of 1911, she killed herself. Lukács was devastated and racked with guilt. "I could have saved her if I'd taken her hand. . . . I have lost my right to life."[13] It would be foolish to reduce Lukács's (or anybody's) ideology to psychology. Still, this heartbreaking affair, and Lukács's self-lacerating judgment on his role in it, may help to clarify some of the mysteries of his thought and action in years to come. It gives us an idea why he felt so guilty—guilty as he repeatedly said, of murder—and why he had such a deep need for confession, repentance, mortification, atonement. It gives a personal urgency and emotional depth to the idea (advanced in *Theory of the Novel* in 1915) that modern humanity's basic problem is "the torment of a creature condemned to solitude and devoured by the longing for community." (And it suggests why it was Ernö Seidler, Irma's brother, who—along with Béla Kun—recruited Lukács into the Hungarian Communist party at the end of 1918.)

V

What does Lukács leave us with, in the end? The sketches and interviews that make up *Record of a Life* offer no final epiphany, but only more layers under layers and wheels within wheels, more of Lukács's enticing and infuriating blend of blindness and insight, of bad faith and transcendent inspiration. He says, with an apparently straight face, "I am perhaps not a very contemporary man. I have never felt frustration or any kind of complex in my life. I know what these mean, of course, from the literature of the twentieth century and from having read Freud. But I have not experienced them myself.'' Yet even as he says this, he recognizes, fugitively, how much of his life's energy has gone into repudiating his thoughts and burying his feelings. "It has cost me nothing," he says, thereby suggesting the depth of its real cost. He is still intermittently swallowed up by the totalities he created for himself half a century before; thus, when asked what he said to himself during the monstrous excesses of Stalinism, he replies that "the worst form of socialism was better to live in than the best form of capitalism.'' And yet, just a few pages before and after, he shows a bitter clarity about the so-called socialism he has served for so long. When the Warsaw Pact armies invaded Prague in 1968, he told István Eörsi, "I suppose that the whole experiment that began in 1917 has now failed, and has to be tried again at some other time and place."

Lukács comes to believe, in his last years, that only a "complete rupture" with Stalinism will enable the Communist movement to reclaim its creative powers; but he sees no "objective forces" that might fulfill this hope. In the end he condemns all Communist regimes for betraying the original promise of Communist revolutions, "genuine socialist democracy . . . democracy of everyday life.'' He sees capitalist and communist powers at home in a détente of domination, oppressing both their own and foreign people. He hopes—not in his lifetime, he knows, but someday—for a convergence of freedom. "Both great systems in crisis. Authentic Marxism the only solution." These were virtually the last words he wrote before he died.

Georg Lukács is one of the real tragic heroes of the twentieth century. Tragic in the price he had to pay—indeed, the price he fought to pay. Heroic in the demands he made on modern art, on modern politics, on the whole of modern life—demands he affirmed to his life's end. It seems uncanny that he was here, in our midst, only yesterday. He seems too big for these times, times when people in both capitalist and socialist countries are demanding so little: big cars, villas in the country, trips abroad, pension plans. These are updated models of the things Lukács grew up with and learned to see through. Maybe after more of the people who haven't grown up with these things have had a crack at them they, too, will learn to see through the many forms of comfortable reification that pass for life. Maybe we will live to see the day when the people who don't want to be commodities in a market, even luxury commodities, and the people who don't want to be items in a plan, even top-priority items, will discover each other, and struggle together for what Lukács called "democracy of everyday life."

Notes

1. Georg Lukács, *Record of a Life: An Autobiographical Sketch*, ed. István Eörsi, trans. Rodney Livingstone (London: Verso, 1983). First published under the title *Gelebtes Denken* (*Lived Life*).

2. Georg Lukács, *History and Class Consciousness*, trans. Rodney Livingstone (Cambridge, MA: MIT, 1971).

3. In 1981, the Lukács Archiv's scholarly collective published a four-volume anthology of criticism of *History and Class Consciousness* under the title "HCC in the Debates of the 1920s."

4. See Morris Watnick, "Georg Lukács: An Intellectual Biography," *Soviet Survey* (January-March 1958), pp. 60–66; (April-June 1958), pp. 51–57; (July-September 1958), pp. 61–68; (January-March 1959), pp. 75–81.

5. See Georg Lukács, "The Ideology of Modernism," in *The Meaning of Contemporary Realism*, trans. from the German John and Necke Mander (London: Merlin, 1962), pp. 17ff.

6. For the definitive treatment of the Lukács-Naphta connection in particular and the relationship between Lukács and Thomas Mann in general, see Judith Marcus, *Georg Lukács and Thomas Mann: A Study in the Sociology of Literature* (Amherst: University of Massachusetts, 1987).

7. Georg Lukács, *The Theory of the Novel*, trans. Anna Bostock (Cambridge, MA: MIT, 1971).

8. Quoted in Michael Löwy, *Georg Lukács: From Romanticism to Bolshevism*, trans. from the French Patrick Camiller (London: NLB, 1979), p. 128.

9. Georg Lukács, "Bolshevism as a Moral Problem," trans. and introd. Judith Marcus Tar, *Social Research* 44, 3(Autumn 1977):416–24. According to Marcus Tar, the Hungarian article first appeared in *Szabadgondolat* (*Free Thought*), mid-December 1918. *Szabadgondolat* was the official journal of the "Galileo circle," an organization of the radical intellectuals at the University of Budapest. Its editor, Karl Polanyi, put together a special issue on Bolshevism and asked Lukács for a contribution.

10. *Editors' note*: written and first published in Hungarian, "Tactics and Ethics" was in fact written in February 1919, that is, two months after Lukács's conversion. See *Georg Lukács: Political Writings 1919–1919*, ed. Rodney Livingstone, trans. from the German Michael McColgan (London: NLB, 1972), pp. 3ff.

11. Lukács, "Bolshevism," p. 424.

12. For details, see Zoltán Tar, introduction to *Georg Lukács: Selected Correspondence, 1902–1920*, ed. and trans. Judith Marcus and Zoltán Tar (New York: Columbia University, 1986), pp. 11ff.

13. For Lukács's account of his feelings and frame of mind, see *Selected Correspondence*, p. 162. Lukács's frame of mind and guilt feelings following Irma Seidler's suicide have been best expressed in his dialogue entitled *Von der Armut am Geiste* (*On Poverty of Spirit*), published in 1912.

11

Lukács and Hungarian Culture

By Ferenc Tökei

Georg Lukács and Hungarian culture is a vast subject. All I can really do on this occasion is to throw some light on certain aspects of a rather complex problem that in my opinion have not been given the attention they deserve by Lukács scholars either in Hungary or in other countries.

My starting point is a simple question: Was Lukács a thinker in the Hungarian tradition or a German philosopher who happened to live in Hungary? The question may seem absurd to some and superfluous to others—after all, the whole world is aware that the important facts and periods in Lukács's life were closely linked to Hungary (at least in part). Moreover, Lukács's lifework, in the eyes of Marxists and non-Marxists alike, is of general significance and of a standard that gives it international importance. The question is really not absurd, since it is well known that Lukács was also part of the German philosophical tradition; he wrote his principal works in German, and, what is more, he spent a great deal more time and effort on German than on Hungarian literature. His lifework can therefore also be regarded as part of German culture. Nor must it be forgotten that Lukács, the scion of a Budapest Jewish *haute-bourgeois* family, as a young man at the turn of the century sharply turned against the Hungary of that time, and against the gentry and pseudo-gentry interpretation of what being a Hungarian meant. All his life, Lukács emphasized his solitude as a thinker in Hungary and, true enough, also in Germany. Following a stay in Florence and Heidelberg (between 1908 and 1917), he lived in exile between 1920 and 1945, first in Vienna, then in Moscow, Berlin, and again in Moscow. He was one of the leaders of the Association of German Proletarian Writers while in Berlin. There is therefore every reason to wonder how deep and how strong the threads were that tied

153

Lukács to Hungary and Hungarian culture—in other words, in what sense one may look on him as a Hungarian writer, and on his work as something Hungarian culture can be proud of. To put the question this way makes it clear, I think, that it is not superfluous to examine what being Hungarian meant for Lukács. After all, if there were strong ties between Lukács's work and Hungarian culture, then the facts of Hungarian history and the characteristic features of Hungarian culture must be borne in mind when trying to understand Lukács's work even on the most elementary level. It seems to me to be one of the most serious weaknesses of the large and increasing volume of literature dealing with Lukács that scholars are not able to understand the actual relationship between him and Hungarian culture. Even in Hungary there is still a great deal of uncertainty in this respect; few of the prejudices involved have been overcome as yet, and research into the problem can be said to be only in its initial stages.

I

Perhaps Lukács himself is the right person to provide an answer. In 1970 he published a selection of essays, written in Hungarian, on Hungarian subjects.[1] In a preface specially written for this volume in 1969, he described how he saw his relationship to Hungarian culture, and the way in which it developed. I should like to quote at length from this autobiographical sketch, particularly where he refers to his origins and early oppositional attitude:

It is well known that I was born into a capitalist family living in the *Lipótváros*[2] in Budapest. I would like to say that since early childhood I was thoroughly dissatisfied with the *Lipótváros* way of life of those days. And since my father's business activities brought us into daily contact with the city's patriciate and gentry, this rejection was automatically extended to them. Consequently, I was ruled from an early age by sentiments opposite to the whole of official Hungary. Corresponding to my immaturity, this opposition extended to all areas of life, from politics to literature, and was obviously expressed in some kind of callow socialism.

It does not matter how childishly naive I consider it now, a posteriori, that I uncritically generalized this antipathy and extended it to all phases of Hungarian life, history and literature alike (with the sole exception of Petőfi);[3] it is certain that those views then dominated my way of thinking. The serious counterforce, the only firm soil that then existed for me alone in which I could dig my toes, was the modern European literature of those days, and I became acquainted with it around the age of 14 or 15. I was touched primarily by Scandinavian literature (mainly Ibsen), the Germans (from Hebbel and Keller to Gerhart Hauptmann), the French (Flaubert, Baudelaire, Verlaine) and English poetry (first of all Swinburne, then Shelley and Keats). At some later point, Russian literature became very important to me. These works provided me with the means to countervail the dominating Jewish as well as the gentry and pseudo-gentry attitude. This not entirely accidental conjunction of circumstances led to my attempt at spiritual liberation from the spiritual servitude of official Hungary, taking on the accents of a glorification of the international modern movement as against what I looked on as boundless Hungarian conservatism, which under those circumstances I identified with the entire official world of the time.[4]

Lukács then goes on to speak of two Hungarian contemporaries whose uncompromising moral attitude had a positive effect on him, describes his role in the Budapest theatrical life of the time, and then continues:

It was at that stage that I discovered that important negative circumstance that I would take part in literature only as a theoretician and not as a creative author. The practical consequences of this lesson took me away from stage work itself; I began to prepare for theoretical and historical research into the essence of literary forms and turned toward scholarly and philosophic work. This again made me more acutely aware of the importance of the contradiction between influences from abroad, mainly German ones, and Hungarian life. It is hardly surprising that under those circumstances my starting point could only be Kant. Nor can it be surprising that when I looked for the perspectives, foundations, and methods of application of philosophic generalization, I found the theoretical guide in the German philosopher Simmel, not the least of reasons being that this approach brought me closer to Marx in certain respects, though in a distorted way.

My interest in the history of literature carried me back from the "great names" of the present to those mid-nineteenth-century scholars in whose writings I found methods of a higher order in the understanding of society and history. I deeply despised Hungarian theory and literary history from Beöthy[5] to Alexander.[6] But important counterweights were to appear soon, acting against this theoretical one-sidedness. Ady's[7] volume *Uj Versek* (*New Poems*) was published in 1906; in 1908, I read the poems of Béla Balázs[8] in *Holnap* (*Tomorrow*),[9] and within a short time we were linked by both personal friendship and a close literary alliance.[10]

II

This takes us to a decisive moment in Lukács's life, decisive also when it comes to understanding Lukács's work. The friendship between Lukács and Balázs was important in itself, even more so owing to the fact that Balázs and Béla Bartók cooperated closely in their work. But more important still was Lukács's encounter with Endre Ady's great poetic oeuvre, one of the great achievements of early twentieth-century Hungarian literature, which unfortunately is almost inaccessible to those who do not read Hungarian.[11] This encounter proved to be decisive for Lukács's philosophy. It would be difficult to formulate it better than Lukács did himself:

My encounter with Ady's poems was a shock, as one would call it today. It was a shock the effect of which I began to understand and to digest seriously only years later. My first experiment in the intellectual exploration of the significance of this experience occurred in 1910, but it was only much later, at a more nature age, that I was really able to grasp the decisive importance of this encounter for the evolution of my worldview. It may mean sinning against the chronological order of things, but I believe this is the right place to give account of the nature of Ady's influence.

To sum things up briefly: although the German philosophers appeared to be ideologically subversive—and I include not only Kant and his contemporary followers but Hegel too, under whose influence I came only years later—they remained conservatives as far as the evolution of society and history was concerned; reconciliation with reality (*Versöhnung mit der Wirklichkeit*) was one of the cornerstones of Hegel's philosophy. Ady had such a determining influence precisely because he never, not for a single moment, reconciled himself to Hungarian reality or, on that basis, to the overall reality of the epoch. A longing for such a view of the world had been alive in me since adolescence without my being able to generalize these feelings conceptually. I did not for a long time understand the clear expression of the very same attitude in Marx—even after I had read him several times. Consequently, I was unable to make use of him to oppose Kantian and Hegelian philosophy in a basic way. But what I did not perceive in Marx struck my heart in Ady's verse. Ever since I became familiar with Ady's work, this irreconcilability has been present in all my thoughts. . . . Admittedly, I did not become conscious of this—at least not to the extent that its importance demanded. For clarification, may I quote a few lines of Ady, which he wrote much later: In the poem "Hunn, uj legenda" ("The Hunn: A New Legend"), Ady describes his attitude to life, history, what was yesterday, what is today, and what will be tomorrow: "Vagyok . . . protestáló hit és küldetéses vétó / Eb ura fakó, Ugocsa *non coronat*" (I am . . . the faith that protests and a veto that has a mission / Only the dog has a master, Ugocsa will not crown). It is indeed strange that a feeling about the world could have had such a broad and deep influence on me . . . transforming the whole world of my ideas without my having attained as yet any true understanding of the world around me or having formed definitive ideas about it. This experience also resulted in my considering the great Russian writers, first of all Dostoevsky and Tolstoy, as true revolutionary factors in my developing worldview that, slowly but surely, took the direction where the internal transformation of man became the expressed focus of social transformation, and where ethics became more important than the philosophy of history. This, then, became the ideological foundation of my *Weltgefühl* (feeling of the world), which, in the last resort, grew out of my experience with Ady. All this did not, of course, mean the total elimination of an objective sociohistorical foundation. On the contrary! It was exactly at this stage of my development that French syndicalism started to exert an influence on me. I was never able to see eye to eye with the social democratic theory of those days, especially with Kautsky. Thanks to Ervin Szabó,[12] my knowledge of Georges Sorel helped me to develop the combined Hegel-Ady-Dostoevsky experience into a sort of ideology that I then considered to be revolutionary; this is what made me stand in opposition to *Nyugat* and what it represented;[13] it also isolated me within the *Huszadik Század* circle[14] and placed me in the position of an "outsider" in the circle of my later German friends as well.[15]

This passage makes it quite clear that the encounter with Ady's poems had a decisive effect on Lukács's development; it was not, however, enough in itself to ensure that he should think of himself as a Hungarian. In a 1966 interview Lukács stated that Ady's work *Uj Versek* (*New Poems*) really changed him; "roughly speaking," said Lukács, "this was the very first Hungarian literary work that allowed me to find my way home, the first I could fully identify with.'' This fact should by no means be interpreted as a wholesale identification, cautioned Lukács: ''What I now think of the Hungarian literature of the past is another question and the result of long experience. At that time, I must admit, I felt no inner relationship with classical Hungarian literature. I was creatively influenced only by world literature, mainly by German, Scandinavian, and Russian literature—in addition to German philosophy, which influenced me throughout my life. The way the Ady experience moved me did not essentially diminish or change this German influence. It neither put an end to it, nor did it take me back to Hungary. One could say that, at the time, the Ady poems meant Hungary to me.''[16]

Lacking close ties with Hungary, Lukács almost became German, as he reminisces in his 1969 preface:

> The experience of meeting Ernst Bloch (1910) convinced me that philosophy in the classical sense was nevertheless possible. I spent the winter of 1911–12 in Florence coping with the impact of this experience; I wanted no distraction while trying to work out an aesthetic theory as the first part of my philosophy. In the spring of 1912 Bloch payed me a visit in Florence and did his best to persuade me to accompany him to Heidelberg, where the atmosphere was most congenial to our work. All this must have made clear that by now nothing stood in the way of my settling in Heidelberg for an extended period, even permanently. Although I always preferred life in Italy to that in Germany, the hope of finding understanding was stronger. I went to Heidelberg without knowing how long I might live there.[17]

Lukács spent the years 1915 and 1916 in Budapest serving in the Auxiliary Military Service. During this time, a group of like-minded friends surrounded him, first forming the so-called Sunday Circle, followed by an interesting experiment at (public) education, called the Free School of the Humanities. To a certain extent, however, Lukács already felt somewhat isolated, even among his friends, because of his revolutionary left-wing attitude. While most of those friends later had positive things to say about the stimulating effect and high-spiritedness of their discussions, Lukács's evaluation is less positive. While he claims that his early work ''no doubt played a certain role'' in the formation of this circle, and acknowledges that it became important later ''thanks to the role played abroad by some of its members'' (Mannheim, Hauser, Frederick Antal, Charles de Tolnay)[18] Lukács nevertheless thought that ''its influence in Hungary is often overestimated . . . for the very same reason.'' He added ''It was not really important to me since it was essentially linked to a way of thinking and acting that I had already outgrown.''[19]

III

Then the events occurred that proved to be the decisive experiences of Lukács's life: the 1917 Russian and the 1918–19 Hungarian revolutions.

Lukács, "by chance," was caught by them in Budapest. Lukács stated fifty years after those events that the Russian Revolution "and its reverberating echo at home" gave him the first inkling of what the answer to his questions might be. The road to be followed was shown to him first in Hungary, but "it was no ideologically conscious homecoming; it was not a necessary consequence of my evolution. Seen objectively and intellectually it was mere chance" and, as such, it was a help, a "fate pointing toward the true path." Lukács concluded this train of thought by saying that "even if my staying at home before and during the revolutions was purely chance as far as the immediate causes were concerned, it created entirely new contacts for my life which, after years of internal struggles, produced an entirely new attitude in me."[20]

Lukács understood right away that a popularly based revolution could only be a socialist revolution in twentieth-century Europe. Not long after the founding of the Communist party of Hungary in November 1918, Lukács joined it and became one of its leaders. This meant giving up his past ways of thinking and undertaking a thorough study of Marxism. He became a People's Commissar of Culture in the Hungarian Republic of Councils. At that point he found out that Hungary was not destined to be the country of revolutionaries without a revolution, but that the elite and the masses could be united in revolution in Hungary also. "The cultural policy of the Hungarian proletarian dictatorship was," in Lukács's words, "the first attempt to unite on the part of all those forces in Hungarian society that truly wished to progress and that sought a genuine renewal."[21]

I am inclined to argue that this decisive change meant that by becoming a Communist Lukács was clearly tied to his native country, Hungary; that his becoming an internationalist at the same time meant a strengthening of his ties to a particular nation. This is certainly not a chance conclusion but necessarily follows from the nature of what has been said. To be sure, the Hungarian Republic of Councils was suppressed after only a few months of existence, and Lukács was forced to live in exile. He began to study Lenin seriously in his Vienna exile, initiating a period in his thinking that lasted more than ten years. As he himself said, in the 1920s he tried to reconcile a "right-wing epistemology" with "left-wing ethics," resulting in a "messianic sectarianism." It is interesting that this "messianic sectarianism" was manifested, in the first place, in his philosophic views and in his attitude toward international questions; as regards the problems of the Hungarian working-class movement, he supported the Landler faction[22] as against Béla Kun,[23] and in opposition to his own theoretical views. Landler's more realistic ways of thinking serves as a basis for overcoming the "leftishness" that Lenin also criticized.

Following Landler's death, Lukács formulated the so-called Blum Theses,[24] which saw the future of the Hungarian working-class movement in a democratic dictatorship of the working class and the peasantry. Lukács's theses were rejected by the party leadership at the time, and Lukács himself was removed from his position in it. But this failure did not put a distance between him and Hungary; on the contrary, it made the links closer still. Lukács said of the importance of the theses for his own development that it was here that "in my case a general theory allowing for further generalization grew directly out of a proper observation of reality, that is, where I first became an ideologist who took his cue from reality itself, what is more, from Hungarian realities."[25]

Lukács therefore was ready and willing, consciously and finally, to accept his role as part of Hungarian culture precisely at a time when, following his removal from the responsibilities of political office, he tended to concentrate his work on German as well as French, English, and Russian literary questions. I hope I will be forgiven for the extended quotation that follows, but Lukács's own words best express what is involved here; moreover, as with the preceding quotations, these autobiographical musings have not been translated into English until now:

The Blum Theses put an end to my political career and took me away from the Hungarian Communist Party for a long time to come. At the same time, as a direct consequence of the crisis, my theoretical and critical work as an aesthetician received a new impetus. I was able to take an active part in the struggle against literary sectarianism on the German and Russian fronts; I was able to lay down the theoretical foundations of socialist realism, in uninterrupted but, needless to say, concealed opposition to the Stalin-Zhdanov views then prevalent. This took me to the Seventh Congress of the Comintern, which came out with the first public statement summing up the popular front policy and at the same time reopened the door to the Hungarian CP for me. When, after this congress, the paper of the Hungarian popular front, *Uj Hang* (*A New Voice*), appeared, I became an active contributor right from the start, once again working with József Révai.[26] We had been apart for a long time. It was then that, for the first time since I became a Marxist, I discussed Ady and the Babits of *The Book of Jonah*.[27] It was then that I attempted to criticize the false antithesis between *urbánus* (urban) and *népi* (populist)[28] writers from the point of view of a true Hungarian democratic popular front. I wrote those articles as a Marxist Communist, but those papers never centered on the opposition of Marxism and bourgeois ideology but on a united Hungarian popular resistance to the Horthy regime. This meant a break with the critical practice of Hungarian Communists, in which arguments expressed in Hungary were judged by Marxist standards. When arguing against the *urbánus* group, I pointed out the distortions caused in the Hungarian development of revolutionary democracy by liberal prejudices, such as the rejection of radical land reform in the interest of the undisturbed capitalist development of large estates. These were differences between liberalism and democracy, and not between socialism and democracy, and both Révai and I recognized and supported consistently the spontaneous plebeian democratic faith of the *népi* writers; we only reproached them for often expressing those ideas inconsistently (making concessions to reaction in opposition to the people). But I, for instance, showed that their ideology in some important respects was dangerous to Hungarian democratic evolution, even by Tolstoyan and not Marxist standards. In this way I joined the mainstream of the best traditions of Hungarian literature. Csokonai and Petöfi, Ady and Attila József,[29] all took this starting point with activities that grew out of the people's attempts to determine their own fate. If Hungarian literary criticism and history—apart from such exceptions as János Erdélyi long ago,[30] Ady later, and György Bálint[31] in the Horthy era—did not proceed along this path, this does not cast doubt on the validity of this particular way of posing the question, nor does it lessen its depth and significance in the life of the Hungarian people. Because of this radical change in my internal evolution, my return home in 1945 in no way looked like the coincidence to which I owed my presence in Hungary during the 1918 revolution. On the contrary, this was a fully conscious decision in favor of returning home against concrete offers made to attract me to places where German was spoken.[32]

IV

Lukács's self-analysis must be looked on as decisive with regard to his relationship to Hungary, and he clearly and unambiguously declared himself to be Hungarian. Following his return to Hungary he passionately threw himself into cultural and literary life and wrote a number of important papers that dealt with basic problems of Hungarian culture. Summing up this last, more than twenty-year period of his life, he said,

> If I wished to characterize this whole period ideologically, I must note that in addition to Ady the influence on me of the plebeian democratic nature of Bartók's art (*Cantata Profana*) became stronger and stronger. I would of course give a misleading picture of the totality of my activities, including the part dealing with Hungarian problems, it I made it appear as if Hungarian cultural and literary topics then dominated my thinking and activities. This definitely was not the case. Just to give a few examples: at the time of my preoccupation with Ady's *Uj Hang*, I wrote my book about the young Hegel; after the liberation in 1945 I worked on *The Destruction of Reason* and *The Specificity of the Aesthetic* as well as my *Aesthetics*, and I am presently about to formulate the philosophical nature of social existence. The bulk of my ideological activities always dealt with general philosophic questions. This must necessarily go beyond Hungarian reality. Not even a member of the greatest group of people on earth would be able to think philosophically (including, of course, thinking about aesthetics) merely on the basis of his own national experience.[33]

Every page of the volume of selected treatises on Hungarian culture and literature bears out Lukács's statements in the preface. A close reading of the anthology proves beyond any doubt that Lukács's theoretical and critical work is in accord with his self-analysis. What needs to be done, I think, is to draw attention to certain particularly interesting aspects of it.

In 1908 young Lukács still could write that Ady "had no need of tradition," that he did not accept the dominant Hungarian values nor did he "join

any existing trend,'' and that it was precisely to this that Ady owed his greatness as a poet.[34] In another article Lukács said that it was a ''tragedy'' that
Ady was Hungarian.[35] One year later, in *The History of the Development of
Modern Drama*, Lukács voiced his opposition to the vulgar interpretation of
the ''international modernist movement'' and spoke of Mihály Vörösmarty's
fairy play *Csongor és Tünde*[36] as the ''most alive, and perhaps only genuinely
organic Hungarian play.'' It is argued that ''it was not chance, not a meeting
of fortunate outside and inner circumstances, that proved successful in this
instance; rather, it was the conscious and artful welding of Hungarian folk-
humor and the mood and techniques of Shakespearean comedy. The main reason why Hungarian fairy-comedy ceased to be organic later on was that it lost
its once present connection with Hungarian life.''[37] Looking ten years ahead,
Lukács predicted the events of 1919, stating that Ady was ''conscience,
trumpet, and fighting song, and the standard around which all can gather if
there should ever be a fight.''[38] That same year, writing about a volume of
short stories by Zsigmond Móricz,[39] Lukács exclaimed ''One can only speak
of this book with genuine joy. It contains true Hungarian stories, and Hungarians in the simplest, most common, and most complete sense of the term.''[40]
Reading such an evaluation, one might well wonder whether Lukács did not
somewhat exaggerate when he said in his preface that he had ''no inner relationship'' to Hungarian literature at that time.

In 1918, when Mihály Babits accused Béla Balázs and Lukács of being
''German,'' Lukács argued and proved the point that Babits wanted to protect
Hungarian literature against philosophic ''depth.'' He showed how retrograde
the Hungarian stiff-upper-lip and *nil admirari* attitude was. Lukács asks
whether it is proper to say that there will not be ''and there must not be any
philosophic depth in Hungarian literature of the future just because there was
none in the past.'' He also inquires whether ''the Hungarian soul should have
any reason to be afraid of depth.''[41] It is evident that Lukács even at that time
was fighting the same fight as Ady and Bartók, the leading spirits in Hungarian cultural life.

A picture of Lukács without his relationship to Hungarian culture would be
a pretty anemic one, even when taking a look at his activities in the 1920s. In
1925, for instance, only two years after the publication of *History and Class
Consciousness* and right in the middle of his ''messianic sectarianism,''
Lukács published a short article on Mór Jókai,[42] who dominated post-1867
Hungarian literature. Lukács argued that for several reasons Jókai's work represented what is best in the Hungarian literary tradition:

> Jókai's narrative style is still fully interwoven with the old Hungarian manner of
> telling a tale that is humorous and imaginative and anecdotal, a style that only
> loosely links up events. As against his contemporaries, Zsigmond Kemény and
> József Eötvös,[43] who insist on forcing the style of the foreign novels of the time on

nascent Hungarian prose, Jókai's style grows organically out of the Hungarian life of his own period. In this respect, his prose can justifiably be compared to Petöfi's prosody. Though it is undeniable that this manner of writing is full of loose and undisciplined elements, . . . this was nevertheless the only road along which Hungarian narrative prose could progress right up to Zsigmond Móricz, while the artificial prose of Jókai's contemporaries remained an episode in the development of Hungarian literature.[44]

V

All his life, Lukács remained true to the simple principle that ''the true greatness of poets rests in their being welded to the life of their nation.''[45] What is more, in his own work this principle was to be put into practice in an increasingly consistent manner. This is why his internationalism has nothing to do with cosmopolitanism; and that is why his criticism of the *népi* and *urbánus* movements of the 1930s is still valid today. He explains the real achievements of both as the effect of the 1919 Hungarian revolution, and that is an interesting point even in the context of world literature. By and large, Lukács considered the *népi* movement to be the more important of the two, precisely because of the close links with the peasant masses and the life of the people. In 1947 he came across an article in which the *népi* writers were viciously slandered—while writers of Jewish origin (the *urbánus*) were unduly praised. Lukács set out to prove that the author of this article applied two different standards in an unprincipled way and reprimanded him as follows:

This method and attitude have their own social background. . . . To put it briefly, what is involved is the literary and cultural role of the so-called *Lipótváros*. Béla Zsolt[46] describes its style with great love, applying positive standards only, allowing at the most for certain ''tragic'' features. But that social and national lack of roots which the *Lipótváros* culture meant for Hungarian writers of Jewish origin at the time [i.e., at the turn of the century], only rarely grew into a genuine tragedy. The break with genuine Hungarian folk culture bred the false extremes of snobbery and literary prostitution. There were of course writers . . . who preserved their human and literary integrity. . . . But one cannot, without applying two separate standards, argue that genuine tragedies like János Vajda's or Lajos Tolnai's took place—not to mention that of Kálmán Mikszáth.[47] It is the great merit of Ady and that of the *Nyugat* revolution as a whole, with all its limits and contradictions, that they started to demolish these barriers. The real work of demolition was, however, done by the class struggles of the counterrevolutionary period, and by *népi* literature that arose as part of that struggle. Until then, there were only a few writers here and there . . . who rose above the dilemma of snobbery and literary prostitution. The counterrevolutionary period produced a new type of writer, liberated from the *Lipótváros* culture; there were not too many of them, perhaps, still enough . . . and they were of a quality that commands respect. . . . In the case of more than one outstanding writer alive today, that ideal and artistic, meaningful, and formal engagement in the great social and national problems of the Hungarian people that destroys the differences of origin in the eyes of all men and women without prejudice, became part of their flesh and blood—and this is what helps to pull out the ideological roots of anti-Semitism. . . .

At the time of the first revolutionary uprising of the Hungarian nation, Hungarian Jewry had only reached a stage of development that could supply thousands of brave soldiers for the fight for freedom.[48] The social backwardness of Hungary made it impossible for this fight for freedom to become manifest in Hungarian Jewry in an ideological form. Heine, for example, was the true representative poet in Germany—a more developed country. . . . Nothing like that could happen in the sultry atmosphere of the 1867 *Ausgleich* and of the pseudo-gentry ghetto, *Lipótváros*. The breeze of the revolution was needed to bring that about. That is what started with *Nyugat*, and continued at a higher level of social development in the period between the two world wars. As Marx correctly says: "The soil of counterrevolution is also revolutionary."[49]

There are not many in Hungary who could deliver such a scathing critique of *Lipótváros* culture with greater justification, and therefore with greater persuasive force, than Lukács, who was born and bred in the *Lipótváros* but who became a revolutionary and found his way home to his country through that revolution.

Writing of Ady's importance and influence on him, Lukács said in 1969, "Those who were not satisfied with the *Ausgleich* [1867] . . . did not consider the situation from a specifically Hungarian point of view."[50] The passages I have quoted at length give a good indication of how one ought to read this sentence. Lukács elaborates: "I have not lost touch with Ady, not even for a day, since reading *Uj Versek* more than sixty years ago. *This is part of the story of my life* [italics added]. And without wishing to exaggerate my importance, I cannot really consider myself as typical of Hungarian development."[51] We might take this with a grain of salt; it is my suspicion that Lukács in this case did not use the term "typical" in the sense of his own aesthetics, but in the everyday sense of the word; his language would have been more exact if he had said "average." I am convinced that, taking the term as used in aesthetics, Lukács was the most typical manifestation of Hungarian culture—though he was, of course, no more average than Ady, Bartók, or Attila József.

It is certainly worth investigating how Hungarian culture managed to accomplish a whole series of achievements of international significance in the twentieth century. This seems to me necessary for a proper understanding of the achievement itself. All that I have outlined is, of course, no more than one of the necessary preconditions of asking the right questions. This is also true even as it regards a proper understanding of Lukács's lifework.

Notes

1. György Lukács, *Magyar Irodalom—Magyar Kultura* (*Hungarian Literature—Hungarian Culture*), *Válogatott tanulmányok* (Budapest: Gondolat, 1970), pp. 695ff.
2. *Lipótváros* was a fashionable residential district in Budapest, located on the left bank of the Danube, in Pest; it was favored by the nouveau riche, mostly Jewish,

bourgeoisie. *Lipótváros* also symbolized a certain ambivalent attitude common in those circles: on the one hand, a frantic nouveau riche desire to be noticed at all costs; on the other, a heightened sensitivity to cultural matters, which was rare in the traditional Hungarian ruling class. The district—no longer called by its old name—is still favored by Jewish professional and business groups.

3. Sándor Petöfi (1823–49) was one of Hungary's greatest and most beloved poets, who played an important part in the 1848–49 Hungarian revolution and War of Independence. He was killed in battle at the age of 26.

4. See Lukács, preface to *Magyar Irodalom*, pp. 5–7.

5. Zsolt Beöthy (1848–1922) was a novelist and literary critic who became an influential Hungarian literary historian of the positivist school. He was a professor at the University of Budapest and a member of the Hungarian Academy of Sciences. From the 1890s on he was a staunch opponent of progressive movements and was instrumental in defeating Lukács's academic aspirations at the University of Budapest.

6. Bernát Alexander (1850–1927), philosopher and aesthetician, was a professor of the history of philosophy at the University of Budapest (and father of the renowned psychoanalytic pioneer Franz Alexander). He was the mentor of a whole generation of Hungarian humanists; as editor of the official journal of the Philosophical Society, *Athenaeum*, he furthered many aspiring scholars such as Karl Mannheim and Lukács. He translated many works by Kant, Spinoza, Hume, Descartes, and Diderot into Hungarian.

7. Endre Ady (1877–1919), the most famous twentieth-century Hungarian poet, was a central figure of Hungary's cultural life. His revolutionary poetry and opposition to Hungarian officialdom and provinciality had a far-reaching and lasting impact on a whole generation of young Hungarians.

8. Béla Balázs (Herbert Bauer) (1884–1949) was a poet, playwright, critic, and revolutionary, best known in the West as the first theoretician of the cinema. His friendship with Lukács lasted from 1909 to 1919. He was the initiator of the so-called Sunday Circle and lectured at the Free School of the Humanities. He joined the Communist party in 1919 and fled to Vienna after the collapse of the Hungarian Republic of Councils. He returned to Budapest after 1945.

9. *Holnap* (*Tomorrow*) was an anthology of modern Hungarian poetry published in 1908.

10. Lukács, preface, pp. 7–8.

11. Edmund Wilson, the American man of letters, recounted in a *New Yorker* article (April 20, 1963) how he had first become acquainted with Ady's poetry in French and English translations, all of which he found "rather flat." So he embarked on learning the language of Ady, whose poetry impressed him "as deserving the enthusiasm that is felt for him by most of his compatriots" (p. 190).

12. Ervin Szabó (1877–1918) was a left-wing social democrat who was at one time Lukács's mentor in Marxism. He was a leading member of the anarchosyndicalist opposition within the Second International.

13. *Nyugat* (*West*), a leading periodical of the literary renewal in Hungary, was founded in 1908. Most of the period's literary celebrities were published there, and not only those from Hungary. It was open to representatives of all kind of *-isms*: symbolism, impressionism, naturalism. Lukács always had a strained relationship with the editors of *Nyugat*. Its progressive editorial policy was responsible for the fact that in the early 1910s it had commissioned articles by Sigmund Freud.

14. *Huszadik Század* (*Twentieth Century*) was the leading sociological journal in Hungary between 1906 and 1919. Oscar Jászi was its founding editor. Not only

Lukács but also Karl Mannheim, Karl Polányi, and others were among its contributors.

15. Lukács, preface, pp. 8–9.

16. From "Conversation with Lukács," published in *Emlékezések (Reminiscences)*, vol. 1 of the Hungarian Literary Museum (Budapest: IM, 1967), p. 21.

17. Lukács, preface, p. 13.

18. Arnold Hauser (1892–1978), art historian and sociologist of art, was a member of the Sunday Circle and friend of Karl Mannheim. He emigrated after the collapse of the 1919 revolution and in due time became a professor at the University of Leeds in England. He returned to Hungary shortly before his death. Frederick Antal (1887–1954), art historian, was also a member of the Sunday Circle who left Hungary in 1919. He lived and worked first in Vienna and Berlin, then settled in England in 1934. His best-known work is *Classicism and Romanticism* (1966). He was considered the leading Marxist art historian of his time. Karl Mannheim (1897–1947) is best known as the founder of the sociology of knowledge. He chose Lukács as his mentor at an early age, but their friendship came to an end in 1916. Mannheim attended the Sunday Circle and was a founding member of the Free School of the Humanities in 1917. He left Hungary in 1919, took his Habilitated with Alfred Weber in Heidelberg, and taught at the universities of Heidelberg and Frankfurt am Main. He emigrated to England after the Nazi takeover, and held teaching positions at the London School of Economics and the University of London. Among his works are "Conservative Thought" and *Ideology and Utopia* (1926). Charles De Tolnay (1899–1981), art historian, member of the Sunday Circle, and lecturer at the Free School, left Hungary in 1919, studied in Vienna with Dvorak, and went to live in Paris in 1933. He emigrated to the United States in 1939 and became a professor of art history at Princeton. He returned to Europe in 1965 and became director of the Casa Buonarotti in Florence. He was a well-known Bruegel and Michelangelo scholar.

19. Lukács, preface, p. 14. Cf. *Emlékezések*, 1:31–34.

20. Lukács, preface, p. 14.

21. Ibid., p. 15.

22. Jenö Landler (1875–1928) was a Hungarian-Jewish lawyer and later a leading member of the Hungarian Communist party, especially during the Vienna Exile.

23. Béla Kun (1886–1939) was one of the founders of the Hungarian Communist Party in November 1918 and the leader of the Republic of Councils in 1919. He emigrated to Vienna after the collapse of the Commune and finally settled in the Soviet Union, dying a victim of Stalin's purges in 1939.

24. Reference is to the *Blum Theses*, originally a draft report to the Second Congress of the Hungarian Communist Party, written in 1928.

25. Lukács, preface, p. 18.

26. József Révai (1898–1959) was one of the leading members of the Hungarian Communist party, a leading theoretician, often a counterpart of Lukács, and a one-time member of the Sunday Circle.

27. Mihály Babits (1883–1941) was, after Ady, the most important member of the *Nyugat* group, editor of its review section. Poet, writer, and essayist, he was Hungary's most prominent literary and progressive-liberal-humanist spokesman between the two wars. *Jónás könyve (The Book of Jonah)* is a confessional narrative poem dealing with guilt and responsibility, written shortly before Babits's death of cancer.

28. Allusion is to an urban (Jewish) liberal anti-fascist literary group called *urbánusok*. Its members were indifferent, even hostile, to the literary movement

originating in the countryside; *népiesek* was a radical peasant literary movement, some of whose members blended social criticism with an "irrational" ideology.

29. Mihály Csokonai Vitéz (1773–1805) was a Hungarian poet of the enlightenment, the author of a still popular comic epic, sensitive lyrical poems, and satirical plays. Attila József (1905–37) was Hungary's leading revolutionary poet after Ady's death until his suicide in 1937. He is still a considerable force and influence in Hungarian poetry.

30. János Erdélyi (1814–68), an influential nineteenth-century democratic critic, was one of the first to popularize Hegel in Hungary.

31. György Bálint (1906–43), a Marxist journalist and critic, was one of the bravest and most talented members of the literary Left in the Horthy era in Hungary. He perished in the Holocaust.

32. Lukács, preface, pp. 18–19.

33. Ibid., p. 20.

34. See the article "Dezsö Kosztolányi," in *Magyar Irodalom*, p. 26.

35. Ibid., pp. 34–36. Quotation is from the article "A Holnap költöi" ("The Poets of Tomorrow"), written in 1908.

36. Mihály Vörösmarty (1800–1855) was the Hungarian author of historical epics and lyric poetry. His works display a powerful romantic imagination and considerable beauty. The work in question, *Csongor és Tünde*, is actually a philosophical play in verse, based on a fairy tale, written in 1831 but still popular in Hungary.

37. See Lukács, "A magyar drámáról" ("On the Hungarian Drama"), written in 1909, in *Magyar Irodalom*, p. 38.

38. Ibid., pp. 45 and 51. The article is on Endre Ady, also from 1909.

39. Zsigmond Móricz (1879–1942), Hungary's prominent twentieth-century novelist, was also the author of short stories depicting the misery, tribulations, elementary forces, and dynamics of Hungarian peasant life. He was also the founder of the populist school.

40. See Lukács, "Móricz Zsigmond novellás könyve" ("A Collection of Móricz's Short Stories"), in *Magyar Irodalom*, p. 60.

41. Lukács, "Kinek nem kell és miért Balázs Béla költészete?" ("Who Rejects Béla Balázs's Poetry and Why?"), in *Magyar Irodalom*, pp. 133–134. The article contains some sharp polemics and was written in 1918.

42. Mór Jókai (1825–1904) was one of Hungary's most popular novelists, whose books are still avidly read today; many of them are being turned into movies. He wrote in a high-romantic vein.

43. Zsigmond Kemény, Baron (1814–75), member of the Hungarian lower aristocracy, was a novelist and journalist as well as politician. He was the author of important historical and social novels. József Eötvös, Baron (1813–71), of the same origins as Kemény, was a novelist, journalist, politician, and important figure in Hungarian public life. His realistic novels were widely read not only in Hungary but also in Victorian England.

44. See Lukács, *Magyar Irodalom*, pp. 150 and 151.

45. Ibid., p. 158. Written in 1939, Lukács's article is devoted to Ady, the "Great Bard of the Hungarian Tragedy."

46. Béla Zsolt (1895–1949) was a leading Hungarian-Jewish journalist of liberal persuasion, especially influential in the 1930s.

47. Lukács was in this case very perceptive in pointing out this tragic constellation of talents: János Vajda (1827–97), poet and journalist, was a forerunner of modern city-life poets; Lajos Tolnai (1837–1902), novelist, was a bitter critic of contem-

porary Hungarian life, especially that of the lesser nobility and officialdom; Kálmán Mikszáth (1847–1910) was also a novelist and journalist, whose work is still widely read in Hungary.

48. Reference is to the War of Independence, the armed conflict of 1848–49 between the Habsburgs and Hungary led by the well-known revolutionary figure Lajos Kossuth. The uprising was crushed when the Habsburg monarch called in the armies of the czar. Thirteen generals were executed by the Austrians on October 6, 1849, which has since been one of Hungary's national holidays.

49. See Lukács, *Magyar Irodalom*, pp. 443–44. Entitled "Egy rossz regény margójára" ("Marginal Note on a Bad Novel"), this piece was written in 1947.

50. Ibid., p. 606. The article is devoted to Ady's significance and influence and was written in 1969.

51. Ibid., p. 609.

12

Lukács's Realism: From *Geschichte und Klassenbewusstsein* to the Blum Theses

By Lee Congdon

I

In the midst of the controversy that swirled around *Geschichte und Klassenbewusstsein*, Lenin died. Within a few weeks of his passing, the Verlag der Arbeiterbuchhandlung (Vienna) published Lukács's *Lenin: A Study of the Unity of His Thought*, which, if it had done nothing else, should have dispelled any notion that the author had recanted his Hegelian heresies. The core of Lenin's thought, he wrote, was the actuality of the revolution, which meant "treating each particular question of the day in concrete association with the socio-historic whole, as moments in the liberation of the proletariat."[1] Critical of utopianism, Lenin was a realist, but one who knew that there was always "something more real and therefore more important than *isolated* facts or tendencies: *the reality of the total process*, the totality of social development."[2] And what was this reality in the era of the actuality of the proletarian revolution? Lukács's answer was extremely inventive. The bourgeoisie, living in the age of the rise of the proletariat, had ceased to be a revolutionary class; indeed, in an effort to prevent or at least forestall its loss of power, it had forged an alliance with the defeated feudal-absolutist class. As a result of this devil's pact, suggested to Lukács by modern Hungary's semifeudal condition, the proletariat's initial task was to effect the full realization of the bourgeoisie's historical responsibilities.[3]

Lukács was quick to add that the revolution in the making was not purely bourgeois, any more than it was purely proletarian. The "real revolution is the dialectical transformation of the bourgeois revolution into the proletarian

169

revolution.''[4] The realization of the bourgeois revolution, that is, entailed its supersession. The proletariat was, then, the legatee of the revolutionary bourgeoisie. It followed from this that the privileged standpoint of the proletariat could not be separated absolutely from that of the revolutionary bourgeoisie, and that therefore the proletariat would be well advised to attend to the history and literature of its revolutionary forebears.

In the final chapter of the book, Lukács summed up Lenin's ''revolutionary *Realpolitik*.'' The Bolshevik leader knew, he wrote, that only utopians separated the final aim from the movement toward it. Socialism was not to be conceived of as a completed condition, a state of ''being'' in the future, but as a process of becoming. Knowledge of that process was the privilege of those who participated in the moment-by-moment struggle. For Lenin, Philosophy was practice, the freeing of the tendencies and possibilities locked in the present and transparent to proletarian class consciousness.[5]

Inspired by Lenin, Lukács threw himself into Hungarian Communist politics with renewed energy. Throughout 1924, he worked side by side with Jenö Landler on a plan to create a new and legal party, the Socialist Workers' party of Hungary. The party was to serve as a political home for social democratic schismatics of the Left, but its activities would be directed by the illegal Hungarian Communist party. Although the Kun faction strongly opposed the plan, it received official approval from the Fifth Congress of the Comintern. Along with Landler and József Révai, Lukács formulated a political program and, on April 14, 1925, the new party was formally constituted. Its central political slogan was ''the republic,''[6] the idea being that before the proletarian dictatorship could realistically be placed on the political agenda, the bourgeois revolution would have to be completed.

Lukács's absorption in Hungarian political realities awakened in him an unwonted interest in the Hungarian past. This interest became all the more intense as world revolution became an increasingly remote prospect and Stalin began to propound the doctrine of ''socialism in one country.'' In reexamining the history of his homeland, Lukács focused his attention on the abortive 1848–49 revolution, Hungary's would-be equivalent of the French or bourgeois revolution. Perhaps, he reasoned, the roots of the Soviet Republic's fall could be discovered in this earlier failure.

Lukács's ideas about that epochal event were largely inspired by the posthumous publication of Ervin Szabó's *Social and Party Struggles in the 1848–49 Hungarian Revolution*. Szabó, the father of Hungarian Marxism, attributed the failure of the revolution to its conservative social character. Because, in his view, Lajos Kossuth had moved steadily to the political Right, he had frustrated a democratic social revolution, one that would have entailed far more attention to an agrarian transformation. Szabó lionized, therefore, the publicist Mihály Táncsis and the poet Sándor Petöfi, both of whom were inspired by the most radical moments in the French Revolution.[7]

Lukács followed Szabó's lead, especially in the pages of *100%*, a legal Communist journal published in Hungary from 1927 to 1930. He too now believed that the agrarian question had been of fundamental significance, not only in 1848–49, but also in 1919. The Soviet Republic, he was now persuaded, had paid insufficient attention to the Hungarian peasantry's legitimate aspirations.[8] Lukács was more inclined than Szabó, however, to view the failure of the 1848 revolution in tragic terms. Perhaps, after all, the revolution was premature. Thus, while he held Táncsis and Petöfi in high esteem, he was not ready to identify an authentic tradition of revolt. Following Szabó, he acclaimed Petöfi's plebeian politics and revolutionary poetry while characterizing the second half of the nineteenth century as an age of epigones and second-rate apologists for the *Ausgleich*. Only after the turn of the century, he argued, did a literary revolution gather around the modernist journal *Nyugat* (*West*). But by restricting the revolution to literature the journal showed its true—compromising—colors. Among the *Nyugat* writers, only Endre Ady, the brilliant journalist and poet, revived Petöfi's social and political radicalism.[9]

Lukács had always admired Ady, and he reacted sharply against the attempt by contemporary Hungarian cultural leaders to co-opt the poet for the conservative national renaissance.[10] It is, however, far from clear that he had the best case, for if there can be no doubt concerning Ady's radical social and political views. his lasting significance is due to his complete identification with the Hungarian nation and its history. Furthermore, it is misleading to assert, as Lukács did, that Ady's "thought and poetry was not, in its essence, romantic."[11] Indeed, Lukács's enthusiasm for the radical Hungarian poets constituted evidence that his own romanticism was not, as he insisted, a thing of the past. Even József Révai conceded that Ady's verse could not provide that insight into the social totality that Lukács demanded of "realist" writers.[12]

II

It is well to bear this in mind when examining Lukács's closely argued attacks on those left-wing and even Marxist movements that competed with revolutionary realism for the allegiance of the proletariat and the radical intelligentsia. In his most famous essays of the decade, on Ferdinand Lassalle and Moses Hess, he attempted to exorcise forever his own youthful utopian romanticism by identifying it with bourgeois class consciousness in the age of bourgeois decline. Yet by retracting his spiritual and intellectual pilgrimage from Fichtean utopianism to Hegelian dialectics, he merely contrived to chart a course from one form of romanticism to another. For if it is true, as I believe, that "romantic philosophy is . . . primarily a metaphysics of integration, of which the key principle is that of the 'reconciliation,' or synthesis, of whatever is divided, opposed, and conflicting,"[13] Hegel was the quintessential romantic. Just so, Lukács's Hegelian Marxism was romantic both in its abstract design and in its idealist conception of reality.

Lukács had a few kind things to say of Lassalle because the flamboyant social democratic leader was himself attracted to Hegel, and his work, like that of Lukács, was inextricably intertwined with his relationship with women, especially with Countess Sophie Hatzfeldt. All the more unfortunate, then, according to Lukács, that Lassalle had turned to Fichte's activism in an effort to transform the Hegelian dialectic into a philosophy of revolution. This was a profound error, for although Fichte professed a more revolutionary disposition than Hegel did, that disposition was purely utopian. For him, the present constituted the third of five world-historical ages—the age of absolute sinfulness; as such, it was negative through and through. The final two ages described by Fichte in *Characteristics of the Present Age* constituted the utopian future and were to witness the realization of that formal "ought" that had for so long stood over against reality, the "is." But precisely how was history to pass from one age to the next? How was utopia to be achieved? Here, Lukács believed, Fichte's philosophy of history revealed its Achilles' heel.[14]

If, Lukács reasoned, Hegel's "reconciliation with reality" ultimately became reactionary in politics and contemplative in philosophy, it yet made possible an understanding of the connection between logical categories and the structural forms of bourgeois society. By rejecting the utopian ought and focusing philosophy on the understanding of the present, grasped dialectically, Hegel had pointed the only way of knowing that which was alone knowable about the future—the tendencies in the present that impel history forward.[15] That understanding should not, to be sure, be passive, Lukács told Anna Lesznai in 1928, "but an active meshing with the historical current and thus a seizure of fate, the humanization of the world order."[16]

By correcting Hegel with Fichte, Lassalle unfittingly fell into the trap of reading history as the record of absolute disjunctions and fundamental antinomies; thus, contrary to his intention, he came increasingly to regard what is as immediately given and what ought to be as totally other. The very antinomic structure of his thinking betrayed its essentially bourgeois character. Perhaps most damaging, this structure made it necessary for Lassalle to regard the bourgeois and the proletarian revolution as two completely distinct phenomena, blinding him to the fact that they were related moments of a single process. Naturally, then, he failed to recognize that in the present age, the proletariat had inherited the task of completing the bourgeois revolution, before the latter passed dialectically on. In the final analysis, he could be nothing more than the theorist of the bourgeois revolution, the age of which was now past.[17]

Lukács took on similar themes in his long and remarkable essay on Moses Hess, that fascinating precursor of Zionism who was Lassalle's chief organizer in the Rhineland. Here too Lukács discussed the problem of the relationship of the bourgeois to the proletarian revolution and rejected the utopian, Fichtean, views he himself had espoused during the Great War. Like Lassalle, he insisted, Hess had attempted to impart of Hegelianism a Fichtean character, thus obscuring Hegel's "splendid realism," his recognition that the present was given its distinctive character by what it once was and what it would be. It was that which always pointed dialectically beyond itself. Hence, "reconciliation with reality" implied an affirmation not of the world immediately present, but rather of the world to come that was already present as living potentiality—of a romantic reality. Even if, Lukács continued, the pull of his bourgeois consciousness led Hegel to allow the present to lose its inner dynamic, his method was not thereby discredited.[18] By reverting to Fichte, Hess was reduced to condemning the alienated present from an abstract, moral point of view—according to Lukács, a quintessentially bourgeois standpoint.[19]

In the age of the proletarian revolution the only correct standpoint was that of the proletariat, for from it one could see that reality was not completely negative and that its progressive possibilities could be realized by means of critical, practical activity. This was an extremely important point with respect to the fundamental problem of alienation, for in a real sense, Lukács believed that alienation was overcome in the active struggle to overcome it.[20] As the party led that struggle, it constituted itself and its ever-expanding *Gemeinschaft*.

Now, since alienation was rooted in the very social, and hence economic, structure of bourgeois, capitalist society, a critique of political economy, such as Marx had carried out, was at the same time a critique of alienation and an important moment in the process that is the overcoming of alienation. In short, Marx had surpassed Hegel by being able to adopt the standpoint of the proletariat and by substituting a materialistic for an idealistic dialectic.[21] Yet even here Hegel was not greatly outstripped, for in many respects, Lukács maintained in 1928, the author of the *Phenomenology* had advanced, however unconsciously, "in the direction of materialism."[22]

III

Lukács's campaign against the utopian Left was not restricted to a critique of political thinkers; he viewed the literary avant-garde with the greatest hostility as well. During the Soviet Republic, he had, it is true, named Lajos Kassák to the Writers' Directory, but even at that early date he perceived in the avant-garde a variety of utopianism. By insisting on a complete and radical break with bourgeois culture, the avant-garde was unable to transcend a rigid dualism, and by refusing to connect itself with the progressive national literary tradition, it condemned itself to irrelevancy. Although he did not say so at the time, Lukács agreed with Béla Kun, when, in 1919, the latter characterized the literature of Kassák's journal *Ma (Today)* as "the product of bourgeois decadence."[23]

Lukács's literary-cultural theory thus paralleled his political conception. Just as he admitted of no absolute disjunction between the bourgeois and the proletarian revolutions, so he refused to sanction any between bourgeois and proletarian culture. At the existing stage of historical progress, the culture of the revolutionary bourgeoisie (late eighteenth and early nineteenth centuries) continued to be relevant because it constituted the only soil in which the new, proletarian culture could be nurtured and grow. All attempts to create a new culture at a stroke were as futile and undialectical as all efforts to bring about heaven on earth in a single apocalyptic moment.

This idea was of enormous significance for Lukács's critical career and for Marxist theory in general, for it insisted that in culture as well as in politics, Marxism was the inheritor, rather than the destroyer, of what was best in the Western tradition. Indeed, it was precisely Lukács's "sense for continuity and tradition" that so attracted Thomas Mann[24] and many another non-Marxist. It also led to a seeming contradiction—a revolutionary with conservative literary/cultural preferences, a Communist for whom the literary past, or at least an important segment of it, was very much alive. This never disturbed Lukács, however, for he recalled what Mann had written in a long essay of 1922 entitled "Goethe and Tolstoy." By then a convert to the Weimar Republic, the German bourgeois writer argued that radical politics could, and indeed should, go hand in hand with cultural tradition. Germany, Mann maintained, would not realize its proper destiny until "Karl Marx has read Friedrich Hölderlin."[25]

So much for the revolutionary bourgeois culture, but what of proletarian culture? Lukács attempted to answer that question in a pivotal essay of 1926, *"L'art pour l'art* and Proletarian Literature." There he reflected upon the tragedy of writers living in late, declining bourgeois society. Because they viewed reality in its immediacy, they were unable correctly to perceive life's deeper possibilities, particularly with respect to the authentic relationship of individuals to one another, always, for Lukács, "the subject matter of literature."[26] Those who did not attempt to escape reality altogether by means of form experiments (*l'art pour l'art*) often opted for a "didactic art," conjuring up "abstract-romantic utopias" or providing glimpses of life in its brute surface immediacy.[27]

Lukács was inclined to identify all of these decadent literary trends with romanticism, but it is clear from the context that he had in mind a romanticism of despair and blind revolt—what, in 1907, he called romanticism *à rebours.* At that time, he had perceptively observed that the romanticism of writers such as Baudelaire, Flaubert, and Ibsen differed markedly from that of the early nineteenth-century romantics. Whereas the latter were inspired by a great faith in humankind and the world, the former had lost their faith and had become bitterly disillusioned. They despised their own time, but they felt themselves to be impotent in the face of it. Hence, they turned from life, fearing disappointment; romantic sensibility was rechanneled. Instead of belief, there was radical doubt about everything.[28]

It was precisely this turn from life, this "sympathy with death," that had defined the sensibility of the young Thomas Mann, the author of *Buddenbrooks*. Only after the Great War, when he was shaken by the increasingly nihilistic politics practiced by the enemies of the Weimar Republic, did Mann eschew romanticism *à rebours*. In 1922, he surprised many by defending the new order and arguing that true romanticism led through sympathy with death to affirmation of life.[29] This idea was also to be central to *The Magic Mountain*. In the celebrated section entitled "Snow," Hans Castorp learns the lesson that Mann himself had learned: death must never be permitted to have dominion over our thoughts.[30] Naturally enough, then, Lukács exempted Mann from his critique of latter-day bourgeois writers.

He was even less critical of Leo Tolstoy. "There are," he wrote in *100%*,

> other great writers who criticized sharply the existing social order (Flaubert, Turgenev, Ibsen), but they called attention only to the consequences of the basic arrangements, while Tolstoy always points to the basis itself. . . . He does not take as his point of departure the inner spiritual problems of his characters, but rather he regards the inner spiritual problems that afflict protagonists as the result of material conditions.[31]

Despite Tolstoy's explicit and reactionary program, this insight lent his work a profound significance.

Lukács's celebration of Tolstoy may seem at first sight to pose a problem, for there is no doubt that his literary criticism was structured by a very schematic historical periodization that owed a great deal to the course of Central European history. The proletariat's authentic heritage was that bequeathed to it by the rising bourgeoisie, a class that was revolutionary vis-à-vis the feudal order and therefore historically prescient prior to 1848. After that tumultuous year, the bourgeoisie betrayed its democratic calling and entered its period of compromise and decline. As a consequence, the literature of the period could only reflect that decadence, whether it took the form of naturalism, *l'art pour l'art*, or the avant-garde. How, then, could Lukács account historically for Tolstoy's success? The answer he gave was that Tolstoy's Russia was still in its precapitalist phase; retarded development in Russia offered him the kind of literary/ideological possibilities that had been available to bourgeois Western European writers before 1848.[32]

But what, finally, of proletarian literature? On this question Lukács had little to say in the mid-1920s. Indeed, it could not have seemed very pressing in
the Central and Eastern European context of retarded development. What
could the proletarian revolution offer the development of art, he asked rhetor-
ically at the time. "Very little," came his reply, because the age of the proletarian revolution was still very much in its initial stages.[33] In an obvious lecture to himself, he wrote that

> the mighty upheaval that we are experiencing, that the revolutionary proletariat is
> carrying out, revolutionizes—in the first instance—the *immediate-sensuous* reality
> (the subject matter and form of literature) less than one would believe from a
> superficial glance. This explains the "disillusionment" with the Russian Revolu-
> tion of those intellectuals who expected from it the immediate solution to their spe-
> cial existential problems.[34]

All the more reason, then, to focus attention on the literature of the great age
of the revolutionary bourgeoisie, a literature that was more relevant to the existing stage of historical development.

IV

Lukács's famous Blum Theses (1928) must be read in connection with the
literary theory he was working out in the 1920s.[35] Prepared for the Hungarian
Communist party's Second Congress, they represented a summing up of his
romantic realism. According to Blum/Lukács, the principal problem confronting the party was the Bethlen government's betrayal and liquidation of
bourgeois democracy and the Social Democratic party's unprincipled collaboration. In view of this situation, the Communist party's immediate task should
be to lead the struggle for a republic and the full realization of bourgeois democracy. This could best be accomplished by establishing a democratic dictatorship of the proletariat and the peasantry as a "mediation," a transitional
phase on the road to proletarian power.[36] However paradoxical it sounded, the
proletariat had to be engaged in a struggle against the bourgeoisie in order to
complete the latter class's Jacobin tasks. This was so because the bourgeoisie
had betrayed its own best self, succumbing to reaction and, increasingly, to
fascism. For Lukács, of course, it was necessary to associate fascism with
bourgeois decline; otherwise it might have been difficult to distinguish between Fascist and Communist violence.

Lukács emphasized the peculiarity of Hungarian development, which combined the old feudal form of land distribution with a relatively developed form
of capitalism. This unholy alliance between landowners and capitalists had to
be confronted by an alliance of the proletariat and the peasantry, taking its
stand on a program of full democracy.[37] Thus, Lukács held that the full realization of bourgeois democracy was the proper goal of the Communist party in
underdeveloped countries as well as in the developed capitalist states. The

latter had turned their backs on bourgeois democracy, however much they preserved its form; the former had not yet placed democracy on the agenda. In both cases, the responsibility for bourgeois democracy devolved on the proletariat and its party.[38]

Lukács was careful to insist, however, that although a democratic dictatorship did not go beyond bourgeois society in its "immediate content," it was to be viewed as a mediation within a total process, "a dialectical form of transition toward the proletarian revolution—or the counterrevolution."[39] He cited Lenin, as he did so often, to the effect that there was "no Chinese wall between bourgeois and proletarian revolutions."[40] Even years later (in 1956), he was still insisting that the democratic dictatorship was a "special transitional form" of the bourgeois democratic revolution.[41]

When compared with utopian revolutionary demands, the Blum Theses defended a remarkably moderate agenda. Yet the boast that they constitute an example of the Popular Front idea *avant la lettre* will not withstand scrutiny. By separating capitalism and democracy so completely, Lukács was led to identify the former and its bourgeois sponsors with fascism or proto-facism. And because social democrats all over Europe worked within the existing system, he lent his name to the preposterous charge that social democracy could be equated with fascism.[42]

Whatever their errors and merits might have been, the Blum Theses were attacked by Kun and the party leadership and, Landler having died the same year, they were rejected. In a letter to the Central Committee, Lukács repudiated them, an act of "self-criticism" that he subsequently admitted to be insincere. After this defeat, he withdrew from active politics to concentrate all of his energies on Marxist aesthetics and literary criticism.

It is only natural to ask why Lukács exercised self-criticism while continuing to believe that he was right. By his account, he did so because he knew that the German party had expelled Karl Korsch in 1926 and he did not wish to give Kun an opportunity to excommunicate him, thus removing him from any effective struggle against fascism. But there was more to it than that. For Lukács the party was a microcosm of a new, emerging social order, a totality within which human beings, no longer subject to the atomizing effects of capitalist society, could meet at last. One is reminded of the old Hungarian proverb, "Outside of Hungary there is no life; and if there is, it is not worthwhile" (*Extra Hungariam non est vita; Aut si vita, non est ita*). For "Hungary," Lukács, the political and existential exile, had substituted "the party."

Notes

1. Geoge Lukács, *Lenin: Studie über den Zusammenhang seiner Gedanken* (Neuwied and Berlin: Luchterhand, 1967), p. 11.
2. Ibid., p. 16.

3. Ibid., p. 18.
4. Ibid., p. 46.
5. Ibid., pp. 69–71, 83.
6. Georg Lukács, *Curriculum Vitae*, ed. János Ambrus (Budapest: Magvetö Kiadó, 1982), pp. 177–78.
7. Ervin Szabó, *Társadalmi és pártharcok a 48–49-es magyar forradalomban* (Bécs: Bécsi Magyar Kiadó, 1921), p. 81.
8. Miklós Lackó, *Szerep és mü* (Budapest: Gondolat, 1981), pp. 92–93.
9. Aladár Tamás, ed., *A 100%: A KMP legális folyóirata, 1927–1930* (Budapest: Akadémiai Kiadó, 1977), p. 193.
10. See Lackó, *Szerep*, pp. 54–55, 93–94.
11. See Tamás, *A 100%*, p. 191.
12. See Lackó, *Szerep*, pp. 84–85.
13. M.H. Abrams, *Natural Supernaturalism* (New York: Norton, 1971), p. 182.
14. Georg Lukács, "Die neue Ausgabe von Lasalles Briefen," *Archiv für die Geschichte des Sozialismus und der Arbeiterbewegung* 11(1925):403–5.
15. Ibid., p. 405.
16. Cited in Erzsébet Vezér, *Lesznai Anna élete* (Budapest: Kossuth Könyvkiadó, 1979), p. 96.
17. See Lukács, "Die neue Ausgabe," pp. 414–15, 423.
18. Georg Lukács, "Moses Hess und die Probleme der idealistischen Dialektik," *Archiv für die Geschichte des Sozialismus und der Arbeiterbewegung* 12(1926):113, 116–17.
19. Ibid., pp. 125–26, 138.
20. Ibid., p. 145.
21. Ibid., pp. 148–52.
22. Tamás, *A 100%*, p. 298.
23. József Farkas, ed., *"Mindenki ujakra készül. . ."*: *Az 1918-19-es forradalmak irodalma.* (Budapest-MTA, 1967).
24. Cited in Judith Marcus-Tar, *Thomas Mann und Georg Lukács* Cologne and Vienna: Böhlau, 1982), p. 20. Cf., for an extended discussion of the problem, Judith Marcus, *Georg Lukács and Thomas Mann: A Study in the Sociology of Literature* (Amherst: University of Massachusetts, 1987).
25. Thomas Mann, *Essays*, trans. H.T. Lowe-Porter (New York: Vintage, 1957), p. 177.
26. Karl August Kutzbach, ed., *Paul Ernst und Georg Lukács: Dokumente einer Freundschaft* (Emsdetten: Lechte, 1974), p. 177.
27. Ibid., pp. 178–79.
28. Georg Lukács, *Ifjukori Müvek, 1902–1918*, ed. Árpád Timár (Budapest: Magvetö Kiadó, 1977), pp. 90–105.
29. Thomas Mann, *Order of the Day*, trans. H.T. Lowe-Porter et al. (New York: Books for Libraries, 1969), pp. 43–44.
30. Thomas Mann, *Der Zauberberg* (Frankfurt am Main: Fischer, 1967), 2:523.
31. Cited in Lackó, *Szerep*, pp., 83–84.
32. See Tamás Ungvári, "Brecht és Lukács vitája a harmincas években," *Valóság* 21, 9(1978):34–35.
33. See Kutzbach, *Ernst und Lukács*, p. 179.
34. Ibid.
35. See Miklós Lackó, "A Blum-tézisek és Lukács György kulturafelfogása," in István Szerdahelyi, ed., *Lukács György és a magyar kultúra* (Budapest: Kossuth Könyvkiadó, 1982), pp. 93–101.

36. Georg Lukács, *Történelem és osztálytudat*, ed. M. Vajda (Budapest: Magvetö Kiado, 1971), pp. 675–76.
37. Ibid., p. 687.
38. See Lackó, '' A Blum-tézisek,'' pp. 94–95; cf. Tamás, *A 100%*, p. 299.
39. Lukács, *Történelem*, p. 678.
40. Ibid.
41. Lukács, *Curriculum Vitae*, p. 195.
42. Miklós Lackó, *Válságok—választások* (Budapest: Gondolat, 1975), pp. 186–87.

13

On Lukács's Later Political Philosophy

By József Bayer

The intellectual development of Georg Lukács often took radical turns and was subjected to self-correction; nevertheless, what stands out more and more over time is the basic continuity of his thinking. Lukács himself was aware of the twofold character of his philosophy. In spite of frequent self-criticisms and the splintering of his career into markedly different periods, toward the end of his life he remarked, "In my case, everything is the continuation of something else. I do not think that there are any nonorganic elements in my development."[1] Even what he considered to be his most crucial transformation—his becoming a Communist—was no exception to that statement. In his later autobiographical sketch, he evaluated the possible resumption of his early tendencies, saying, "Marxism: a qualitative change but no rupture in my development, unlike in many others."[2]

Nor did the termination of his "political" period, with the renunciation of his Blum Theses and his retreat into the mere "ideologist's" position, bring discontinuity into Lukács's political philosophy, as might be expected. Naturally enough, for a long time to come he did not engage in any explicitly political analysis on a strategic-theoretical level, especially in relation to his own (Communist) movement; but the continuity of Lukács's thought remained so strong that his views on literary policy as late as 1949 still attracted accusations that they bore the mark of the same old political stance expressed in the Blum Theses—a charge not altogether unjustified.

However, we must look into the background of that Lukácsian turn away from the Blum Theses for much more than the subjective motives he himself admitted—among them, that his political talents seemed to prove insufficient.[3] The relationship between theory and practice changed objec-

181

tively within the Communist movement as soon as the prospects of the world-wide socialist revolution dwindled and gave way to a preoccupation with the problems of building up socialism in a single country—or, in Lukács's later usage, the "nonclassical"[4] form of establishing socialism politically, pressed by the urgent need to make up for underdevelopment, led to necessary changes in the theoretical perspective by upsetting the harmony of theory and practice so characteristic of the movement's beginning, and by finding cogent expression in the Engelsian program of "scientific socialism."

As a natural step in his quest for universality, Lukács soon retreated into areas like aesthetics and the history of philosophy in which universality could best be sought through the struggle for a cultural heritage and continuity. He could manifest the antisectarian attitudes that had surfaced in the Blum Theses, only in indirect ways that were easily labeled "partisan" in a politically obsessed atmosphere that directly subordinated any sort of overt intellectual activity to the needs of political agitation and legitimation.

Thus, even though the place for politics is left empty in Lukács's philosophical system from that moment on,[5] this does not mean an absence of a political philosophy; to the contrary, politics exerts an influence even in Lukács's "purely" theoretical or ideological writings. That influence is indeed felt not only in pointedly political pronouncements, such as those in his anti-Fascist journalism, but also in his more abstract aesthetic and philosophical works, especially when they come under sharp ideological criticism.

However, the following discussion focuses on some elements of the political philosophy of the late Lukács, mostly based on writings and other statements made after the Twentieth Congress of the Communist party of the Soviet Union. At that time, more or less giving up his "philosophical illegality," Lukács again commented openly on what he judged to be vital political issues. Moreover, politics changed its role and regained its importance in Lukács's later philosophical system.

I

We have already noted Lukács's universalistic approach, which for him meant that the significance of the Twentieth Congress was to be measured against world history. In his address to the Political Academy on June 28, 1956, "The Struggle between Progress and Reaction in Today's Culture," the aged philosopher seized the opportunity to analyze the event in its full strategic significance, dismissing any lurid overtones and seeing it as the starting point of a long-term process of reorientation. Lukács still interprets the struggle of socialism against capitalism as the basic contradiction of the entire world-historical period. But, self-critically recalling Lenin's critique of leftist extremism, he proceeds to declare that the direct application of the world-historical scale to actual political problems is not only wrong theoretically but could lead to grave political consequences. The dialectic of progress and reaction is much more complex than that. Leaving the validity of the great theoretical principles unaffected, the fundamental contrasts of our age may take on often contradictory concrete forms, which are likely to extend over a long period. We must understand these in their specificity and develop our political strategy accordingly. In the past years, Lukács adds, the strategy of the fight for progress was not directly linked with the problem of capitalism versus socialism, at least in two cases. One of these was the question of fascism and antifascism, on which he remarks,

> Countless serious strategic errors committed by our parties originated from the fact that the truths of the revolutionary period of 1917 and immediately after . . . were transposed without any criticism or examination of the new situation into an era in which the fundamental strategic problem was not the immediate struggle for socialism but the fight between fascism and antifascism.[6]

Lukács here is not only criticizing Stalin and the Comintern's earlier strategic errors but, in view of the sectarian position expressed in the Blum Theses about fascism and social democracy, he implies a thorough self-criticism too.

This experience lends additional importance to the second question, that of the proper attitude toward war and peace and the issue of coexistence. Lukács saw this issue as the root of all the fundamental strategic questions of our age, and he kept this opinion till the end of his life. He criticized Stalin's politics for its inconsistency on this matter (as he did later with Chinese politics of similar intent during the cultural revolution), and indeed he adjusted his own political and theoretical viewpoints to the perspective of peaceful coexistence opened up by the Twentieth Congress. According to this perspective, the world-historical dimensions of the struggle between capitalism and socialism still remain valid; but no concession is to be made to reactionary pressure or sectarian-dogmatic reflexes that would immediately reduce every actual question to a large-scale world-historical controversy and apply pressure to settle the question prematurely. Peaceful coexistence is not just a tactical necessity made possible from a military point of view. It is a long-term strategy for giving socialism a chance to compensate for its handicap through a long, organic unfolding of its powers, not only in socialist but in capitalist countries. Coexistence means above all that both social systems may follow their inner laws of development. It is on this basis that their dialogue may start, introducing peaceful competition in areas of political, economic, or cultural performance and improving the conditions of meaningful human life, all in order to determine which way is more commendable to humankind.

Lukács's conception is diametrically opposed to those who consider socialism merely a particular sociopolitical arrangement best suited to the nature of a particular group of countries—an arrangement to which there could in fact be a perhaps more efficient capitalist alternative. He conceives of socialism as a universal response and solution to the crisis in which world capitalism involves the whole of humankind, its contradictions affecting the capitalist center and the peripheries alike. Lukács can see no road to harmony; as he puts it in a later writing,

> Unlike the preceding economic formations, both [contemporary] systems are fundamentally of a universal character. Both could emerge only on the basis of the whole world's becoming an inextricably unified configuration economically and therefore politically. Both have the immanent tendency to shape the world to its own model of life; and neither can abandon that objectively necessary aspiration without giving up its own self.[7]

In this way, the ideological conflict between the two world systems is but an expression of a deeper, world-historical conflict that cannot be banished simply by sending it to the devil. Quite the contrary, it is through transposing the conflict onto the ideological plane (i.e., replacing the military threat, economic discrimination, or political offense against sovereignty with "ideological influence" based on real social, economic, and cultural achievements) that it will become possible to settle the conflict in a humane and acceptable way that will best serve the future of humankind.

II

This conception, which Lukács espoused later on several occasions, was not a passing fancy but the basic definition of a whole era, one unlikely to vary with transitory changes in world politics. (Those who give up easily had better look for another ideal.) From that moment on, it was always within that wide world-historical-philosophical context that Lukács carried on his constant search for a *tertium datur* that would replace false extremes in both theory and practice and take on many possible forms and expressions. Despite capitalism's perceived capacity for reform, which was made obvious further by the decades of prosperity following World War II, Lukács maintained that capitalism's structural changes only meant its more complete unfolding and not its death, and that these changes were all very well explained by the method of classical Marxism (as the more complete domination of relative surplus value as opposed to the domination of absolute surplus value). He also pointed out that it will be through its own intrinsic contradictions that capitalist society will finally start to search for a socialist solution, a search that we may be able to influence only ideologically at best. This conception is a *tertium datur* both in that it contrasts with dogmatic Marxist postulates of a totally unchanging capitalism and with bourgeois claims of its complete disappearance.

As regards socialism, Lukács is very optimistic about its potential development, though he is not overwhelmed by any ideology of "quantity." He insists that socialism itself needs to undergo a qualitative change so that all of humankind will see it as a promising alternative. Lukács's political ideas are elaborated accordingly. Among them are the urgent need for the renaissance of Marxism; the restoration of its scientific content to serve as the ideology guiding the adequate practice (a *tertium datur* opposed to the unattractive extremes of dogmatism and revisionism); a properly conceived political program for class alliance that abandons the Stalinist method of exclusion and returns to the Leninist principles of retaining a basically critical attitude but encouraging collaboration in practice for the common cause; and, an open cultural policy free from bureaucratic manipulation that nevertheless does not yield to the manipulative tendencies inherent in culture's becoming a commodity. Finally, as a consequence of the economic reforms necessitated by the termination of the period of extensive industrialization, Lukács finds it timely to raise again the question of an original socialist democracy, another *tertium datur* between Stalinism and a manipulative pluralist bourgeois society.

III

No doubt all these questions retain their relevance even now. It is another consideration how far Lukács himself was able to provide consistent, concrete, and valid responses to them. As is well known, toward the end of his life Lukács expressed his thoughts on these topics in many interviews and articles as well as in his correspondence; but in view of his strict scientific and systematic standards, we can hardly use those pronouncements to try to reconstruct some unified political theory. In his old age, Lukács concentrated his energies on what he considered to be the most important task of all, the philosophical foundation of the renaissance of Marxism, together with the reconstruction and application of the genuine Marxist Weltanschauung and method. Those efforts resulted in the grand syntheses of "The Specificity of the Aesthetic" and "Towards the Ontology of Social Being." Thus, the value of his "occasional" utterances seems to originate less in their theoretical coherence than in the fact that they reveal the deepest political mission of his great theoretical enterprises.

For example, the slogan of the "renaissance of Marxism" is not only based on a purely theoretical need; it reflects aspirations to renew socialist practice entirely and to break with Stalinist methods of giving priority to tactics over strategy and to propaganda over theory. Consequently, Marxism is to perform its ideological function once more as a science and should serve as the guideline for a renascent practice. While still arguing for continuity in the field of culture, Lukács becomes an advocate of discontinuity in politics, once he's got rid of direct political responsibility. He envisages the development of socialism through a series of radical reforms, which would now be easier to implement than to postpone. We can at least say that the experiences of the recent past do not refute that conjecture. At the same time, it is true that Lukács had no concrete, politically feasible plans for those necessary reforms.

Lukács was known to be a firm supporter of economic reforms in Hungary rather early. The main elements of his conception can be found in his earliest interview with *L'Unita*,[8] in which he says that what is needed is a theoretically based planned economy resting more on the Marxian theory of reproduction and taking into account the specific features of socialist reproduction that ultimately differ from those of capitalist reproduction (as in the area of cultural reproduction). He also says that the bureaucratic model of a planned economy should be replaced by a less centralized structure relying on proletarian democracy and more mass initiative; therefore, to facilitate the introduction of the reform, discontinuity should be accentuated and the masses should thus be made interested in change.

Any socialist reform policy that deserves the name can embrace such a program, abstract as it is, especially if it remains without further political concretization. (By the way, this is the origin of the charge often voiced by some of the renegades among Lukács's disciples that the "establishment" appropriates Lukács for its own purposes.)[9] As a matter of fact, in spite of the historical and strategic dimensions of his political conception, it cannot be said that Lukács possessed some directly applicable political theorem or even a political ideology with a mobilizing force. Actually, he did not seek to provide one. Lukács forever remains a "pure ideologist." He himself makes a definite distinction in the *Ontology*, contrasting "pure ideologies" with political ideologies, the latter being meant to grasp the practicalities of decisive moments at the crisis stage. Speaking of pure ideologies, he states,

> Every important philosophy wants to present an overall picture of the state of the world in which it tries to synthesize interrelations from cosmology to ethics so that those interrelations may show even timely decisions to be necessary moments of decision determining the fate of mankind.[10]

Quite naturally, the practical implications of Lukács's Marxist philosophy surpass the possibilities of such a "pure ideology." We even find that political problems receive more and more emphasis in his last works. In a piece still published only in part, Lukács interprets the process of increasing socialist democracy in a historical perspective as a crucial question of development.[11] Socialist democracy, a fundamental and indispensable practical precondition to building socialism, is not just an extension of bourgeois democracy; it is its opposite, for "it is not an idealistic superstructure surmounting the spontaneous materialism of the bourgeois society but the material motion of the social world itself.'' Lukács then continues, ''Socialist democracy must indeed pervade the whole material life of men; it must represent the social character of man from everyday life to crucial social questions as the product of everyone's own activity.'' Lukács analyzes the different answers to the historical dilemma posed by the ''nonclassical'' way of socialist development, asking ''What should the relation be in the transitory period between the economic practice merely trying to make up for economic underdevelopment and the acts and institutions that are already directly related to socialist democracy and to directly improving proletarian democracy?'' As he did so often before, Lukács lays stress on the basic discontinuity separating the Leninist and Stalinist methods; and he also urges a return to the Leninist method of experimentation, for it ''could even now be our useful defense against planners' phantasms which, owing to their apodictical nature often based on haphazard extrapolations, cannot foresee the real tendencies.''[12] Lukács recommends both the revival of the wide-ranging forms of the masses' own activities and the conscious organizing and guiding role of the party in the process of democratization.[13]

IV

Notwithstanding the numerous deep insights and the fruitful methodological inspiration embodied in this particular work, as a whole it shows the philosopher wrestling with a set of problems that cannot be dealt with solely by means of philosophy. Obviously Lukács did not intend to offer more than methodological principles and stimulation to later ''substantial'' research. He left many a question open, in no way to be considered settled, awaiting continued critical reflection. Thus, in Lukács's conception, socialism is a society in which the spontaneous, autonomous motion of the economy is controlled by a unified social teleology. We can hardly expect to find an answer on a purely philosophical basis to the crucial question of socialist democracy as to how that teleology arises, and which social processes contribute to defining it as well as to making it unified or even social. Nor can the ''education of educators'' as the essential content of democracy, the ''democracy of everyday life,'' be discussed merely on the philosophical plane of total reproduction, independent of analyses of the social structure and the division of labor, the resulting value differentiation, and the mediating institutions, together with the corresponding ideological conflicts. Finally, what is the real role of knowledge, especially institutionalized knowledge, in defining social teleology as compared with political motion and institutions? Even the great conception of the renaissance of Marxism suspends that question simply by not considering it a problem from the point of view of democracy. We get no help either from Lukács's ambiguous relationship with the special social sciences.

His often repeated statement of the Marxist principle of the unity and mediation of theory and practice only remains a desideratum in this "politological" essay of the philosopher.

None of these points detracts from Lukács's credit for calling attention again and again to democracy as a central question of socialist development so that—as he put it—the "objectively" socialist relations may also become "subjectively" socialist in the course of a long-term process of democratization. We are warned only that concrete solutions and applications cannot be derived from Lukács's philosophy directly, without critical appraisal, scientific investigation, and political efforts.

It seems, however, that the shift in emphasis toward political questions mentioned at the beginning of this paper did not essentially influence the theoretical structure of Lukács's later chef d'oeuvre, the *Ontology*. There the treatments of politics within the framework of the theory of ideology and the ontology of the ideal moment does not constitute a qualitative change in what we earlier called the "empty place" of politics within Lukács's philosophical system. This again reflects the changed historical relationship between theory and practice in the peculiar kind of orthodox Marxism to which Lukács adhered throughout. Achieving a renewed harmony between theory and practice and a more fruitful mediation will be the work of a new generation of Marxists, who can nevertheless greatly profit from the philosophical heritage of the Hungarian thinker of reason, emancipation, and humanism.

Notes

1. István Eörsi quotes Lukács, "Az utolosó szó jogán," in *Uj Symposion* (Novi Sad/ Yugoslavia) 17, 195–96(July-August 1981):256.
2. Georg Lukács, *Curriculum Vitae* (Budapest: Magvetö, 1981), p. 36.
3. Cf. Jörg Kammler, *Politische Theorie von Georg Lukács* (Darmstadt and Neuwied: Luchterhand, 1974), p. 333.
4. Georg Lukács, *A társadalmi lét ontológiájáról (On the Onotology of Social Being)*, vol. 1 (Budapest: Magvetö Kiadó, 1976).
5. László Sziklai, *Lukács és a fasizmus kora (Lukács and the Era of Fascism)* (Budapest: Magvetö, 1981), p. 151.
6. Georg Lukács, "Der Kampf des Fortschritts und der Reaktion in der heutigen Kultur," in *Schriften zur Ideologie und Politik*, ed. Peter Ludz (Neuwied and Berlin: Luchterhand, 1967), p. 607.
7. Georg Lukács, "Probleme der kulturellen Koexistenz," *Forum* (Vienna), April-May 1964.
8. "The Economic Reform in Hungary and Socialist Democracy," interview with Georg Lukács, *L'Unita*, August 18, 1966.
9. Ágnes Heller, "Lukács's Later Philosophy," in *Lukács Reappraised*, ed. Ágnes Heller (New York: Columbia University, 1983), p. 181.
10. Lukács, *A társadalmi lét ontológiájáról*, 2:542.
11. Georg Lukács, *Demokratisierung heute und morgen* (Budapest: Akadémiai Kiadó, 1985).
12. Preceding quotations from György Lukács, *Lenin*, (Budapest: Magvetö, 1970), pp. 226, 222–23, 217, and 220 respectively.
13. Lukács, *Demokratisierung heute und morgen*.

14

Naphta or Settembrini?—Lukács and Romantic Anticapitalism

By Michael Löwy

Georg Lukács was probably the first thinker to use the concept of romantic anticapitalism; the term appeared in his writings of the 1930s. Although he never developed a systematic definition of the concept, some elements of its meaning are implicitly present in his philosophical and literary works. First of all, Lukács perceives romanticism not as an aesthetic or literary category, but as a broad cultural configuration, present in politics, philosophy, sociology, political economy, religion—as well as in art and literature. Second, he sees both the link between romanticism and capitalism and the difference between the romantic and other forms of anticapitalist consciousness; its criticism of the modern bourgeois civilization is based on precapitalist social and cultural values.

I

In my opinion, romantic anticapitalism is one of the main styles of thought of modern times, and one of the most influential Weltanschauungen in European culture since the end of the eighteenth century. At the time of Lukács's spiritual formation—the beginning of the twentieth century—it was the dominant worldview in German as well as Central European intellectual life.[1]

Nothing is more perplexing and contradictory than romantic anticapitalism; its enigmatic ambiguity is marvelously represented through the fictional character of Leo Naphta, one of the protagonists in Thomas Mann's *The Magic Mountain*. A Jesuit Communist (of Jewish origin) and the archenemy of the liberal humanist, Lodovico Settembrini, Naphta celebrates the struggle of the

Fathers of the Church against capitalism, and is sympathetic toward the romantic movement with its "fantastic double meaning," incorporating both reactionary and revolutionary tendencies.[2] Lukács has frequently been presented as the real-life model for Thomas Mann's literary creation, and there is at least partial truth to this assertion.[3]

Max Weber stressed in several of his writings that capitalism and industrial society are characterized by the "disenchantment of the world" (*Entzauberung der Welt*), in that the supreme feelings and values are replaced by rational calculation of benefits and losses. Romantic anticapitalism, which finds one of its most typical expressions in a fascination for religion and mysticism, is a form of revolt against this *Entzauberung*, and a desperate attempt at "reenchanting" the world by restoring to the cultural universe the qualitative values eradicated by the machines and the accounting books.

The so-called Max Weber circle in Heidelberg of the 1910s was one of the main centers for the irradiation of neoromantic ideas in the academic milieu. The attraction of Russian literature and Russian religious thought was for its members a sort of an expression of their distancing themselves from the excessively rationalized spirit of Western capitalism. The two members of this circle who are most representative of this general state of mind in its most extreme, most radical, and eschatological form are two young philosophers of Jewish origin: Ernst Bloch and Georg Lukács.

The ambiguity of romantic anticapitalism manifests itself in the development of contradictory streams out of a common matrix: conservative, even reactionary (later, Fascist) trends as well as utopian and revolutionary ones. To this last category belong not only Lukács and his friend, Bloch, but also many expressionist writers, the Frankfurt School, the Bavarian revolutionaries of 1919 (Gustav Landauer, Ernst Toller, Erich Mühsam, and Eugene Levine), and participants in the 1919 revolution in Hungary. Thomas Mann lived in Munich in 1919 and was a keen observer of the revolutionary events there; one can find in his recently published diaries a sympathetic interest in the writings of Gustav Landauer, for example, and less sympathetic remarks about other (mostly Jewish) revolutionaries. (It has been suggested that Gustav Landauer may be another possible source for the Naphta figure.)[4]

Romantic anticapitalism is the key to the understanding of Lukács's youthful writings as well as to his sui generis path to Marxism—in radical opposition to the orthodox historical materialism of the Second International. In his pre-Marxist period (up to December 1918), Lukács dreams of a romantic utopia that combines *Kultur, Gemeinschaft*, religion, and socialism as spiritual substances held together in a sort of elective affinity existing beyond the prosaic, shallow, *enzauberte* world of bourgeois society. Romanticism is the immediate focus of Lukács's first literary and philosophical reflections. In 1907 he envisages the project temporarily entitled *Die Romantik des XIX.*

Jahrhunderts. The following main chapters were planned: (1) Goethe and Fichte; (2) The Tragedy of Romanticism (Schelling, Schlegel, mysticism); (3) The Old and New Romanticism (youth as reaction); (4) Germany and France (*Sturm und Drang* and French romanticism); (5) The Pre-Raphaelites (artistic romanticism and socialism); (6) Romanticism *à Rebours* (types, Schopenhauer, Kierkegaard, Baudelaire, Flaubert, and Ibsen). In his notebooks of that period, one can also find excerpts from Novalis, Schelling, Schlegel, and Schleiermacher.[5] But as this book project shows, Lukács's interest was not limited to German literature and philosophy. Rather, it is the whole cultural universe of romantic anticapitalism that attracted him. One source of inspiration that becomes increasingly important for his development is the Russian literature in its political-religious dimensions: Tolstoy and, above all, Dostoevsky. In an interview he gave me in 1974, Ernst Bloch recalled the "tremendous role" of Russian culture, of the "spiritual universe of Tolstoy and Dostoevsky"—in a word, "the imaginary Russia"—for German intellectuals at the beginning of the century. This was even more true for his friend, Georg Lukács[6]—or, for that matter, for Bloch himself. Both he and Lukács regarded the Russian writers as representing and articulating the aspiration to overcome the desperate and godforsaken individualism of Western Europe, and the striving for the "new man" and a "new world."[7]

If Lukács criticizes German romanticism in his *Soul and Form* (in the essay "The Romantic Philosophy of Life"), he does so because of the paradox that romanticism's rejection of the existing world was not radical enough; while it had created an organic and unified world, poetic and spiritual, it had identified it with the real one. For Lukács, the only way toward an authentic work of art is through the sharp separation of heterogeneous spheres, which means "the creation of a new and unified stratification of the world finally cut loose from reality."[8]

The Theory of the Novel (1916) is permeated with romantic nostalgia for the blessed times "whose paths [were] illuminated by the light of the stars," the ages of the epic, which were characterized by the perfect matching of acts to the inner requirements of the soul.[9] Its eternal archetype is Homeric Greece; the Christian Middle Ages—Giotto and Dante—represent for Lukács the new Greece, the last manifestation of an organic *Gemeinschaft*, of the natural unity of the metaphysical spheres. In opposition to the romantics, however, Lukács does not believe that restoration is possible or even desirable: in a closed world we could not breathe, after having discovered the creativity of the spirit. The failure of the romantics results from this impossibility of returning "to the times of the chivalrous epos." Instead of harking back to the past, Lukács dreams of a utopian future, an earthly paradise, a "breakthrough towards a new epoch of world history," beyond the present bourgeois society and industrial/capitalist civilization—the era of "absolute sinfulness"

(*Epoche der vollendeten Sündhaftigkeit*)—that is, toward a new world of which Tolstoy is the herald and Dostoevsky possibly the new Homer or the new Dante. The aim is not to reestablish the old Greek or medieval closed world but to create a new community whose artistic expression would be a "renewed form" of the epos.[10] In this concept, the backward-looking romanticism transforms itself in a decisive spiritual metamorphosis into a utopian romanticism oriented toward the future, albeit fascinated by that "mystical Russia," the "dream of a Russia," to which Bloch refers.

After joining the Hungarian Communist party in mid-December 1918[11]—a decision that cannot be properly understood without his previous romantic anticapitalist stance, and his participation in the Hungarian Soviet Republic of 1919—this romantic dimension by no means disappeared from Lukács's thinking. During this period up to the publication of *History and Class Consciousness*, it is fused with Marxism in a highly original and intellectually subtle manner; the most accomplished product of this combination is his essay "The Old and the New Culture" (1919), which was published while Lukács was the Deputy People's Commissar for Education and Culture in the Hungarian Revolutionary Government. This writing confronts the organic *Kultur* of Greece and the Renaissance (which seems to have replaced the former Giotto/Dante configuration), when life and production were dominated by the *künstlerische Geist* (artistic spirit), with the total mercantilization of art and culture by capitalism. The process of revolutionizing production by means of capital requires the manufacturing of so-called novelties through a rapid transformation of the form or quantity of the product, a process that has no relation to aesthetic or use values. What we have is the tyrannical domination of fashion. (One can find similar insights in certain writings of Walter Benjamin dealing with "fashion" and the "false novelty" of the commodity.) To be sure, fashion and culture are concepts that, according to their essence, exclude each other (*dem Wesen nach ausschliessende Begriffe*). With the general mercantilization of life, culture, in the authentic meaning of the word, begins to decline; in a word, capitalism is culture-destructive (*kulturzerstörend*). Lukács perceives socialist revolution as a cultural restoration: organic culture again becomes possible. In a typical romantic-revolutionary way, Lukács understands socialism as the reestablishment of the cultural continuity disrupted by the advance of capitalism; the utopian future (the "new culture") provides a bridge toward the precapitalist past (the "old culture") above the void of the capitalist present ("nonculture").[12]

A few years later, in *History and Class Consciousness* (1923), Lukács seems to have distanced himself from this romantic anticapitalism; he now asserts that after Rousseau, the concept of "organic growth" took on an increasingly "reactionary accent," as a battle cry against reification, from German romanticism to the historical school of law, to Carlyle, Ruskin, and others. At the same time, however, he recognizes and appreciates that authors like Carlyle understood and described well before Marx the "anti-human (*widermenschliches*) essence of capitalism, its destruction and oppression of everything that is human." Still, a trace of romantic nostalgia sometimes appears in this work; for example, Lukács at one point compares the capitalist submission of all forms of life to mechanization and rational calculation with the organic life process of a *Gemeinschaft* such as that to be found in the traditional village. As a matter of fact, the main theme of the book, the critical analysis of reification (*Verdinglichung*) in all of its forms—economic, juridical, bureaucratic, cultural—is to a large extent inspired by German neoromantic sociology: Toennies, Weber, and Simmel. Of course, Lukács reformulates the sociological motives in the framework of a Marxist critique of capitalist reification. In other instances, he proceeds the other way around: starting from certain passages from *Das Kapital*, he develops a very insightful criticism of the mechanization of labor and the quantification of time, whose affinities with romanticism are undeniable. For the neo-Kantian critics of Lukács, like Coletti, this kind of analysis proves that the Hungarian philosopher replaced Marxism with Bergsonian romanticism. On the contrary, one could argue that it was possible for Lukács to present this line of argumentation precisely because there is a romantic anticapitalist aspect in Marx himself; looking at it this way, it could be asserted that the "young Lukács" was trying to recover the lost romantic dimension of Marxism.[13]

Lukács's literary writings of the early 1920s contain some highly significant references to romantic anticapitalist writers in general, and in particular to the author who, in his view, represents the most radical utopian rejection of bourgeois Western civilization, Dostoevsky. In the 1922 article "Stavrogin's Confession" published in the *Rote Fahne* (the daily of the German Communist party), Lukács celebrates Dostoevsky because he represented a utopian world, a world in which all was abolished that characterized capitalist society in its mechanical, inhuman, soulless, and reified aspects. And in another article of 1923, it is possible to hear an echo from the last chapter of *The Theory of the Novel*, where it is stated that Dostoevsky is the forerunner of that human being in a future society who has already been liberated "socially and economically" and is able "to fully live his inner life."[14]

Only toward the end of the 1920s did Lukács's thought become openly hostile to romanticism—a change that did not take place without contradictions and sudden turnabouts, as his writings of the following few years show. This new position is probably linked with his "forced reconciliation" with Stalinism, which had its starting point more or less at the same time. We are talking here of the Stalinist Five-Year-Plan (1928–33), which claimed industrialization the alpha and omega of "building socialism" and certainly had no room for romantic nostalgia. Recollecting his way of thinking as a militant Communist in 1930, Arthur Koestler writes in his autobiography, "When I have said that I fell in love with the Five Year Plan, this was hardly an exaggeration. . . . Marxist theory and Soviet practice were the admirable and ultimate fulfillment of the nineteenth century's ideal of Progress, to which I owed allegiance. The greatest powerdam of the world must surely bring the greatest happiness to the greatest number."[15]

But the relation between Stalinist dogma and Lukács's attitude toward romanticism is more complex; we shall see that ten years later he again becomes sympathetic to romantic anticapitalist writers. One could also try to establish a link between his cultural views and the upsurge of Nazism that he perceived—along with many others—as the logical outcome of the romantic reactionary tradition in German culture. But then again, the parallel is far from obvious and cannot explain his astonishingly different interpretations of Dostoevsky in 1931, 1943, and 1957.

II

One has the impression that for many decades Lukács's soul was torn between two tendencies: the dominant one is the classical *Aufklärung*, the democratic-liberal and rationalist ideology of "progress" (which, by the way, he tries to reconcile with the harsh realities of the Soviet state), but the other, the romantic anticapitalist temptation, emerges time and again at some unexpected moments.

The term "romantic anticapitalism" appears for the first time in an article on Dostoevsky in 1931; here, Lukács categorically throws the great Russian writer who inspired his own romantic-revolutionary youthful ideals into the dustbin of "reactionary literature." According to this essay, written in Moscow, Dostoevsky's influence has mainly to do with his capacity to transform the problems of the romantic opposition to capitalism into the "inner," spiritual problems, thereby helping a large segment of the petty bourgeois intelligentsia to "deepen" their Weltanschauung into religious pseudo-revolutionarism (*religiöselnde Salonrevoluzzerei*)—a concept that today would presumably include his own as well as Ernst Bloch's early writings, at least those up to 1919. In his youthful writings Lukács always linked Tolstoy and Dostoevsky (stressing, however, the latter's superiority); in this essay he now hails Tolstoy as the representative of the "classic tradition of the rising, revolutionary bourgeois class" (a strange definition for a writer who despised urban luxury and admired the way of life of the poor peasantry) as against Dostoevsky, whose writings express "the romantic undercurrents of the petty bourgeoisie." At his worst, Dostoevsky is nothing but "the writer of the 'Hundred Blacks' and czarist imperialism" (sic); at his best, he is the poet of a "section of the romantic-anticapitalist petty bourgeois intellectual opposition," a social segment that oscillates between Right and Left, but for whom "a wide avenue opens to the Right, to reaction (today: to fascism) and only a narrow and difficult path to the Left, to revolution." The conclusion of this fascinating piece of dogmatic frenzy is that with the inevitable decline of the petty bourgeoisie, "Dostoevsky's fame (*Ruhm*) will ingloriously (*ruhmlos*) vanish."[16]

With this article begins a pattern of analysis that can be found in most of Lukács's references to romantic anticapitalism: on the one hand, the recognition of the contradictory character of the phenomenon, and on the other, the tendency (at times utterly one-sided) to consider its reactionary, and even Fascist, predisposition as the dominant one. Little wonder that this essay on Dostoevsky roused the anger of his one-time friend of the romantic-revolutionary times, Ernst Bloch; it contributed to the cooling off of their relationship.[17]

In the framework of this paper it is impossible to examine all the milestones in Lukács's movement toward romantic anticapitalism, which turned out to be a tortuous, strange, and opaque process. I will, therefore, limit myself to mentioning only those examples that I consider most significant and illuminating.

In an essay published a few months after the Dostoevsky piece, Lukács again refers to the existence of a direct link between German fascism and the "theoretical arsenal of romantic anticapitalism." But at least he makes here the distinction between the "subjective honesty still present in Sismondi and the young Carlyle" and the manipulations of Fascist propaganda.[18] Lukács cannot ignore the fact that his own evolution toward Marxism and revolution has its roots in romantic anticapitalist culture. Instead of thus qualifying his analysis, this very fact makes him practice some harsh self-criticism in an essay on the cultural origins of fascism, written in Moscow in 1933. According to this manuscript, *History and Class Consciousness* is a "dangerous book" that contains some weighty concessions to the idealistic bourgeois worldview. After insisting on the continuity between this German idealist culture and fascism, Lukács adds, "As a follower of Simmel and Dilthey, as a friend of Max Weber and Emil Lask, as an enthusiastic reader of Rilke and Stefan George, I lived through myself all the evolutionary process described here. . . . I had to witness the fact that several of my early friends, sincere and convinced romantic anticapitalists all, were carried away by the tempest of fascism."[19] Lukács refuses to discuss the decisive link between the romantic anticapitalist vision and his own path to the cause of revolution as well as that of many German intellectuals of the same romantic background (particularly those of Jewish origin), such as Ernst Bloch, Ernst Toller, Gustav Landauer, and Walter Benjamin.

This manuscript of 1933—a kind of first draft to the book *The Destruction of Reason*—tries to accomplish a more general and systematic analysis of the renaissance of romantic anticapitalism starting with the end of the nineteenth century. Although he classifies as "romantic reactionaries" (or even as fore-runners of fascism) all the various currents of cultural criticism against capi-talist society, Lukács makes an important distinction between two periods of neoromanticism: (1) the period before 1914 with its affinity for the *Frühromantik*, in which there still exists the possibility of ambiguity, permit-ting a "leftist" interpretation (this period is represented by Nietzsche, Toennies, Simmel, Max Weber, the *Lebensphilosophie*, Ricarda Huch); (2) the post–World War I period, which claims allegiance to *Spätromantik* and is openly reactionary, if not Fascist (Heidegger, Ernst Jünger, Spengler, Alfred Bäumler, Freyer, Rosenberg). The evolution from the first stage to the second takes the form of a growing tendency toward irrationalism and myth.[20] This hypothesis is interesting but hardly sufficient for explaining the post–World War I evolution of such leftist thinkers as Herbert Marcuse, Erich Fromm, and many others whose links to the neoromantic culture are well established.

Lukács is particularly interested in the case of Nietzsche. He writes an arti-cle in 1934 about "Nietzsche as the Forerunner of Fascist Aesthetics," pres-enting the author of *Thus Spoke Zarathustra* as a follower of the tradition of anticapitalist romantic criticism. Like other writers of this school, Nietzsche is said to "oppose each and every time the manifestations of the nonculture (*Kulturlosigkeit*) of the present." Like all the romantic critics of human deg-radation by capitalism, Nietzsche struggles against fetishized modern civiliza-tion by holding up against it "the culture of more primitive economic and social stages," states Lukács. He does not seem to be aware of the fact that this kind of cultural criticism—which effectively puts Nietzsche into a retro-gressive mold—may also, in another context, take a revolutionary form; for instance, in his own article of 1919, "The Old and the New Culture." His only concession toward Nietzsche is to grant him sincere intentions that were subsequently degraded by the Nazi manipulators of his ideas: "Fascism has to abolish all that is progressive in the bourgeois heritage; in the case of Nietzsche, it must falsify or negate all the moments that show in him the exis-tence of a subjectively sincere romantic critique of the capitalist culture."[21]

A similar approach is taken by Lukács toward expressionism. In his well-known essay "The Grandeur and Decadence of Expressionism" (1934), he relates this artistic movement to romantic anticapitalism and draws a parallel with Simmel's *Philosophy of Money*. Utterly disregarding the revolutionary dimension of expressionism, Lukács sees it only as "one of the diverse bour-geois ideological currents that would later result in fascism; its ideological role in paving the way was neither greater nor smaller than that played by various other currents of the time."[22] Three years later, the Nazis organized the infamous exhibition of "degenerate art," which contained works by nearly every well-known expressionist painter. In a note added to the article in 1953, Lukács remained quite unperturbed by this fact: "The Fact that the National Socialists later rejected expressionism as a form of 'degenerate art' in no way affects the historical truth of the analysis set out below.''[23]

This position led Lukács to a polemical confrontation with his former friend and alter ego, Ernst Bloch. In 1935, Lukács wrote a critical review of Bloch's *Heritage of Our Time*; in his review he argues that since Bloch uncritically rallies to the defense of romantic anticapitalist ideology, his conception of Marxism is "fundamentally wrong." Curiously enough—although quite insightfully—he compares Bloch with "the social-democrat Herbert Marcuse," as he calls him, who tries to oppose the "authentic" *Lebensphilosophie* (of Dilthey and Nietzsche) to the false one of the Fascists.[24] In his debate with Bloch of 1938 (as well as in other writings) Lukács distinguishes between the sincere "subjective intentions" of certain expressionist artists and the "objective" (reactionary) content of their work. One of the examples he mentions as illustrating this contradiction happens to be his own youthful writing: whatever the intentions, he states, "*The Theory of the Novel* was a completely reactionary work," full of idealistic mysticism. He regards in retrospect even his *History and Class Consciousness* as a "reactionary" work on account of "its idealism."[25] In this essay, entitled "Es geht um den Realismus" (1938), Lukács develops an argument that is perhaps the basic historicophilosophical premise of his one-sided approach to romantic anticapitalism: he refers to the danger of "demagogic poisoning" of popular culture as a result of the decomposition of previous forms of everyday life in capitalism, a process that may "in itself be progressive in economic terms." This belief in the essentially progressive and beneficial nature of capitalist development prevented him from grasping the subversive and potentially revolutionary dimensions of criticism that looks back with nostalgia to past forms of social life or cultural values.

It seems therefore that following the Dostoevsky article of 1931, Lukács employs a dogmatic analytic pattern that emphasizes almost exclusively the reactionary aspect (which certainly existed) and the pre-Fascist disposition of the romantic anticapitalist culture. A few years later, however, in some of the essays of the Moscow period written between 1939 and 1941, there emerges a surprisingly favorable assessment of certain romantically inclined critics of capitalism (for example, Balzac and Carlyle). Arguing with some Soviet literary critics who celebrated the "progressive bourgeois" tradition and denigrated Balzac's reactionary ideas, Lukács opts for rejecting what he now considers to be "liberal-bourgeois mystification," that is, "the mythology of a struggle between 'Reason' and 'Reaction,' or as another variant, the myth of the fight of the enlightened angel of bourgeois progress . . . against the black devil of capitalism." In Lukács's opinion, the insight of a Balzac or Carlyle into the nature of capitalism—especially into its culture-destroying character—cannot be mechanically separated from the totality of their worldview (their conservative ideology included) according to the good old Proudhonian method of disassociating the "good" and the "bad" side of economic and social facts. In the works of these writers, the clear-sighted criticism of capitalism is intimately linked to their idealization of the Middle Ages: Balzac's art is so penetrating precisely because of his romantic anticapitalism and not in spite of it.[26]

The article Lukács wrote on Dostoevsky in 1943 is even more impressive. In it, he not only thoroughly revised his former outrageously negative assessment of the writer but also displays an astonishing degree of understanding of the revolutionary possibilities inherent in romantic anticapitalism— notwithstanding the fact that the term itself never appears in the article. According to Lukács, Dostoevsky's works express the "rebellion against the moral and spiritual deformation of the human being as the result of capitalist development"; they are also a powerful "protest against all that is false and distorted in modern bourgeois society." Against the backdrop of this inhuman world, Dostoevsky dreams of a Golden Age long past, represented symbolically by archaic Greece as imagined by the painter Claude Lorrain in his picture *Acis and Galatea*. The spontaneous and savage revolt of Dostoevsky's characters has in each case an unconscious relation to such a Golden Age. As for Lukács, "this revolt is the poetic and historically progressive grandeur of Dostoevsky; here a light truly has shone forth from the darkness of the misery of St. Petersburg; a light that illuminates the road for the future of humanity."[27] One could hardly imagine a more striking formula to capture the romantic-revolutionary Weltanschauung than Lukács's image of the Golden Age of the past that illuminates the path to a utopian future. It is also obvious that he made this formula his own in this 1943 writing.

The question is, however, for how long? In a preface to a volume of essays on Russian realist writers, dated February 1946, Lukács still hails Dostoevsky as a progressive figure; he also inverts the pattern of explanation that he used in the 1930s: while recognizing the reactionary and mystical elements in Tolstoy's and Dostoevsky's subjective intentions (*subjektive Meinungen*), Lukács insists that the really important aspect is their objective and historical meaning. Lukács states,

> The important moment is the human and artistic link of the writer with a great progressive popular movement. . . . Tolstoy's roots lie in the peasantry, Dostoevsky's in the suffering plebeian segments of the cities, and Gorky's in the proletariat and the poorest segment of the peasantry. But all three of them are rooted with their deepest soul in this movement that was both searching and fighting for the liberation of the people.[28]

During the first years following the end of World War II, the previous antiromantic attitude again becomes dominant. It is easy to follow the development of this trend by comparing the different interpretations offered by Lukács to explain the enigmatic and provocative fictional figure of Leo Naphta, the Jewish-Jesuit-Communist-obscurantist-conservative-revolution-character of Thomas Mann's novel *The Magic Mountain*. In 1942, he brands Naphta's ideology as "reactionary demagogy" and admits at the same time that Mann used this character to bring out "the seductive (spiritually and morally) character of romantic anticapitalism" and "the correctness of certain elements of its critique of present-day social life."[29] Only a few years later, Lukács calls the "Jesuit Naphta" the "spokesman of the reactionary, fascist and anti-democratic *Weltanschauung*." His analysis this time resembles a sophisticated version of that very "mythical struggle" between the "enlightened angel of bourgeois progress" and "the black devil of capitalism" to which he ironically referred in his 1941 article. The central motif of *The Magic Mountain* is defined as the "ideological struggle between life and death, health and sickness, reaction and democracy" in the intellectual duel between the Italian humanist and democrat Settembrini and the Jewish pupil of the Jesuits, Leo Naphta, this "spokesman of a Catholicizing pre-Fascist ideology."[30] Such a one-sided and crude simplification cannot even begin to do justice to the fascinating ambivalence of the Naphta figure; it reduces Naphta's complex and paradoxical romantic anticapitalist, religious-revolutionary ideology to the conservative and obscurantist dimension that undeniably is part of Naphta's ideological baggage.

This narrow and impoverished approach to the romantic culture leaves its imprint on subsequent publications of Lukács; its best-known expression is *The Destruction of Reason* (1954), which presents the whole history of German thought from Schelling to Toennies, from Dilthey to Simmel, and from Nietzsche to Max Weber as one vast assault of "Reaction" on "Reason" and all romantic currents "from the Historical School of Law until Carlyle" as a development leading inevitably to a "general irrationalization of history" and consequently, in the last analysis, to the emergence of Fascist ideology. Critics in general consider this book simply a Stalinist pamphlet. The matter is not quite so simple: the leitmotiv of the book is not a confrontation—in the manner of Zhdanov and his followers—between "proletarian" science (or philosophy) and "bourgeois" science but only between "reason" and "irrationality." Its main limitation is, in my opinion, that it ignores what the Frankfurt School called "the dialectic of Enlightenment," that is, the transformation of reason into an instrument in the service of a myth, of oppression and alienation. Paradoxically, the concept of romantic anticapitalism hardly appears in the book. The romantics and their followers are simply treated as reactionaries and irrationalists. One of the few authors who is explicitly referred to as a "romantic anticapitalist" is Ferdinand Toennies, who appears in a relatively favorable light:

> Admittedly, if we compare Toennies with the older Romantic anti-capitalists, we will notice the particular and subsequently important nuance that he was not voicing a desire to revert to social conditions now surmounted, and certainly not to feudalism. His position provided the basis for a cultural critique which strongly emphasized the problematic, negative features of capitalist culture, but which also underlined that capitalism was ineluctable and a product of fate.[31]

In Lukács's view, however, the antithesis of *Gemeinschaft* and *Gesellschaft*, which is the central theme of Toennies's sociological work, is but a distortion "in a romantically anticapitalist, subjectively irrational way" of the "case-facts of capitalist development ascertained by Marx."[32]

At each and every stage of Lukács's intellectual evolution, the nature of the special relationship to Dostoevsky is symptomatic of his general attitude toward romantic anticapitalism. In the late 1940s, anathema clearly dominates his treatment of Dostoevsky and is still echoed in the following passage of one of his worst pieces of writing, *The Meaning of Contemporary Realism* (1957): while giving credit to the critical force of the Russian writer, for making his characters suffer the "characteristic inhumanity prevailing at the early stages of capitalism which leaves its imprint directly on interhuman relations," Lukács sees the essential point lying somewhere else: Dostoevsky's protestation "against an inhuman capitalism transforms itself right away into a critique of socialism and of democracy, based on an assimilating-sophistry and an anticapitalism of the romantic kind." The evolution started by Dostoevsky will be systemized by Nietzsche and will lead in the last analysis to fascism: "This refusal of progress and democracy developed progressively until it resulted in the social demogogery of Hitlerism."[33] This kind of abstract reasoning becomes absurd as it establishes a sort of irreversible and compelling ideological continuity from Dostoevsky to Hitler; needless to say, it is also unable to explain the decisive and in-depth influence of the Russian writer on so many revolutionary intellectuals—the young Lukács included.

During the following years we hear nothing further on this topic. In his great writings of the 1960s, the *Aesthetics* and the *Ontology*, the question of romantic anticapitalism is not raised, and all the references to romantic culture are of a neutral nature.

In the last five years of his life (1966–71), Lukács presents a more balanced and more open approach to romantic anticapitalism, and his discussion takes place almost always in the framework of his recollections of his early work. In the 1967 preface to his republished *History and Class Consciousness*, he acknowledges, for example, that "ethical idealism with all its romantic anticapitalist elements" brought him something "positive," and that these elements were integrated into his new (Marxist) worldview, albeit with "multiple and deep modifications."[34] And in an interview given to Wolfgang Abendroth in 1966, Lukács admitted that "today, I do not regret that I took my first lessons in social science from Simmel and Max Weber and not from Kautsky. . . . [This] was a favorable circumstance for my own development.''[35]

As was the case before, Lukács's attitude toward Dostoevsky is characteristic of his general approach. In the preface to the Hungarian edition of his collected essays, entitled *Utam Marxhoz* (*My Road to Marx*), published in 1969, Lukács mentions his youthful romantic anticapitalist rebellion, which was directed against the basic foundations of the established system and was to a large degree ''inspired by Dostoevsky.''[36] In another preface of the same year for the essay volume *Hungarian Literature, Hungarian Culture*, his recollection of his attitude in 1917 again includes this reference to Dostoevsky:

> I integrated into my universe the great Russian authors, first and foremost Dostoevsky and Tolstoy, as decisive revolutionary factors. . . . It was at this moment of my development that French anarchosyndicalism influenced me considerably. But I never could accommodate myself to the social democratic ideology of the time, and particularly not to Kautsky.[37]

III

All these autobiographical remarks provide ample and illuminating examples of the degree to which during the years of his intellectual and political *Bildung* (education and development) he was inspired by various forms of romantic anticapitalism, ranging from German sociology to Russian literature, and how he used it in his fight against the liberal-rationalist or positivist-utilitarian ideologies that were dominant at that time, including their social democratic version. The same spirit then led him to support those radical and revolutionary movements that contested the power of the bourgeois order: first, it was anarchosyndicalism, followed by Bolshevism.

From the late 1920s up to the mid 1960s, however, a curious ideological blindness took hold of Lukács; during this time, he seems to have perceived in the diverse manifestations of romantic anticapitalism solely their reactionary, irrationalist or pre-Fascist aspects—with the exception of a short period during World War II. How can one explain these astonishing variations in Lukács's approach? How do they—if at all—correspond to internal movements in Lukács's intellectual development? Are they linked—and in what way—to actual historical events and processes such as the ascension of fascism or the use of ''romantic'' notions by Nazi ideologues? And finally, do they represent an obeisance to various turns of the Comintern (and Soviet) political line?

As for myself, I am unable to find simple and sufficient answers to these questions. In any case, this tormented and contradictory path is a mystery to which I have not as yet found the key; it reveals Lukács to us as continuously oscillating in his positions just like Hans Castorp, the hero of Lukács's favorite novel, *The Magic Mountain*, who is torn between two opposing forces: a "liberal Settembrini" and a "revolutionary Naphta." It was denied to Lukács to be able to overcome the antinomies of his own Weltanschauung by means of a dialectical synthesis, the *Aufhebung* of the contradiction between romanticism and Enlightenment.

Notes

1. See Robert Sayre and Michael Löwy, "Figures of Romantic Anticapitalism," *New German Critique* 32(Spring-Summer 1984).
2. Thomas Mann, *The Magic Mountain* (London: Harmondsworth, 1977), p. 694.
3. For a discussion of this aspect, see my book *Georg Lukács—From Romanticism to Bolshevism* (London: NLB, 1979), pp. 56–66. See further Judith Marcus, *Georg Lukács and Thomas Mann: A Study in the Sociology of Literature* (Amherst: University of Massachusetts, 1987).
4. Thomas Mann, *Journal 1918–1921* (Paris: Gallimard, 1985), pp. 88, 89, 106, 108, and 121. Mann writes, "Landauer's book did bring many things, indeed, with which I can sympathize. . . . I was thinking of the possibility of including in my book *Der Zauberberg* some Russian-chiliastic-communist elements" (my translation). For a thorough discussion of these elements in Mann's book, see Marcus, *Georg Lukács*, especially the chapter on Naphta.
5. This document is to be found at the Georg Lukács Archiv of the Hungarian Academy of Sciences, Budapest.
6. See Micheal Löwy, "Interview with Ernst Bloch," *New German Critique* 9(1976):44.
7. See Georg Lukács, "W. Solovjeff: *Ausgewählte Werke*, Band II. (Jena 1916)," *Archiv für Sozialwissenschaft und Sozialpolitik* 42(1916–17):978.
8. See Georg Lukács, *Soul and Form*, trans. Anna Bostock (Cambridge, MA: MIT, 1974), p. 50.
9. Georg Lukács, *The Theory of the Novel*, trans. Anna Bostock (Cambridge, MA: MIT, 1971). The hidden religious/revolutionary presuppositions of this book can be found in the contemporary *Dostoevski Notizen und Entwürfe*, ed. J. C. Nyiri (Budapest: Akadémiai Kiadó, 1985), where Russian literature, mysticism, Jewish messianism, Kierkegaard, Nietzsche, and Sorel are integrated into a romantic and apocalyptic philosophy of history.
10. See Lukács, *Theory of the Novel*, p. 169.
11. For an account of Lukács's "conversion," see Judith Marcus Tar, note to the translation of "Georg Lukács: Bolshevism as a Moral Problem," *Social Research* 44, 3(Autumn 1977):416ff.
12. See Georg Lukács, "Alte Kultur und neue Kultur," in *Taktik und Ethik* (Neuwied and Berlin: Luchterhand, 1975), pp. 136–45.
13. See Georg Lukács, *History and Class Consciousness: Studies in Marxist Dialectics*, trans. Rodney Livingstone (Cambridge, MA: MIT, 1971). See also L. Colletti, *Marxism and Hegel* (London: NLB, 1979), pp. 179, 186.
14. G. Lukács, *Litterature, philosophie, marxisme 1922–23*, ed. Michael Löwy (Paris: Presses Universitaires de France, 1978), pp. 76 and 110.
15. See Arthur Koestler, *Arrow in the Blue: An Autobiography* (London: Collins, 1952), p. 245.

16. See Georg Lukács, "Über den Dostojewski-Nachlass," *Moskauer Rundschau* (March 22, 1931). Lukács here compares Dostoevsky's path from revolutionary conspiration to orthodox religiosity and czarism with the evolution of Friedrich Schlegel, the romantic Republican who then rallied to Metternich and the Catholic church.

17. See Michael Löwy, "Interview with Ernst Bloch," *New German Critique* 9(1976):38–39. Bloch reported saying to Lukács, "My dear friend, my mentor is Dostoevsky and Kierkegaard. . . . What happened to you that you now can write such a sentence as this about Dostoevsky?"

18. See Georg Lukács, "Über das Schlagwort Liberalismus und Marxismus," *Der Rote Aufbau* 21(1931).

19. Lukács, *Wie ist die faschistische Philosophie in Deutschland entstanden?* (Budapest: Akadémiai Kiadó, 1982), p. 57.

20. Ibid., pp. 131–32.

21. Georg Lukács, "Nietzsche als Vorläufer der faschistischen Ästhetik" (1934), in Mehring/Lukács, *Friedrich Nietzsche* (Berlin: Aufbau, 1957), pp. 41 and 53.

22. Georg Lukács, "Grösse und Verfall des Expressionismus" (1934), in *Essays über Realismus* (Neuwied and Berlin: Luchterhand, 1971), p. 120.

23. Ibid., p. 149.

24. Reference is to Herbert Marcuse's essay "Der Kampf gegen den Liberalismus in der totalitären Staatsauffassung," *Zeitschrift für Sozialforschung* 3, 1(1934). Lukács's review has until now remained unpublished. There exists an Italian translation in G. Lukács, *Intellettuali et Irrazianismo* (a cura di Vottoria Franco) (Pisa: ETS, 1984), pp. 287–308.

25. Georg Lukács, "Es geht um den Realismus," in *Essays über Realismus*.

26. Georg Lukács, *Escrits de Moscou* (Paris: Editions Sociales, 1970), pp. 149–50, 159, 167, 235, 243, and 257.

27. Georg Lukács, "Dostojewskij," in *Russische Revolution, Russische Literatur* (Rowohlt, 1969), pp. 148–49. In former references to this article I was mistaken in dating it as having been published in 1936.

28. Georg Lukács, "Vorwort," *Der russische Realismus in der Weltliteratur* (Neuwied and Berlin: Luchterhand, 1964), pp. 11–12.

29. Georg Lukács, "Die verbannte Poesie," in *Internationale Literatur* 4(1942).

30. Georg Lukács, *Essays on Thomas Mann*, trans. Stanley Mitchell (London: Merlin, 1964), pp. 33–35.

31. Georg Lukács, *The Destruction of Reason*, trans. Peter Palmer (London: Merlin, 1980), p. 554.

32. Ibid., p. 595.

33. See Georg Lukács, *Wider den missverstandenen Realismus* (Hamburg: Claasen, 1958), esp. ch. 2 and the essay "Franz Kafka oder Thomas Mann?"

34. Lukács, "Vorwort" (1967), in *Geschichte und Klassenbewusstsein* (Neuwied and Berlin: Luchterhand, 1968), pp. 12–13.

35. Theo Pinkus, ed., *Conversations with Lukács* (Cambridge, MA: MIT, 1975), p. 100.

36. Georg Lukács, "Mon chemin vers Marx," *Nouvelles Etudes Hongroises* (Budapest) 8(1973):80 and 82.

37. Georg Lukács, "Litterature Hongroise, Culture Hongroise," *L'Homme et la Société* 43–44(1977):13–14.

APPENDIX

A Conversation with Georg Lukács

By Franco Ferrarotti

Georg Lukács died on June 4, 1971. I am publishing here the essential passages of a discussion I had with him at my request. The meeting took place on Thursday, November 19, 1970, in Lukács's apartment in Budapest, and lasted from 10 A.M. to about 1 P.M. The conversation was conducted in French, with occasional use of German.

From notes taken that day: the building is by the Danube and overlooks the monument to Liberty that stands on the hill opposite, on the other side of the river. Lukács lives at number 2, on the fifth floor. On the door, simply the name "Lukács György." In the telephone directory, on the other hand, there follows the description "academicus." He himself opens the door; small, thin, with wonderful eyes, the mouth a little fallen in, twisted. He is smoking a huge cigar; from time to time he is racked by a cough, gobs of phlegm seem about to come out of his mouth, the house trembles. But after this brief storm he recomposes himself; nothing has happened; he continues the discussion. I ring the bell exactly at ten; we enter a little dark hallway; I hang up my overcoat; a housekeeper of about 50 helps me with gestures. I go into the study with Lukács, carrying the camera and tape recorder with me.

F.F. My interest is in sociology.
G.L. I too was interested in sociology, for years. I studied with Max Weber, and have good memories of those years. But in general sociology is boring.
F.F. For years my interest has lain in sociology; I have never wanted a university post save as a sociologist, a researcher or professor of sociology. When I began, in the immediate postwar period, sociology in Italy was dead, extinguished, suppressed. . . .

207

G.L.   I have often asked myself about the function and nature of sociology as a science. Can there really be a sociology as an autonomous science? What meaning would such autonomy have? Certainly, there is currently talk of an interdisciplinary approach. But I ask myself if that is enough. I have the impression that behind the need for interdisciplinary study there is hidden a great conceptual confusion.

F.F.   From the earliest years, when I had begun the battle for the rebirth of sociology in Italy, it seemed clear to me that a truly critical sociology, that is, one scientifically based and politically oriented at the same time, could only be realized by simultaneously leaving behind both neo-idealism, as we knew it in Italy in its Crocean version, and fragmentary empiricism, which through a long tradition was triumphant in the United States.

G.L.   It is not only a question of this. I have often asked myself what relation there is between sociology, philosophy, economics, and history. This relationship is important, and must at any event be kept alive. If the sense of this relation is lost and one limits oneself to speaking of an interdisciplinary approach in sociological research, I believe one cannot avoid falling into a position of fragmentary technicism. In this regard I think the influence of the United States has not been very positive.

F.F.   I have never believed in a purely technical sociology, one reduced, that is, to pure technique, as practiced in the United States. Nor yet, however, do I believe in mere combinations like the formula ''Marxist sociology,'' which seem to me simplistic. . . . Perhaps one should found a critical sociology.

G.L.   Agreed. But one must understand why American sociology is not enough, why it accepts being reduced, and in fact reduces itself, to pure technique. It is true that American sociology understands nothing, or almost nothing, of the general movement of society. . . . This occurs because American sociology has cut its link with economics. How can one understand a society without taking its economic structure into consideration? Sociology cannot be an independent science. It is not possible to study society in little bits. Marx's method, which Stalin simply inverted, lies in the analysis of the whole of society, its style, its movement, its rhythm of development. It is necessary to understand how the fragmentation of the social sciences was possible. Perhaps one should try to recompose them unitarily. Here, there is a precise bourgeois tradition that it is possible to identify historically beyond any reasonable doubt. I believe this bourgeois tradition lies in taking the specialization of the sciences to the point of transforming it into separation. The separate sciences are no longer capable of understanding society as a unitary whole; they become instruments of mystification.

F.F.   I have two problems in this respect. One is theoretical; the analytical approach, the careful and well-defined outlining of the objects of study, are basic methodological requirements, and respond to real heuristic demands. A second problem concerns the possibility—or impossibility—of recovering the results of many sociological studies carried out in past decades. Must we throw everything away, or are some results, however partial and incomplete, salvageable; that is, can they be used, if only in a radically different perspective?

G.L.   Let me reply first to the second problem. I believe that some results of current, or academic, sociology, especially as it is practiced in the United States, can be saved; they are gains, that is, contributions of information that are important. For example, some of the studies reported in Galbraith's books seem to me interesting. Naturally this involves specialist studies, without a comprehensive theoretical framework, without, that is, a general theory of society. They are, thus, studies that never reach the heart of problems but stop halfway, dealing with society as though it were a chance mass of disconnected facts. However, though incomplete, these results of bourgeois sociology are available for critical use. I believe, indeed, that one must use critically partial contributions, including those of people like Galbraith. To the extent to which they describe actual situations, internal developments of capitalism, they are important. Capitalism has changed; it changes, one might say, day by day, even though its fundamental character remains unchanged. As Marx used the classical economists, especially Ricardo, so one must learn to use, from a Marxist point of view, the contributions of bourgeois sociology.

F.F. But bourgeois, or academic, or vulgar sociology, so to speak, is not without its overall theoretical framework, even if it is implicit. . . .

G.L. No. Bourgeois sociology does not have a theoretical framework in a real sense, does not manage to overcome the givenness of the specific datum, does not avoid vulgar empiricism. For this basic reason, bourgeois sociology has no cognitive value in the real sense. But there are in it particular analyses that can be taken up critically and used. These analyses are partial contributions of information and knowledge, but essentially well-grounded ones.

F.F. This seems contradictory to me.

G.L. It is not contradictory. For example, the character, nature, and manner of proceeding of capitalism today present new aspects. Bourgeois sociological analyses, although partial, indeed necessarily partial, at times document these aspects very well. Let us take a particular subject. In the last century, for the whole of the nineteenth century, the market, the capitalist forces, concerned all in all important but limited sectors of economic life and social life. In particular, the logic of capitalism was felt at work in the key sectors of industry; especially in the iron and steel industry, heavy industry, *schwere Industrie*. Today capitalism is quite different. Today it affects, involves, concerns much more closely, indeed, conditions all aspects of life. From the partial capitalism of the previous century we have moved on to generalized capitalism. In this sense, far from being exhausted, one might say that Marxism has not even begun. In any case, paradoxes aside, one must complete Marxism; one must study what Marx never studied through and through.

F.F. I don't understand. Earlier you said that Marx is still essential for the revolutionary movement because he is the only guide, the only theoretical framework the movement has. Now instead you say this framework must be completed; thus, this framework is not complete.

G.L. I mean something different. The framework is complete. Marxism as the need and arrangement of the global study of society, as interpretation of society in its globality, its totality in view of its structural and cultural—that is, historical—transformation, is truly complete. However, it is complete as method, that is, as a mode of analysis and a criterion for establishing the theoretical hierarchy of the constituent factors of society. The completeness of the method does not necessarily imply that in Marx one can find everything; that is, rather, all specific contents that only long, patient study, carried out on the basis of Marxist method so as to attack the global, historical meaning of social evolution, could bring to light. Here the Marxists have erred greatly, have taken the easy way, have confined themselves to repeating things they had not understood, or have made questions of tactics prevail over, and against, theory. For me it is clear that Marx never seriously studied the Asian, African, or Latin American economy. And yet, and yet. Just think: in his polemic with Trotsky, Stalin invented a Chinese feudalism. A genuine bestiality. The really astounding thing is that this invention should have been accepted by Mao.

F.F.   I agree regarding the nonsystematic character and the occasional gesture made by Marx and Engels toward non–Western European modes of production. However, the controversy surrounding the "Asiatic mode of production" has a whole history within Marxism, and insofar as it allows us to get rid of every hypostasis of necessary and rigidly sequential stages, unilinear in human evolution, it seems to me important.

G.L.   Yes, it is important. But the really urgent and important things to be done are different.

F.F.   In other words, you think that sociology should be schooled by Marx, should learn the lesson of Marxism well.

G.L.   The trouble is that today there are no Marxists. One must recognize that at this moment we have no Marxist theory. Believe me: today one has to do what Marx did for the capitalism of his day. However, we must do it both for today's capitalism and for socialism.

F.F.   For socialism?

G.L.   Yes, for socialism too. Socialism also needs continuous critical, demystifying analysis. And, notice, this must be done on a world scale. No one is doing this, no one thinks of it. Thus, what happens is simply grotesque. As the Marxists have no theory, they are condemned to run along behind present reality. For example, when so-called spontaneous movements occur, student movements, youth protests, and so on, then the Marxists run along behind these things and try to account for them post facto, rationalize their surprises. . . . It is ridiculous. It is the price one pays for the lack of a theory.

F.F.   But the youth movements, especially the student movement, both in the socialist countries and in the West, cannot simply be considered fleeting fashions. They are phenomena certainly treated superficially by the majority of sociologists, psychologists, psychiatrists, and pedagogues, who are concerned with them, one might say, more to read in them the confirmation of their own prejudices than to understand them; but they have structural roots in the struggle against the bureaucratization of social and personal life, they have a profound significance to be reflected upon.

G.L.   However, I absolutely do not mean to say that student movements and youth protest movements in general are without significance; I am saying that without a general theory of society—and Marxism is still today the only genuinely general theory of society we have—these movements cannot be interpreted correctly. Then, in these movements there spring forth especially, if not exclusively, the picturesque and strange aspects, which are misleading and not in any event essential. On the other hand, since the Marxists have not creatively extended Marxist theory in the analysis of contemporary social phenomena, they are thus shown to be forced to run along behind the present, what makes news, case by case, in a fragmentary—that is, wholly anti-Marxist—manner.

F.F.   The remark that Marxism has not been creatively extended to involve current problems seems to me very serious. It means that there has been an interruption in development. How? Since when?

G.L.   I have said that Marxism as a general theory of society has in fact suffered an interruption. It has stopped. One can say that Marxism understood (as it should be understood) as a general theory of society and history no longer exists, has been over for a while. For this reason, there exists, and will still exist for a long time, Stalinism. Much nonsense has been talked about Stalinism. However, in reality things are quite simple. Every time practice is placed before and even against theory, Stalinism is produced. Stalinism is not only a mistaken interpretation and a faulty application of Marxism. It is in reality its negation. There are no more theorists. There are only tacticians.

F.F.   What's that? And Suslov? And the official theorists in the Soviet Union?

G.L.   Official Marxism in the Soviet Union, or in the other socialist countries too, is very often a poor thing. Under the label of Diamat [dialectical materialism], mediocre professors think they can explain all the problems of the world through the mechanical application of some simplistic formula, repeated ad infinitum like a phrase from some catechism, which they smuggle in as Marxism. Fortunately, Marxism does not come into this at all. These paraphilosophical exercises respond to the practical needs of the didactic organisms, propaganda, etc., but have nothing in common with Marxism. We are still Stalinists.

F.F.   Then Stalinism does not signify the aberration of a tyrant, nor yet the institutional distortion and deviation of the Soviet regime, as determined by the moral deficiencies of a particular individual, however powerful?

G.L.   Stalinism cannot be understood by making use of the categories of moralism. As I have already said, we are still Stalinists in the sense that we do not know how to do for today's capitalism what Marx did for the capitalism of his time. We do not have, that is, a general theory of society and its movement. We have only tactics, and we use meaningless words.

F.F.   I can understand the tactical worries for those Marxists who have arrived at and won power. Does your criticism also apply to the Marxists of those countries, for instance those of the capitalist West, where the Communist parties are in opposition?

G.L.   I believe so. There are indeed political situations that greatly amaze me. Faced with them, I am perplexed. For example, the discrepancy between the great organizational strength of the Italian Communist party and its slight theoretical weight has always surprised me. There must be a reason, but I don't know it. There is no doubt that Togliatti was a politician of the first water, a great tactician, but perhaps his curiosity regarding theory was limited. . . . They tell me he had the habits of a good clerk.

F.F.   The Italian Marxist leaders have a precise cultural matrix: their education is generally humanistic in the traditional sense. Their Marxism has been filtered through the original Hegelian mediation of Antonio Labriola and then also through Benedetto Croce's neo-idealistic one. This involved a Marxism that did no fieldwork, and that also had relations with economics that were, all in all, weak: a Marxism more for pure politicians and literary men than for scientists. . . . Togliatti was moreover a great admirer of Croce and Giolitti. It may be that in all this there entered a good dose of calculation; that is, by accepting the line from Labriola, De Sanctis, Spaventa, to Croce, and for good or ill approving it, he hoped for a painless insertion of Marxism into the national cultural tradition. For operations of this kind it seems clear to me one does not want to refine a palate. Rather, one needs good tactical gifts.

G.L.   Precisely. But now we are left on our own with tactics. Objective conditions change and we do not know what to do. We follow behind the protests of the young and student movements without understanding them. We call the Arab countries socialist; without hesitation we identify as such organisms that call themselves, for example, the Arab socialist union. All this makes one laugh.

What is "socialist" in the Arab world? No one knows, and no one can know, perhaps because there is nothing socialist. At most one might talk of an attempt at national, and even nationalist, identification. But not of socialism. I have already said in addition that in Marx there is very little about the economy of the non-European regions of the world; no more than a few sentences . . . Africa, Asia, Latin America. One must study these countries and their economies in a Marxist perspective and with the method of Marx. Otherwise there are only abstractions, there is no serious analysis.

F.F   But is not the moment of abstraction perhaps the basic one for the construction of general theory?

G.L.   Certainly it is. I should be the last to deny the importance of the moment of abstraction in the name of a misunderstood materialism or misunderstood empirical need. What the positivists do not understand is precisely this: the facts must be interpreted; thereby they must be transcended. The process of abstraction is fundamental for the construction of general theory. And without general theory, the facts are and remain meaningless.

F.F.   Yes, agreed; but the problem at bottom is different. The problem concerns what it is that comes first. For me, the fundamental reason for the lack of empirical studies in a certain Marxism for literary people, or ideal-Marxism, is the deep-rooted conviction—wholly idealist—that the facts are important only as an accompaniment, that there is no transition from empiricism to the logicotheoretical schema, that the most important thing is the theoreticoconceptual apparatus that the individual scholar works out at his desk, for his own purposes on the basis of his own problematic awareness. . . .

G.L.   No, absolutely not. The problem as you pose it is badly put and becomes insoluble. That is, it becomes a false problem, an idle one. It is not a matter of establishing what comes first and what comes after. There is not a before and an after. To proceed in this manner involves a hypostasizing of the terms of the problem and an inevitable falling back into metaphysics. Thus, the problem becomes insoluble. I do not understand all this worrying about facts. Facts, being. . . . One can only say that the facts are indeed, a fact; that there is being, and so—all right. There is no need to establish hierarchies between being and consciousness, or problematic awareness, as you say. I am well aware you are now thinking of Marx's phrase that "being determines consciousness" and not vice versa. Yes, certainly, Marxism recognizes and indeed bases its own historical materialism on the priority of social being over consciousness, but it is a priority sui generis that should not be taken literally. . . . There is trouble if it is understood in the sense of a hierarchy between being and consciousness, still worse in the sense of a subjection of consciousness to being. At bottom, it is only thanks to consciousness that we have social being, that we can intervene in social being and transform it. Indeed, consciousness is the only instrument we have to dominate social being, to remove ourselves from its empirical weight.

F.F.   Thank you for these clarifications. Now I understand better how it is that neither you nor any of your disciples have ever undertaken any empirical research in the real sense. Even when you speak of the problems of everyday life and it seem you are starting a delimited social study, not with the results taken for granted beforehand, in reality you go on speaking *sub specie philosophica*, you never gain ground, you use facts if and to the extend to which they square with your general philosophical outlook. I understand too your hostility toward sociology, which seems to me not limited to the acritical and descriptive sociology of the American type, and seems to me to involve also sociology of the critical kind, politically oriented, based on well-defined and methodologically controlled empirical research, even if sustained and guided by a general theoretical framework. The primacy recognized in your concrete scientific work for consciousness necessarily leads you to undervalue empirical research into objective conditions. Furthermore, it leads you, equally necessarily, to psychologize social being—whose existence depends, according to you, on its being recognized as such by consciousness—and thence on to spiritualistic unreality, if not indeed to the mystical ravings of extreme subjectivism.

G.L.   I am wholly in disagreement with what you have said.

F.F.   I am not surprised. The fact is that the meaning of empirical research completely escapes you. For you, research only supports what is already known on the subjective conceptual level. Essentially, you deny that important novelties can spring forth from research, such as to compel the renewed discussion of the theoreticoconceptual scheme. Thus, the creative function of research escapes you.

G.L.   Not at all. I have no difficulty in recognizing the basic importance of well-grounded analysis against gratuitous, arbitrary abstractions. Is it not perhaps here that the scientific character of Marxism should be seen? Moreover, Marx himself considered his youthful writings as purely ideological, purely philosophical in the traditional sense. He himself considered his truly important work to be *Capital*, that is, the analysis of capitalist society in Europe in his epoch. However, a scientific analysis is not a positivistic one, which is the slave of facts, instead of interpreting them coherently. And naturally neither is it an idealist analysis.

F.F.   I do not at all deny the importance of theory: I am raising the problem of how to proceed to its construction. For me the datum of objectivity is the essential starting point. And it is in that too that I see the scientific, not utopian, character of Marxism.

G.L.   Certainly, Marxism is distinguished from the other bourgeois explanations of society because it is a scientific explanation, which avails itself of dialectical, not metaphysical, metaphysicalizing, concepts. Marx's critique of classical political economy, especially Smith's and Ricardo's, is an example of scientific criticism. Classical political economy was a static economics, essentially unable to take into account the movement of society. In Smith and in Ricardo, economic analysis is only a group of fixed concepts that refer to given realities, treated as natural data, nonmodifiable (the market, labor, the commodity, etc.). Marx takes up these realities in their specific historical determinateness and redefines them in dialectical terms and concepts capable of taking into account the historical movement, without eternalizing by reifying it, any particular phase. This restores his history to man, and in Marx history once more becomes culture, consciousness, the creation and responsibility of man, of social consciousness, which masters, grasps, and transforms social being. The scientific element in Marxism is provided by the use of dialectical, nondogmatic, or metaphysical concepts, and by its characteristic ability to take on, on the basis of its own general theory, the viewpoint of totality, as against the sectoral and partial approaches of bourgeois science, which is, of course, a pseudo-science. The only real science is based on totality. By this I repeat that there should be no hierarchy between being and consciousness, and that in any case practice has no meaning without theory.

F.F.   I agree as regards the use by Marx of dialectical concepts, but there seems to me no doubt that precisely in *Capital*, not to speak of the *Introduction to the Cri-*

tique of Political Economy, Marx's starting point is never indeterminate social being. Rather, it is the specific historically determined situation of the economic interests and motives connected with it. The economic, or structural, level is decisive, I believe, for the Marxist explanation of society.

G.L. However, as you say, the economic level must never be isolated from all the rest. By themselves, economic motives do not explain anything. One must always be careful of the risk of mechanically interpreting Marxism. The positivistic interpretation of Marxism is the premise, political and philosophical, of opportunism and also of Stalinism.

F.F. On the other hand, does not putting everything on the same level in the name of totality expose one possibly to the risk of constructing an empty totality? That is, of falling into the trap of idealistic mystification?

G.L. Yes. This is a real risk. However, it is useless to hope to get out of it by counterposing structure to superstructure, *Unterbau* to *Überbau*. This is still a precritical mode of thought, undialectical. Basically one could also say that it is simply still a prescientific mode of thinking, at least in the sense that it makes a myth of the separateness of moments that are essentially aspects of a unitary process.

F.F. I should like to understand your concept of science better.

G.L. Science is the historical proceeding of consciousness, which transforms being.

F.F. I do not agree.

G.L. I shall explain more fully: no one is threatening the objectivity of objects. It is scarcely necessary for me to say that this objectivity is wholly independent as regards the subject. It exists and develops according to its logic, which is independent of the wills, aspirations, desires, goodness, or wickedness of men. Marx's explanation of capitalism is scientific precisely because it clarifies the logic on whose basis the system moves and develops independently of the good or ill will of the individual capitalists. Science means the end of anthropomorphism, it is the mirroring of objective reality. But this mirroring is not just a fact simply experienced: the contribution of man is essential. In this sense, science has nothing of the absolute, the impersonal, about it. It is a historical product, that is, one produced by individuals operating in history. Before Marx, Hegel had already recognized that men literally self-create themselves through their productive activity. The scientific categories are not unchangeable, as the positivists and neopositivists believed, and believe; they too are tied to historical development.

F.F. To assert the de-anthropomorphizing nature of science and at the same time theorize the self-creation of historically operating individuals seems to me contradictory.

G.L. It is only contradictory from a nondialectical, positivist viewpoint, or one of ingenuous realism. The historical character of science, discovered by Marxism, makes it a human undertaking in the full sense and a potential instrument of liberation. Certainly, science thereby loses its halo of absolute, everlasting certainty.

F.F. I agree as regards science as a historically determined undertaking, and thus not neutral but political. But why only in the West? This is Max Weber's problem. Further, the scientific problems and the use of research pose a political problem, historically dated and determined. However, the schemata, or the bases, of scientific reasoning—problem, hypothesis, testing—within a given historical horizon have their own validity, which leaves aside historical contingency.

G.L. This simply means that Marxism should not be dogmatized. There is a critical impulse in Marxism that works on Marxism itself as specific doctrine. I have already said that Marxism must be pursued, that we need to bring to fulfillment Marx's work. Marcuse tried this, but according to an essentially utopian schema. Marcuse is incapable of scientific analysis, he has lost sight of the working class, and has not understood the basic importance for a Marxist scientific analysis of the relations of production. His idealization of the subproletariat is wholly romantic and devoid of a serious basis. On the other hand, the moment of scientific analysis is basic. There can be no truly revolutionary politics without a preliminary scientific analysis that refers to the framework of the general theory of history and society. For the revolutionary movement today, this is the strongest, most urgent, demand. We do not have a policy because we do not have a theory. We have to go forward day by day improvising bad solutions to real problems, making do one day at a time. A lot of tactics but no strategy; small politics; opportunism. One goes ahead without knowing where one is going. For this reason I said we are still all Stalinists. Without a genuine general theory of society and its movement, one does not get away from Stalinism. Stalin was a great tactician. He grasped at once what it was best to do in a given situation. He made some *coups*. For example, Stalin was certainly right as against Liebknecht and Rosa Luxemburg. Later, the pact with Hitler and the handshake with Ribbentrop were perfectly justified. From the point of view of tactics, it was a case of pure and simple necessity, as we know today, and it is one of the great historical merits that Stalin immediately understood it. But Stalin, unfortunately, was not a Marxist. If you will permit me a paradox, I would say that Stalin was rather a Trotskyite. I shall tell you a story. Between Lenin and Trotsky there arose some disagreements; they had different opinions regarding the role and tasks of the unions. According to Trotsky, the unions should pose as their primary task the construction of the state and thus behave in every situation and in regard to every problem as an organ of the state. For Lenin, on the other hand, the unions should present themselves as mass organisms and consider their task that of defending the immediate interests of the workers involved in production. The evolution of the Soviet state thus tells us that Stalin was a Trotskyite, at least in this respect, naturally without knowing it. But the fact is that Stalin has not yet been surmounted. The essence of Stalinism lies in placing tactics before strategy, practice above theory. This can be seen everywhere in the international Communist movement. Togliatti, for example, as I have already said, was a great tactician, perhaps the greatest, but a nothing as a theorist. Only for Gramsci would one need a separate argument, very complex; however, it is certain that the Italian Communist party does not have the theoretical weight it should have, given its organizational force, which is imposing. A headless greatness. However, here too in Hungary, in Poland too . . . we have learned to produce some things; on the practical plane agriculture is going fairly well, but industrialization in general is not going well, it is behind, coordination is lacking, raw materials do not reach the enterprises in time, the plans stay on paper. We must learn to connect the great decisions of popular political power with personal needs, those of individuals. There is no doubt that abstract planning creates anarchy. The bureaucracy generated by Stalinism is a tremendous evil. Society is suffocated by it. Everything becomes unreal, nominalistic. People see no design, no strategic aim, and do not move; the problem of individual incentives becomes insoluble.

It is perfectly useless to refurbish the idea of individual profit of the capitalist type, or invoke market forces. We are still thinking of capitalism as it was in the last century, the nineteenth century, but the market of the nineteenth century is dead! . . . it is useless to invoke it; it no longer exists. On the other hand, in the political and intellectual climate dominated by Stalinism, the taste for considering the great alternatives is lost. What society do we want to build? A bureaucratic-socialist society? Or an individualistic society of mass industrial consumption and production? Or again, a pluralistic, decentralized society with low economic productivity? These questions seem useless, vain. Indeed, they are useless because they are strategic questions Stalinism cannot pose; it prefers to live by the day. Stalin not only was not a Marxist, but inverted, overturned Marxism by putting tactics before strategy. We are all still Stalinists because we do not have a Marxist theory of capitalism today, and for this reason we do not even have a real policy, one based, that is, on a strategic design.

F.F.   But how in Marx are the scientist and the politician coherently linked?

G.L.   In my view, in Marx the concretization of research always depends on and comes after the general theory. Thus, the scientist and the politician help each other in turn. Today we have no policy because we have no theory that tells us what to do in different circumstances. On the contrary, we are always surprised by events.

F.F.   What can one do today toward the exit from Stalinism and the return to Marxism in the Soviet Union?

G.L.   Little; very little; almost nothing. As they have put practice before theory, our Soviet friends are forced to use Marxism as an instrument of rationalization of immediate political demands. For example, the dispute between the Soviet Union and the Chinese has nothing to do with Marxism. It is purely a conflict of political tactics that cannot be resolved, as there is no general Marxist theory.

F.F.   To what do you attribute the lessening, the nonexistence, of a general Marxist theory applied to contemporary conditions?

G.L.   To the fact that we are losing ground and that things seem to escape us. There are new phenomena about which we have nothing to say. We are waiting for the great crisis of capitalism, but capitalism has had no more crises of great significance after that of 1929, as presently capitalism has taken possession of the whole of social life. It doesn't please us to say it, but it is the truth. The mass consumption by the workers has become very important as a means of eliminating the crises of capitalism. We have passed from the structural, objective market provided with an important, in many respects revolutionary, function as Marx and Engels recognized, as against the idiocy of rural life and tradition in general, to the manipulated market of this century. Our analysis stopped, but capitalism has continued evolving. We stopped with Lenin. After him, there is no more Marxism. In the socialist countries, too, the lack of a theory and especially the lack of a Marxist analysis of contemporary capitalism prevent the real construction of socialism. Planning is too abstract. They are words. The evolution of capitalism has meanwhile experienced radical, qualitative changes. I have already said it, but I want to be more specific. For example, in the course of the last century, the length of the working day was an important question; it went from fourteen to thirteen to twelve to ten hours, and so on. Today the same question is posed differently; it is not so much the length of the working week that is important, but rather knowing and planning what the workers do during nonworking time, that is, how they use their famous "free time," what they consume, where they go. . . . In the last century, in his projects and speculations, the capitalist never took into consideration the workers' capacity to consume, as this could in fact be quietly forgotten. Capitalism was then interested above all in basic investments, in big industry. Important sectors of collective life were of no interest to it. Today, capitalism is deeply interested in the whole of social life, from ladies' boots to cars to kitchen implements to means of amusement. . . . It is a qualitative change about which we know very little. In this respect the partial results of some bourgeois studies should be used critically. However, often these results are abstract and valueless, as they lack historical dimension and neglect the data of economic evolution. For example, one can easily study a country's schools. But without this country's history and economy, studying its school system is abstract, it has no value.

F.F. A study of this kind, in any event, with the economic and historical dimensions, should be carried out in all countries; it should be a study on a world scale.

G.L. Certainly, yes. A world counteralienation and countercapitalism are needed.

F.F. Whose is this task? The intellectuals'?

G.L. This task concerns the whole working class. The intellectuals have no responsibility, no position, nor any longer a privileged consideration. Certainly, the working class has changed; it changes its internal composition just as capitalism continuously changes, while remaining in essence identical to itself. One must keep in view the evolution of the division of labor, and the repercussions of productive technology on professional roles and the mode of presentation of class struggle.

F.F. I believe one can say that in modern industry work with a high intellectual content is increasing with respect to those that require a simple expenditure of muscular energy. At the same time, the number of intellectuals is increasing, and the links that involve them in various ways in capitalist enterprises are becoming tighter. Can one also consider the intellectuals as a separate social group and variously privileged, or are they wage laborers like all the others?

G.L. No, it does not seem to me that intellectuals are simple wage laborers like all the others. The so-called proletarianization of the intellectuals does not at all make them similar to genuine proletarians. The fact is that the intellectuals have indeed got special responsibilities. Here, for example, they can have no real power, play an important part in political decisions, but they go on complaining. Like an adolescent with his first girl, he is proud of her, wants to show her off, but is also ashamed of her. The relation with power is ambiguous. And then official propaganda continues to speak of the "dictatorship of the proletariat." However, the intellectuals who pass themselves off as workers become ridiculous. How can one forget that Marx and Engels too were intellectuals, and were bourgeois? So too Lenin came from a bourgeois intellectual family. Socialist consciousness, as Lenin taught us, does not arise spontaneously from within the working class; it is brought to it from without, from the revolutionary intellectuals. The way this happens varies, naturally, from one epoch to another, but there is no mechanical spontaneousness in it, no fatalism.

F.F. However, if, as I believe, it is true that Marx's greatest discovery was that of the political nature of culture and science, does it not seem to you that there is a paternalistic risk of continuing to view culture and science as the fief of a narrow stratum of intellectuals, tendentially exclusive and corporate, supposed to put culture at the service of the masses, that is, to enlighten them, guide them, as though they were the only authorized trustees of the genuine revolutionary word?

G.L. I believe one must at all costs avoid paternalism, which is always an authoritarianism that is hidden and thus more insidious. But the fear of paternalism should not make us close our eyes to the importance, in specific circumstances decisiveness, of the role played by great personalities in history. What would have happened in 1917 in Russia without Lenin? Can we be certain that we would have had, in his absence, the October revolution? Socialism is what men make of it. It depends on them to prevent the construction of socialism from being hampered and ultimately suffocated by bureaucratization.

The discussion comes to an end. It is nearly one in the afternoon. While we are talking, the housekeeper comes in with two cups of coffee on a green ceramic tray and some irregularly shaped sugar lumps on a saucer. She does not speak; she puts the tray on a trolley, which, still in silence and with great discreetness, she pushes up to the desk, between Lukács and myself. She leaves almost at once, murmuring something like, "It's not sugared." She closes the door again behind her. During the whole, certainly customary, maneuver, Lukács calmly continues talking. Now he cautiously sips at the coffee by taking a little in the coffeespoon, which he sucks in a curiously infantile way. Later, having assured himself that it is not too hot, he sips it little by little. Especially toward the end, the conversation has been a rapid, heady mixture of French and German, with words and whole sentences in English and other languages, in the fashion of the kind of Esperanto that was the mark of the great, cosmopolitan mid-European intellectuals before World War I, and that one hears so well in the letters of Marx and Engels. Even in moments of total disagreement, the eyes of the great old man continue to hold me, shining with liking, almost winking as if at a secret understanding, as a mark of complicity between us, in which I sense a confused mixture of intellectual solidarity, common hopes, and an instinctive impulse of affection that goes well beyond the duties of hospitality toward a passing stranger. Unexpectedly, diffidently, Lukács confesses to not knowing Italian well enough to be able to speak it. He complains that Einaudi has not yet published the translation of his *Aesthetics*, though it has already appeared in Spanish and even in Japanese. After a few sentences of thanks and farewell, I gather together my things and descend to the banks of the Danube, where the morning fog has lifted and the sun is bright.

About the Contributors

Ehrhard Bahr is professor of German at the University of California at Los Angeles. His books include *Georg Lukács* in German and *Georg Lukács* in English written with Ruth G. Kunzer. He has written numerous studies on significant figures in German literary history, among them Goethe, Lessing, Kafka, and Brecht.

József Bayer is a Hungarian political philosopher and the author of books and articles on pluralism. He was recently a visiting scholar at Harvard, Yale, and Columbia University.

Marshall Berman is professor of political science at the City University of New York, and the author of *The Politics of Authenticity, All That Is Solid Melts into the Air*, and numerous articles on politics and culture.

Lee Congdon is professor of history at James Madison University, and the author of *The Young Lukács* and numerous studies on European intellectual history.

Franco Ferrarotti is professor of sociology at Rome University, the editor of *La Critica Sociologica*, and the author of *Max Weber and the Destiny of Reason* and more than twenty books in Italian.

János Kelemen is chair and professor of philosophy at Budapest University, and the author of monographs on Benedetto Croce and George Edward Moore, among others.

Goerge L. Kline is Milton C. Nahm Distinguished Professor of Philosophy at Bryn Mawr College, and the author of *Religious and Anti-Religious Thought in Russia* and many other books and articles on Marxist philosophy.

Harry Liebersohn chairs the History Department at Claremont Graduate School, California. He has published many works on European intellectual history with a special interest in German social thought.

Robert Lilienfeld is associate professor of sociology at the City College of the City University of New York. He is the author of *The Rise of Systems Theory: An Ideological Analysis* and of numerous books on sociology, musicology, and culture.

Michael Löwy is a full-time researcher in the Sociological Section of the Centre National de Recherche Scientifique in Paris and has been a lecturer in sociology at the University of Paris VIII (Vincennes) since 1969. His books include *La théorie de la révolution chez le jeune Marx, Dialectique et revolution*, and *Georg Lukács—From Romanticism to Bolshevism.*

Joseph B. Maier is professor emeritus of sociology, Rutgers University. He was associated with the Institute of Social Research from the mid-1930s until the death of Max Horkheimer. He is the author of *On Hegel's Critique of Kant* and of many works on Latin America. He has written extensively on the Frankfurt School and European intellectual history.

Judith Marcus, on the faculty of Kenyon College, is the author of *Thomas Mann und Georg Lukács* in German and of *Georg Lukács and Thomas Mann: A Study in the Sociology of Literature.* She is co-editor of *Foundations of the Frankfurt School of Social Research* and *Georg Lukács: Selected Correspondence, 1902–1920.* She has written extensively on European social and intellectual history.

Tom Rockmore is chair and professor of philosophy at Duquesne University. He is the author of *Fichte, Marx, and the German philosophy of Tradition* and *Hegel's Circular Epistemology.* He has published numerous studies in English, French, and German.

Laurent Stern is professor of philosophy at Rutgers University and the author of works on Lukács, aesthetics, and the philosophy of language.

Zoltán Tarr, is the author of *The Frankfurt School*, and co-editor of *Foundations of the Frankfurt School of Social Research* and *Georg Lukács: Selected Correspondence, 1902–1920.*

Ferenc Tökei is a member of the Hungarian Academy of Sciences, and the author of *On the Asiatic Mode of Production* and many other books on philosophy and sociology in Hungarian, German, and French.

Name Index